TOLERATION, NEUTRALITY AND DEMOCRACY

TOLERATION, NEUTRALITY AND DEMOCRACY

Edited by

Dario Castiglione
Department of Politics,
University of Exeter, U.K.

and

Catriona McKinnon
Department of Politics,
University of York, U.K.

SPRINGER-SCIENCE+BUSINESS MEDIA, B.V.

A C.I.P. Catalogue record for this book is available from the Library of Congress.

ISBN 978-90-481-6492-9   ISBN 978-94-017-0241-6 (eBook)
DOI 10.1007/978-94-017-0241-6

Printed on acid-free paper

Contents

Acknowledgements

The idea for this book originated from discussions between the editors and the contributors at the Annual Conference of the UK Association for Legal and Social Philosophy on 'The Culture of Toleration', which we organised at the University of Exeter in April 2000. Most of the papers presented at the conference were intellectually stimulating, whilst the discussions that followed them were both lively and tolerant. But the rationale of this volume has developed independently of the conference itself, as we explain in the Introduction.

In the preparation of this volume we have incurred many debts. Thanks are due to the contributors for their enthusiastic participation in the project; to the ALSP for the opportunity to organise the conference at Exeter; and to all participants to the Exeter conference for the stimulating discussions that sharpened our understanding of the debate on toleration.

We are particularly indebted to Bob Brecher, the editor of *Res Publica*, for having advised us throughout the various phases of this project. We need also to acknowledge Robert Lamb's help in the preparation of the final manuscript; the support of the British Academy in the organisation of the ALSP conference through a UK Conference Grant; and, separately, the support of the AHRB (Grant: RL/AN 6410/APN 10467) to Catriona McKinnon and the ESRC (Grant: L21352022) to Dario Castiglione.

DC
CM

Notes on Contributors

Barry Barnes is Professor of Sociology at the University of Exeter. His publications include *The Elements of Social Theory* (UCL Press, 1995) and *Understanding Agency: Social Theory and Responsible Action* (Sage, 2000) and many articles on the sociology of science and knowledge.

Dario Castiglione is Senior Lecturer in Political Theory at the University of Exeter. Recent publications include co-edited volumes on *The Culture of Toleration in Diverse Societies* (Manchester, 2003) and *The History of Political Thought in National Context* (CUP, 2001) as well as a number of articles on European citizenship. He is currently completing a monograph on David Hume.

Robert Paul Churchill is Professor of Philosophy and Director of the Peace Studies Program at George Washington University. He has published a number of papers focusing on questions of human rights, ethics and democracy. He is currently engaged in research projects concerned with global diversity and human rights and the morality of multilateral responses to ethnic cleansing and genocide.

Ingrid Creppell is Associate Professor of Political Science at George Washington University. She is the author of *Toleration and Identity, Foundations in Early Modern Thought* (Routledge, 2003) and has published articles on medieval and modern political thought.

Maurizio Passerin d'Entreves is Professor of Philosophy at the University of Cape Town. He is the author of *Modernity, Justice and Community* (1990) and *The Political Philosophy of Hannah Arendt* (1994). More recently, he has edited a collection entitled *Democracy as Public Deliberation: New Perspectives* (2002), an issue that provides the focus for his current research.

Colin Farrelly is Assistant Professor at the University of Waterloo. He has published a number of articles on contemporary political philosophy and is the author of *An Introduction to Contemporary Political Theory* (Sage, forthcoming). He is currently engaged in writing a book on distributive justice and researching the ethics of genetics.

Graham Finlay is Lecturer in Philosophy at Trinity College Dublin. He has published articles on John Stuart Mill. His research is mainly concerned with moral and political philosophy, its history, and its intersections with epistemology and the philosophy of language.

Anna Elisabetta Galeotti is Professor of Political Philosophy at the University del Piemonte Orientale-Vercelli. She is the author of *Toleration as Recognition* (CUP, 2002) and of other books in Italian on Individualism and Multiculturalism.

Peter Jones is Professor of Political Philosophy at the University of Newcastle. He is the author of *Rights* (Macmillan, 1994) for the series 'Issues in Political Theory' of which he was one of the editors. His current research focuses on the problems posed by diversity of belief and identities.

Frederic Kellogg is the author of *The Formative Essays of Justice Holmes* (1984) and *Justice Holmes and the Philosophy of Judicial Restraint* (forthcoming). His main research interests are the philosophy of law, common law theory and the interpretation of constitutional rights.

Catriona McKinnon is Lecturer in Political Philosophy at the University of York. She is the author of *Liberalism and the Defence of Political Constructivism* (Palgrave, 2002), has co-edited *The Demands of Citizenship* (Continuum, 1999) and *The Culture of Toleration in Diverse Societies* (Manchester, 2003), and edits *Imprints: A Journal of Analytical Socialism*. She is currently working on a book on the theory and practice of liberal toleration.

Saladin Meckled-Garcia is Rubin Research Fellow in Human Rights at the School of Public Policy, University College London. He has published articles on issues concerning equality and international justice. He is currently working on a book on the ethical foundations of human rights.

Glen Newey is Reader in Politics at the University of Strathclyde. He is the author of *After Politics: The Rejection of Politics in Contemporary Liberal Philosophy* (Palgrave, 2000), *Toleration, Ethics and Virtue* (Edinburgh, 1999), and an introduction to Hobbes (Routledge, forthcoming). He is currently working on a book concerning political deception and democracy.

INTRODUCTION

Catriona McKinnon and Dario Castiglione

It is not an overstatement to say that toleration is one of the most important issues for the definition of a moral and political theory with application to modern globalised societies. Toleration is a value which no politician in any liberal democratic society would dare to reject. In the UK, its value is reflected in the learning outcomes of education for citizenship isolated by the Final Report of the Advisory Group on Citizenship (which schools have a statutory responsibility to deliver): children ought to be disposed to the 'practice of toleration', and have the 'ability to tolerate other view points'. In these days of feelings of heightened insecurity prompting suspicion of strangers and departures from the norm, toleration has again taken centre stage as one of *the* values definitive of stable and just liberal democratic societies.

Toleration is a matter of principled restraint with respect to differences which are opposed, either at the personal or at the political level. With respect to the former level, the tolerant person does not use the power she has over others she dislikes and/or disapproves of to interfere with them. However, the tolerant person does not thereby divest herself of her dislike or disapproval; the tolerant person does not transform her dislike and disapproval into warm feelings, and neither does she simply become indifferent to what she hitherto disliked and disapproved of when she practices toleration. At the political level, toleration requires that institutions be designed and laws be framed so as not to damage groups whose characteristics and practices are opposed by the majority or the most powerful, where these characteristics and practices are not unreasonable. That principles of toleration counsel restraint without requiring the resolution of disagreement or the dissolution of opposition makes their practice the holy grail for many liberal theorists in search of principles of justice fit for modern, conflict-ridden societies.

Of course, this emphasis in liberal theory on toleration as an essential pre requisite of stability and ingredient of justice has historical precedent. John Locke's defence of political principle of religious toleration responded to the bloody and interminable Wars of Religion with arguments focused on the irrationality of the attempt to use force to inculcate religious belief.[1] And two centuries later John Stuart Mill—confronted with the

---

[1] John Locke, A Letter Concerning Toleration (Indianapolis: Hackett, 1983) ed. and tr. By James H. Tully.

stifling norms and intrusive laws of Victorian society—was moved to defend a principles of toleration with wider scope than Locke's as the best way of ensuring the continued progress of human kind.[2]

However, these traditional liberal defences of the personal and political practice of toleration—and others like them—are not obviously robust enough to justify toleration to the various and opposed parties constitutive of the diversity within which toleration must operate in the contemporary world. For those who take the permanence of such diversity to be a non-regrettable fact about the human condition,[3] political justifications can no longer appeal to theological premises or to the truth of any one moral theory. Rather, toleration must be justified in a way that eschews appeal to controversial premises which can legitimately be disputed by those to whom the justification is addressed, thereby making principles of toleration acceptable to a more diverse range of people than ever before. The requirement that principles of toleration have this degree of acceptability is, many liberal theorists argue, both a requirement of justice and a pre requisite of stability.

There are at least four clear areas in which liberal theorists committed to this conception of political justification must do some work. First, the sense in which the same principles of toleration might be equally acceptable to diverse and opposed members of liberal democratic societies must be delineated and defended. Many liberal theorists meet this challenge with an account of how the proper exercise of public reason makes principles of toleration acceptable in conditions of diversity. We have addressed this area of contemporary liberal theory elsewhere.[4]

Second, there are problems associated with the achievement of a tolerant society. If it is claimed that a tolerant society is only possible when its citizens are tolerant, then if doubt is cast on the coherence of toleration as an attitude that citizens ought to adopt towards one another, the possibility of creating a tolerant society is undermined. Such doubts are said to be raised by the very formulation of the *idea* of toleration, which gives rise to a paradox: why tolerate ideas, behaviour, and practices that one believes to be wrong? Toleration looks like an 'impossible virtue'[5] because it would appear to be appropriate when an agent has good reason to be intolerant: but why should an agent refrain from acting on her good reasons, as toleration demands? What sorts of reasons, or other considerations, could explain the demands that the virtue of toleration makes in order to trump the agent's (first-order) good reasons? If the individual virtue of toleration is incoherent, then the tolerant society may turn out to be either an impossibility or an

---

[2] J.S. Mill, On Liberty (Oxford: Oxford University Press, 1998), ed. John Gray.

[3] We are thinking here in particular of John Rawls and his followers. At the start of *Political Liberalism* (New York: Columbia University Press, 1993), Rawls claims that the account of political justification he develops there will work on the assumption that reasonable pluralism is a fact, and is "the natural outcome of the activities of human reason under enduring free institutions" (p. xxiv).

[4] Catriona McKinnon and Dario Castiglione (eds), *The Culture of Toleration in Diverse Societies: Reasonable Tolerance* (Manchester: Manchester University Press, 2003).

[5] We self-consciously borrow here from David Heyd's edited collection *Toleration: An Elusive Virtue* (Princeton: Princeton University Press, 1996)

abstract myth. Arguments are needed here to establish either that the achievement of a tolerant society does not require the presence of tolerant individuals,[6] or that the air of paradox surrounding the practice of toleration at the individual level is illusory.

Third, there are a newly emerging set of questions regarding the compatibility of toleration with another value much-loved by many contemporary liberals: neutrality. Neutrality is a property of political justifications; it requires that the justification of any principle or policy be independent of any moral theory or set of values with which another moral theory or set of values might reasonably compete. Liberal neutrality so understood is a matter of ensuring that the acceptance of any political justification does not depend on acceptance of any particular reasonable moral theory or set of values, rather than a matter of ensuring that the principles justified are neutral in their consequences for those affected by them. Understood in this way, the debate about neutrality is clearly connected to the debate about public reason mentioned above: establishing which moral theories and sets of values can be appealed to in political justification consistent with neutrality requires an account of which moral theories and sets of values qualify as reasonable. However, the debate about neutrality and toleration does not simply resolve into the debate about public reason and toleration. Regardless of where the limits of reasonableness are set as a consequence of the first debate, there are aspects of the liberal requirement of neutrality in the construction of political justifications which appear to be in tension with the liberal requirement of toleration. If adopting the standpoint of liberal neutrality requires disowning reasons to use state power to interfere with people one opposes, then it looks like toleration has no role in a truly neutral liberal polity: as was signalled above in description of the second area of enquiry for liberals, toleration is only possible in circumstances in which a person takes the grounds on which she is opposed to others to be informed by good reasons.

Finally, contemporary liberal defenders of toleration must engage with questions about how this cherished value can be realised in and through democratic institutions. Democracy is the only game in town for contemporary liberals, but there are puzzles about whether genuinely democratic procedures can reliably yield principles of toleration, and whether the institutions of constitutional democracies—such as constitutional courts—provide the best model for reasoning fit to encourage toleration in liberal democratic citizens.

The papers in this collection address the last three areas of concern mentioned above; they range across historical, analytical, normative, and jurisprudential perspectives. However, what they share is a concern to identify real problems in the contemporary liberal theory of toleration, and to offer constructive suggestions for ways of thinking about these problems. We turn now to a brief outline of the papers themselves.

---

[6] Bernard Williams defends a version of this view . See "Toleration: An Impossible Virtue?", David Heyd (ed), *Toleration: An Elusive Virtue*, pp. 18-27.

The papers in part 1 address toleration understood as a moral attitude of individuals, and have a place in the second area of liberal enquiry outlined above. In 'Tolerance as a Primary Virtue' Barry Barnes addresses the core of a common understanding of toleration as a virtue by questioning the idea that toleration only applies to our dealings with those who may subscribe to very different values and come from different traditions than us (a view which provides part of the framework for the putative paradox of toleration). A reified view of traditions as ossified and non-dynamic affects how we understand the nature of engagement with others within and outside the tradition to which we belong. Rejecting the view of traditions as ossified—traditions are instead, he argues, the result of a co-ordination exercise as much as any other form of social relationship—Barnes argues that toleration is not an extraordinary (or, as some have argued, 'secondary') virtue, but the very essence of our relations with others. Toleration is something inevitable, but, at the same time, a virtue to cultivate, in so far as it represents the way we pursue our various membership projects by accepting that the views of others whom we consider relevant to a particular project of membership we value are on a par with our own.

In 'Montaigne: The Embodiment of Identity as Grounds for Toleration', Ingrid Creppell challenges a more historical point in the toleration literature. Her account of Montaigne's contribution to the emergence of the idea of toleration suggests that the sceptical and instrumentalist image that is currently dominant in early modern views of toleration is mistaken, at least with respect to Montaigne. In her reading of Montaigne, corporeality—revealed in different ways at social and individual locations, and the demands that come from being both mind and body—informs his understanding of what judging others means. In Montaigne, the tolerant recognition of others is demanded by a humanistic, judgmental appreciation of others using oneself, and one's own humanity, as a measure. This gives our ideas of toleration both a particularistic insight and a universalist reach.

Elisabetta Galeotti's treatment of the putative paradox of toleration in 'Is Toleration a Moral Virtue?' starts with an exploration of the full implications of what she calls the *moral model* of toleration. This, she argues, may go some way towards addressing the paradox of toleration, but is beset by a number of problems, such as that it has to rely on the principle of autonomy and that of harm. She argues that both these principles are underdetermined as the grounds for a full justification of toleration and of its limits. Perhaps more damagingly for the moral model, it often seems be inadequate to capture and help us to make sense of our common experience, and so fails the test of reflective equilibrium which is essential to moral and political reasoning. For Galeotti, the problems posed by the moral model can only be addressed by a *political* approach. Indeed, political toleration asks not that people accept the reasons or action of others to whom they may strongly object, but rather that they reassess and revise their own reasons for opposition and repression in the light of public reason, though she admits that a *moral* understanding of toleration may appear, in private, as a support to political toleration.

The shift to the political perspective brings new theoretical problems relating to, in particular, political neutrality: the papers in Part 2 address these questions, which map on the third area of liberal enquiry identified above. In 'Neutrality and the Virtue of Toleration', Robert Paul Churchill argues that the only conception of toleration worth the name is one whereby a person with reason to oppose others who differ from her restrains herself on the principled ground that she respects the autonomy of others, and so will not interfere with them so as to prevent their wrong doing as she sees it. Churchill argues that this form of toleration requires a degree of virtue among citizens, which cannot be assumed by liberal theorists like Rawls who purport to take seriously the fact of reasonable pluralism. If assumptions about the virtue of citizens are built into the conception of pluralism as reasonable, then 'reasonableness' is far more morally loaded and far less neutral than such theorists would have us believe.

Churchill's scepticism about whether toleration is a value consistent with liberal neutrality is echoed in different arguments made by Saladin Meckled-Garcia in 'Toleration and Neutrality: Incompatible Ideals?'. He argues that liberals who advocate neutrality in the justification of principles and policies cannot at the same time endorse toleration as a political value. To be committed to neutrality is to be committed to the creation of a world in which toleration is unnecessary: a world in which toleration is necessary is a world in which citizens lack the virtues and political attitudes necessary for sustaining truly neutral forms of political justification of institutions and policies. Meckled-Garcia's argument is that toleration and neutrality are incompatible ideals because citizens who act for reasons of neutrality cannot believe that they have reason to use state power to enforce their comprehensive views on others who disagree with them, and this latter belief is what toleration responds to.

In contrast, in 'Toleration and Neutrality: Compatible Ideals?' Peter Jones argues that the problems about toleration and neutrality identified by Meckled-Garcia only arise given an unduly narrow conception of the sorts of reasons which inform the practice of toleration. Jones suggests that it is only if these reasons are understood as second-order reasons which cancel out the first order reasons for opposition to which toleration responds that neutrality appears to demand that toleration be transcended. And, using Joseph Raz's work on first order reasons, Jones argues that there is no requirement that we think of reasons to be tolerant as second-order reasons. (Meckled-Garcia replies to Jones in the *Appendix* at the end of the collection).

Jones purports to establish that toleration and neutrality are compatible ideals. Colin Farrelly takes the debate a step further in 'Neutrality, Toleration, and Reasonable Agreement' by arguing, not only that these ideals are compatible, but that neutralist procedures are inadequate for solving some hard cases in contemporary liberal democratic societies. Making reference to two real-world cases in the Canadian courts related to hate speech and pornography, Farrelly argues that only a liberal theory informed both by the ideal of neutrality and the ideal of toleration (insofar as it reflects values of civility, a sense of justice, and reasonableness) can provide guidance with respect to such cases.

The claimed clash between toleration and neutrality is a relatively recent problem for liberals, because the ideal of neutrality never had the prominence in classical liberalism that it does in contemporary liberalism. Graham Finlay makes this clear in his discussion of J.S. Mill, and the accusations sometimes levelled against him that he was an 'assimilationist' with respect to cultural difference. In 'John Stuart Mill as a Theorist of Toleration', Finlay makes a persuasive case against this accusation, and argues the Mill was a theorist of toleration with respect to cultural difference. Furthermore, and germane to the overall theme of this collection, Finlay argues that Mill's approach is superior to those of contemporary theorists like Rawls who yoke together neutrality and toleration. Finlay argues that defending toleration on non-neutral grounds yields a liberalism fit to address political problems as they appear in the very unreasonable pluralism of the modern world.

Regardless of whether toleration and neutrality ought to appear as twin values in liberal theory, there are hard practical questions for liberals about the place of toleration in contemporary democracies, and about the best way to encourage the practice of toleration in a democratic citizenry. The three papers in Part 3 address these questions.

In 'Is Democratic Toleration a Rubber Duck?', Glen Newey offers a tripartite analysis of toleration, and argues that toleration is an executive virtue. Given this analysis, he claims that toleration cannot adapt to politics in modern democratic conditions. Toleration appeared as an ideal at a time when political decisions were at the discretion of a personalised authority, and the logical structure of toleration cannot be adapted to the democratic form of authority. However, the claim that the logic of toleration is extraneous to the logic of modern democratic politics does not mean that such politics must be the site of continuous confrontation: if more toleration will not suffice as a solution to political problems, there may be other more roundabout ways of limiting confrontation, such as encouraging a less judgmental culture among citizens.

Different conceptions of the way in which both toleration and the encouragement referred to by Newey might be manifested in democratic institutions are addressed by Frederic R. Kellogg in 'The Enforcement of Toleration'. Kellogg isolates two different locations for the public reasoning which sets the limits of toleration for contemporary liberals. On the one hand, with Rawls, we might hold up judicial deliberations in the US Supreme Court as the ideal model for public reason. In contrast, we might follow Frankenfurter and Learned Hand in envisaging public reasoning as a conversation of mutual persuasion between judges, legislators, and the citizenry. Kellogg advocates the latter model.

In the final paper in the collection—'The Fraught Relation Between Toleration and Democracy'—Maurizio Passerin d'Entrèves highlights a problem in the relationship between political toleration as an aspect of neutrality, and democratic principles which are claimed by theorists like Sheldon Leader to embody a 'shareable understanding' of the just society. By grounding demands for political toleration in the acceptance of democratic values and principles, Leader aims to show that the acceptance of political toleration does not depend on the acceptance of liberalism, thereby broadening the scope of political toleration. D'Entreves argues that it is questionable whether democratic values are shareable by all those in a non-liberal diverse society. This scepticism casts doubt on Leader's attempt to prise apart liberalism and political toleration; d'Entreves argues that liberalism is at least a necessary condition for effective political toleration.

PART I

TOLERATION: MORAL AND POLITICAL

CHAPTER 1

TOLERANCE AS A PRIMARY VIRTUE

Barry Barnes

FAMILIAR GROUND

It is surely beyond dispute that tolerance currently counts as a virtue amongst us, and indeed there is probably no supposed virtue to which we devote greater attention. Yet attempts to justify our treating tolerance in this way are known to lead to recalcitrant problems; and the 'paradox of tolerance' is now a recognised focus of interest in moral philosophy and political theory.[1] Considered in an individualistic framework, the difficulty is that tolerance appears to require the acceptance of conflicting beliefs. Individual A believes action (of kind) X to be unethical or immoral, and hence something that she should oppose. And yet, being tolerant, A believes it right not to oppose X enacted by B; since it falls within the limits of what is tolerable. Thus, A's tolerance appears to consist in her acceptance of beliefs that enjoin her to embark upon conflicting courses of action.

The same difficulty arises at the collective level, notably in contexts where members of two different cultural traditions coexist, or seek to coexist. Action X may be wrong or immoral by the standards of culture or tradition A; yet those same standards may enjoin members of A not to oppose the enactment of X in tradition B, and to accept the legitimacy of overarching institutions that protect B and those who enact X therein. Indeed tolerance in this form is a key ordering device in the many kinds of society characterised by complexity or diversity. Different traditions sustain incompatible conceptions of what is right and good in their various 'private' (familial) domains. Yet they also co-operate in the public domain on the basis of a weak shared morality structured around notions like tolerance, in an institutional frame embodying a corresponding degree of toleration. Arrangements of this kind make for peaceful coexistence in societies where 'authentic' moral and ethical action could engender violence and wretchedness for all parties. And indeed, in such

---

[1] Among the sources wherein the paradox is discussed are D.D. Raphael, "The intolerable", in S. Mendus, ed., *Justifying Toleration* (Cambridge: Cambridge University Press, 1988) 137-54, and S. Mendus, *Toleration and the Limits of Liberalism* (Atlantic Highlands, N.J.: Humanities Press, 1989). Raphael indicates particularly clearly how it is universalising tendencies and the inclination to a strongly individualistic rationalism that generate the sense of paradox.

societies 'authentic' moral action is liable to be condemned as fanaticism or fundamentalism, and tolerance encouraged because it is functional or expedient. But that tolerance may be functional in this sense does not necessarily make it any easier to rationalise as genuinely moral or ethical action for an individual member of A or B, or indeed as an ethical or moral imperative in traditions A and B.

Tolerance is routinely characterised as essential to the peace and stability of societies wherein sub-sets of members are primarily committed to distinct and formally incompatible moral and ethical orientations. Thus, Alasdair MacIntyre has contrasted primary virtues, such as courage, or loyalty, conducive to the living of a good life in the context of a single shared cultural tradition, with secondary virtues, like tolerance, fairness and willingness to compromise, that facilitate co-operation across and between traditions.[2] These latter virtues, he implies, whilst they figure prominently in our current moral thought, can only function as guides to moral or ethical action in situations where members have prior commitments to other conceptions of how it is good to live and what is conducive to so living. They facilitate our social relations with members of different traditions oriented to different moral and ethical standards and inclined to cherish different primary virtues. But for an individual to be committed both to these secondary virtues and to the primary virtues of her particular tradition implies irrationality and an inauthentic way of living, since their implications for action are in conflict.

MacIntyre's account was what initially stimulated my interest in this topic, and indeed his historical, anti-individualist account of ethics and morals has furnished much of the frame in which I myself continue to think of these matters. However, as this essay seeks specifically to show, on tolerance I believe him to be mistaken on a matter of fundamental importance. Of course, it is not only those who share MacIntyre's vision of the fallen character of our modern societies who take a jaundiced view of tolerance and fail to do justice to its role in our social life. The view that tolerance is no more than the price to be paid for some other good, an expedient departure from a genuinely moral and ethical orientation, a form of imperfection, a self-denying ordinance that reason is unfortunately forced to accept, is very widespread. And indeed, it is not immediately obvious how tolerance might be embraced as a virtue in any wholehearted and completely unqualified way, and encouraged, not as a regrettable departure from the ideal of authenticity, but as a part of what authenticity necessarily involves.

THE ARGUMENT

People oriented to conflicting ethical standards may indeed orient tolerantly to each other, and reckon it right and proper to do so. Tolerance may indeed exist as a secondary virtue, and may be clearly identified as such especially in the interactions between members of different cultural traditions. But there is much more to tolerance

---

[2] The secondary virtues are discussed in A. MacIntyre, *Secularisation and Moral Change* (Oxford: Oxford University Press, 1967). But, his position has of course since been developed so that societies of coexisting traditions have become, by the time of A. MacIntyre, *After Virtue* (London: Duckworth, 1981), much closer to being atomised 'societies'.

than this, or so I argue. Tolerance is in truth a universal and a necessary virtue, always implicated in efforts to live a good life, even in the context of a single shared cultural tradition. To evoke the work of MacIntyre again: even in the context of the most homogenous culture, wherein the highest achievable level of ethical agreement appertains, tolerance is going to be a virtue, and may even be explicitly extolled as a vitue in the reflective discourse of members.

The rationale for this suggestion is that problems of securing agreement in practice must all the time occur, even when everything is proceeding 'entirely routinely' in the context of a single 'homogenous' cultural tradition. Whatever objective ethical standards individual members of such a tradition are agreed upon will not of themselves elicit a like agreement concerning their particular implications and what specific actions follow from them. Formally speaking, even where there is complete agreement on the relevant standards, participants in a tradition remain distinct and other as far as moral and ethical action is concerned. This crucial point is often obscured by the unduly individualistic way in which moral and ethical actions are described, and in particular by untenable accounts of the relationship between standards and the individuals who are oriented to them.

How are actions related to moral or ethical standards? It is tempting to imagine that a standard divides actions into two sets – moral and immoral actions, let us say for simplicity – and that the division in question is apparent to any rational individual who confronts the standard. But there are obvious problems with this picture. Such is the difficulty of identifying just where such divisions lie, when those standards that are also our laws are concerned, that a large part of the energy of the legal profession has continually to be devoted to this task. And there are analogous difficulties in our everyday encounters with others: disputes about the nature of murderous action may arise with the anti-abortionist next door; or about what constitutes discrimination with the feminist along the street; or what cruelty consists in with the saboteur trying to wreck the hunt. Thus, we find ourselves asking, of standards that we may all alike acknowledge and defend, just what they 'really' imply, and just what it is for us to follow them correctly as specific persons in particular settings. But precisely by asking such questions we acquiesce in an individualistic frame of thought as a regulative ideal. And, whilst a frame of this kind does not blind us to the insecurity of the connection between standards and actions, it merits criticism nonetheless for turning the very nature of this connection into a 'problem' that is said to afflict it. What is actually needed here is a different regulatory ideal altogether, one that pays proper heed to the prompting of our experience and acknowledges that the relationship between standard and action, in so far as any individual person is concerned, is indeterminate.

Reference to everyday examples of the application of standards, and persistent curiosity about what goes on in them, is probably the best route to an appreciation of the indeterminacy referred to here. But the issue can also be addressed by means of formal argument. Suppose we begin, for convenience, with a standard formulated verbally as a general statement with which all of a membership agrees. How do members know what such a statement means or implies, and, in particular, how do they know what actions it implies in specific instances? It is through its salience in particular cases after all that the standard will bear upon the living of members' lives.

Two ways of communicating 'meaning' appear to exist: a member may be told what something means, or shown what it means. But attempts to communicate meaning verbally face an inescapable circularity. They can merely replace one verbal formulation, the standard as initially stated, with another formulation employing different words, wherein the problem of meaning recurs. We need to look, therefore, at how far the meaning, or correct mode of application, of standards can be shown or demonstrated.

What members take standards to imply is indeed actually conveyed in just this way, by exemplification in the practice of the membership. But formally speaking problems inhere in this way of conveying meaning as well. These derive from the familiar difficulties associated with establishing relations of sameness between empirical particulars. In the last analysis, a standard must be acquired and understood as specific instances of its application, that is, as a series of exemplars of actions that do (or do not) accord with it.[3] And further actions in accord with the standard will be actions reckoned by members to be of the same sort as these exemplary actions. However, no particulars, whether states-of-affairs or actions, are ever self-evidently the same as each other, or even the same in some given respect or property. Because they are *empirical* particulars, situated in an indefinitely complex world, they will never be identical: they will always differ from each other in some discernible way and be liable to differ further in not yet discerned ways. Moreover, if it is said that different particulars are the same by virtue of some shared property or empirical characteristic, the problem of sameness merely transfers to the properties or characteristics. All relations of empirical sameness are *intransitive*.[4] Hence, formally speaking, how far particular actions are 'really' the same as existing actions that exemplify standards will be a matter for members themselves to decide, and not something they can 'read off', as it were, from the standards themselves or the concepts incarnate in them. What standards imply is not given by or inherent in the standards themselves or even the previous use of the standards.

The way in which standards, laws, norms and so forth is addressed in parts of philosophy and the social sciences, does indeed constitute something of an oddity. Everyone is all too well aware that what these things 'really imply' is problematic to say the least; that, as Habermas has somewhat inadequately expressed it, "no norm contains within itself the rules for its own application".[5] Yet many of us persist in

---

[3] Exemplification of concepts through ostension and analogous processes is essential if significance is to be injected into language. The systematic arguments on behalf of this point deserve to be more widely known in view of what is now a widespread tendency, particularly in the social sciences, to imagine that the use/meaning of concepts must be given entirely through recourse to other concepts. See, for example, B. Barnes et al., *Scientific Knowledge: a Sociological Analysis* (Chicago: Chicago University Press, 1996) 47-53

[4] The basic problem here is indeed often formulated in the literature as that of the intransitivity of relations of sameness: if A is the same as B, and B is the same as C, it does not follow that A is the same as C. Thus, on opening the wine one can expect to have a bottle of vinegar in, say, a fortnight. Yet on drawing samples at half-hour intervals no taste-difference may be discernible between one and the next. Between samples drawn at shorter intervals not even a spectrometer may find a difference. If the sameness relation were transitive, then wine would be the same as vinegar, and it is not. A good discussion of this standard point is in M.B. Hesse, *The Structure of Scientific Inference* (London: Macmillan, 1974).

[5] J. Habermas, *Moral Consciousness and Communicative Action* (Cambridge: Polity, 1990) p.206.

attempting to understand human agreement in terms of these things, and some even reckon that they account for that agreement. Reference to the intransitivity of sameness goes to the core of what is wrong here, and gives it concise expression. The empiricist criticism of which the rationalist mode of thought stands constantly in need is thereby economically supplied. The differences and the contestation hidden under references to shared objective standards are once more made visible. And that such references do not so much describe what is agreed as co-ordinate the activity of agreement-seeking is made clear.

The technicalities associated with the problem of transitivity can be set aside here, and what is crucial to the present discussion stated very simply. When someone seeks to act in accord with a standard she is aware of existing instances of such actions and seeks to act in 'the same way'. But all she can actually hope to do is to act in analogy with the instances, and there are innumerable ways of so acting. Existing instances can only serve as precedents, and not as determinants, of her action. Different individuals may model their actions on exemplary precedents in different ways. And they may evaluate each other's actions in different ways as well, so actions taken by one individual to be routine applications of an accepted 'objective' ethical standard may be opposed by another precisely as a violations of it, as in the examples referred to earlier. And it goes without saying that ethical disagreement of this kind cannot be resolved by references to standards 'themselves'.

It follows that independent individuals cannot sustain a shared tradition. If we allow them to possess one in our imagination, then we must contemplate their routine actions increasingly diverging, and routine evaluations of those actions losing co-ordination over time and clashing with each other. And all this, as it were, after the tradition has done everything it can to help those involved. If agreement is to exist in and as the continuation of the shared tradition, it must be through the modification of judgements and the adjustment of actions, so that they come sufficiently within range of each other, as it were, to sustain mutual intelligibility and ongoing co-ordination. It may be, for example, that an individual who initially held X to be morally impermissible according to recognised objective standards will re-evaluate it as permissible after all; and for no reason other than that it is evidently so evaluated in the practice of others – powerful others perhaps, or the majority of those others in the relevant situation. Certainly, one way or another, individual conceptions of what standards entail or imply must continually be reconstructed if a shared tradition is to persist, and only individuals capable of such reconstruction may sustain such a tradition.

Thus, reflection on the way that standards are sustained and applied in cultural traditions leads to a conception of traditions, and of the members who participate in them, radically at variance with individualistic accounts of these things. Certainly it contrasts strongly with the familiar caricature of tradition as petrified practices, enacted again and again by automated individuals, in conformity with reified standards or imperatives. But the equally familiar positive picture, in which a genuinely moral or ethical tradition persists through rational individuals separately conforming to its rules and standards, is scarcely any different formally speaking. Both pictures effectively obscure what participation in a tradition actually involves, and misrepresent how and on what basis it persists. Better than these individualistic accounts is a view of traditions as the continuing collective accomplishments of their members.[6] This view recognises that the processes of co-ordination all the time necessary to keep traditions constituted are essential components of those very traditions and must be incorporated into our notion of what traditions are. It offers an ideal vision of tradition, not as fully co-ordinated practices deriving from the shared standards of identical individuals, but as the project of a membership, working against a backdrop of diversity and disorder, that manages to achieve some degree of co-ordination through and as agreement on standards, and on what specifically they imply. Traditions are not expressions of a uniform culture inherited by identical individuals; they consist in variegated and shifting practices that nonetheless represent a partial overcoming of the differences between individual human beings and the variety in their cultural inheritance. It goes without saying that when traditions are carefully studied empirically and historically, they invariably manifest themselves, not as repetition and invariance but as innovation and change.[7]

The picture of tradition as individuals acting alike in conformity with a shared set of objective standards has informed a number of impressive accounts of the nature of moral and ethical order, including those of some profoundly anti-individualistic thinkers. Even Alasdair MacIntyre's account, wherein good actions are those that conform to the relevant standards of goodness, and 'good' denotes just what conforms to those standards, is consistent with that picture. But the picture is flawed. It omits any adequate representation of the specific practices and procedures wherein standards are invoked and exemplified in particular situations. These social practices actually constitute standards as they exist at a given time, and they must be recognised, accordingly, not just as inherent in the efforts of a membership to attain a good life but as inherent in whatever might be regarded as the actual living of it. Once this is understood, it becomes clear that good actions cannot be identified purely by reference to existing objective standards, and that 'good' cannot refer to whatever is implied by or 'really' in accord with those standards. All evaluations of

---

[6] Individualistic caricatures of 'tradition' remain widespread and influential: see, for example A. Giddens, "Living in a post-traditional society", in U. Beck et al., *Reflexive modernisation* (Oxford: Polity, 1994). It is tempting to describe them as 'Enlightenment' accounts, mindful, for example, of Kant's 'motto of enlightenment': *Sapere Aude*, a call for the individual to think for herself; and Habermas's remarks on 'enlightened thinking' as something wherein "insights gained individually and transformed into motives (are) supposed to break the spell of collective powers": see I. Kant, "An answer to the question: what is enlightenment?" in H. Reiss, ed., *Political Writings* (Cambridge: Cambridge University Press, 1991) p.54; and J. Habermas, *The Theory of Communicative Action. Vol. 2, Lifeworld and System: a Critique of Functionalist Reason* (Cambridge: Polity, 1987) p.107. But of course to use such a tag comes close to caricaturing 'the Enlightenment' rather as 'it' caricatures 'tradition', and it certainly fails to do justice to the subtlety and variety of the thought of the period.

[7] A 'perfect copy' of a work of fine art, far from contributing to the tradition to which the work was ascribed would be actively excluded from it. Similarly, a major focus in the sociological study of science and technology as cultural traditions is the problematic character of 'replication'. For example, the successful 'replication' of a scientific experiment normally involves deliberate variations in design and/or the apparatus used, and the 'mere repetition' of what was originally reported (itself problematic) no more counts as a further enactment of tradition than does the copying of a work of art. See, for example, H. Collins, *Changing Order* (New York: Academic Press, 1985), Barnes, *Scientific Knowledge*. I discuss tradition further in B. Barnes, *The Elements of Social Theory* (Princeton: Princeton University Press, 1995) and, with special attention to some of the key points of the present essay, in B. Barnes, *Understanding Agency: Social Theory and Responsible Action* (Thousand Oaks, C.A.: Sage, 2000), Ch. 8.

good actions must now be understood as involving at once a descriptive and a performative dimension, and sufficiently settled agreements about what are good or correct modes of action must be seen as continually arising from, and dissolving back into, something less than that, even in the ideal case. Terms like 'good' and 'right' must be recognised as *operators*, with which participants create, defend, contest the implications of, challenge and even overturn specific shared standards or images of 'the good' or 'the right'. And striving to live a good life must be recognised as part of the very essence of living it.

What now of the individual members who sustain traditions and seek to live a good life within them? They cannot stand separately in fixed relationships to objective standards and 'their implications', even in routinely reproducing their tradition. They must be affected by each other's actions, and each must be disposed to move her own toward those of others, as it were, if co-ordination is to be sustained. In relation to standards they must manifest autonomy, but in relation to each other accountability and susceptibility[8]. They must be understood as regulating each other's conduct by invoking standards, not as regulating their own conduct as separate individuals by subservience to standards. But this implies a specific attitude to the judgements and actions of others, judgements and actions that may initially be seen as erroneous or unethical. However an individual initially evaluates the actions and judgements of others, she has to allow them a status like to her own in the evolving ethical life of the membership. As a member, she has to accept that other members may prove right 'really', despite her own initial individual views. It is necessary that the individual member has both her own view of what genuine moral and ethical activities consist in, *and* a sense that how those activities are viewed by others has a standing on a par with their own. It is necessary, in other words, that participants manifest that peculiar orientation to the judgements and actions of others that we characterise as tolerance. Tolerance in this sense, manifest in the interactions of 'tolerant members', is intrinsic to social life. Those who would aspire to dispense with it, who would seek somehow to fulfil their ethical aspirations by following standards directly, as independent individuals, actually risk the legitimate condemnation of others in terms of those very standards. The very existence of the agreement in practice necessary to the living of a good life depends upon tolerant interaction.

It is only when authentic moral action is thought of as independent rational individuals rigorously implementing the implications of rules or standards that tolerance becomes problematic as a virtue. Such an account opposes tolerance and authenticity and forces us, as it were, to be apologetic about tolerance. But if we take proper account of the continuing problems of co-ordination that must invariably be overcome by any individual who would act ethically and authentically in relations with those in her own tradition, a different picture emerges. Now we can understand that tolerance is conducive to the living of a good life in all conditions and circumstances, and recognise that authentic ethical action by an individual within a

---

[8] These points are developed much more extensively in Barnes, *Understanding Agency*, wherein it is argued that human beings affect each other *causally* in their social relations, and that it is this causal connection that results in the co-ordination of their actions and the alignment of their understandings.

tradition entails acting as a member, respectful and tolerant of other members.[9] Like courage, tolerance is necessary to life as a participant in a cultural tradition, and normal and natural to the human beings who invariably so live. And again like courage, tolerance may be cultivated and developed by and amongst participants as a primary virtue, conducive to the living of a good life within their tradition. There is no paradox of tolerance.

TOLERANCE WITHIN AND BETWEEN TRADITIONS

Always and everywhere, human beings live in collectives and carry forward a shared cultural tradition. Always and everywhere, therefore, they live in tolerant interaction with recognised others, and will continue to do so even if and as they seek to change how they live. This does not mean, of course, that they live without reference to standards and rules, or that there are no limits to what they will tolerate. Rather, it means that in referring to standards and rules they are actually referring to each other's past actions as instantiations of them, and that on the basis of such references they sustain co-ordination and a continuing shared sense of what actions are tolerable and what are not. Should we wish to reify all this into an idealised picture, then we might say that, in all societies, tolerant interaction 'within' cultural traditions sustains systems of standards with associated tolerances.[10] But it is important to recognise that this apparently innocuous picture is offered not as a minor adjustment to current individualistic accounts of cultural traditions, but as an attempt to shift our understanding away from them altogether.

An analogy may help to convey what this shift involves. The term 'tolerance' is widely encountered in the culture of engineering, and its technical sense therein is not greatly different from its everyday sense. An artefact may be assembled from parts manufactured to specific 'tolerances'. Imagine that a part is specified as 'x' cm. long, but that any length between 'x+y' and 'x-y' cm. is regarded as tolerable: any part with a length in this range may be used in assembling the artefact. It is tempting to speak here of 'x' as the ideal length, and of 'y' as specifying what errors or mistakes or lapses will nonetheless be tolerated. But this beguiling image is a misleading one. It suggests that zero-tolerance is the ideal, and that the magnitude 'y' represents a compromise between what the designer would have wished, on the one hand, and the limitations of manufacturing processes and the high costs of achieving accuracy therein, on the other. But in truth a designer who proceeds in terms of zero-tolerance, and only later adjusts to something more 'realistic' if it is necessary, deploys an inadequate ideal vision that may threaten the success of her entire project; whereas one who attends to tolerances from the start, as part of her ideal vision of the artefact, is likely to fare better. Indeed, an innovation in design that allows a

---

[9] It can be asked of any individualistic rhetoric of authenticity that fails to emphasise this, whether it does not thereby inadvertently valorise solipsism at one level and totalitarianism at another.

[10] The vision of traditions deployed in this essay sits awkwardly with some of the vocabulary presently in routine use in relation to them, vocabulary that I have nonetheless continued to use for convenience. There is a danger that to speak of what goes on 'within' traditions may mislead. And again, it is important to recognise that the 'objective' standards of traditions can be no more than inter-subjectively accepted standards, and that even this formulation threatens to mislead.

widening of tolerances can be a triumph in some contexts, and permit the manufacture of something closer to an uncompromisingly engineered product.

The key formal point here is that, sameness being intransitive, exact reproducibility is impossible in principle in any production process. Even the best conceivable engineering must accordingly recognise its own inherent limitations. At times great precision may be called for in engineering processes. But however high the level of precision that is specified, it is also the specification of a corresponding set of tolerances.[11] A conception of an artefact wherein tolerances are essential to its functioning is what is actually required, and of design as something that encompasses tolerances from the start. And similarly, it is a shift away from a zero-tolerance ideal of an authentic ethical life to one wherein tolerances are recognised as essential that is proposed here. Just as functioning artefacts are validly described as interacting parts whose dimensions fall within specific tolerances, so are cultural traditions validly described as interacting participants whose actions fall within specific tolerances. But whereas artefacts have external makers, cultural traditions do not. The tolerances intrinsic to the continued unfolding of a tradition are continually recreated from 'within', by interacting human beings who recognise each other as members of the collective that carries and constitutes it.

Some important features of the rhetoric of toleration are brought to the fore when cultural traditions are properly conceptualised, and the tolerances always incarnate in them are acknowledged. In particular, there is then no danger of overlooking the distinction between the tolerances actually established in a society, and what is said of tolerance and/or toleration in its rhetoric and reflective discourse. With regard to tolerances, it is important to recognise that, whilst particular cases may be widened or narrowed, there is no means of comparing the magnitude of one tolerance with that of another, and hence no means of indefeasibly identifying one society as more tolerant than another. And again, whilst tolerances may be varied they cannot be eradicated; they are bound to continue to exist whether or not members would consciously have it so, and whether or not they are explicitly spoken of. Hence, the reflections on toleration discernible in the rhetoric of a society, and its own accounts of where and in what respects it is tolerant, need careful interpretation. Indeed, whilst such rhetoric may have the form of an argument 'for' tolerance or toleration, or of a call to forego all truck with them in favour of rigour and principle, it will always be put forth in a setting of tolerant interaction that is going to persist. However it is formulated, therefore, it is likely to be best understood as a performative rhetoric, used by parties seeking to modify, or relocate, or shore up, the tolerances incarnate already in specific practices.[12] A rhetoric informed by these kinds of purpose is

---

[11] There is, of course, a regress involved in remaining within tolerances, that is, in conforming to standards of tolerance which cannot themselves be applied other than tolerantly. The regress has to end in a practice. Consider the practice of sorting grade 1 (large) eggs for sale: a mesh suffices for the task even though it will not pass through the same set of eggs if a run-through is repeated, and even though it is subject to wear.

[12] Rhetoric of this kind is part of a discourse that rehearses possibilities well beyond the tolerable boundaries of action, in order, as it were, to encompass, contextualise and hence evaluate the merits of those boundaries. Such a discourse is close to what is often casually referred to as 'free speech', and there is here the beginning of an argument on behalf of 'free speech' as something to be singled out for toleration in any ideal vision of how we should live.

going to be directed predominantly toward sites where there are recognised *problems*, whether because tolerant interaction is tenuous or unstable, or because adverse effects are reckoned to be associated with tolerances that are too narrow, or broad, or ill-defined.

Where are such sites likely to be located? No doubt they may be found anywhere, but in our own complex, highly differentiated and culturally diverse societies they are especially prone to cluster around the points of contact between different cultural traditions. The most remarked problems of tolerance and toleration in these societies do indeed arise where the members of such traditions encounter each other, either directly, or else indirectly through the mediation of the state and its associated institutions. They arise because members of different sub-cultures move all the time beyond them, in contexts wherein radically disparate tolerances are operative, and because what is legally tolerated exceeds the tolerances established in most of those sub-cultures precisely so that all of them may be held in stable relations with the polity. It goes without saying, of course, that a major function of the rhetoric of tolerance in differentiated societies is precisely to press for the modification, generally the widening, of the tolerances of specific problematic sub-cultures so that they move closer to what is legally tolerated. And indeed efforts to encourage 'tolerance' in this specific sense, in the furtherance of peace, may well be ethically defensible, even laudable, political and educational projects in societies such as ours.

Nothing said here, however, has any positive bearing either upon the empirical problem of how to induce greater tolerance between traditions, or the moral and ethical problem of how far such tolerance should extend. It merely affords some modest reassurance to those directly engaged with those problems. If the present argument is correct, then they need not fear the charge that in countenancing tolerance they are sacrificing a genuinely ethical orientation on the altar of expediency.[13] For even within traditions difference must constantly be confronted as a part of a tolerant interaction, and no fundamental distinction can any longer be drawn between what must appertain within traditions and what may appertain between them, as far as the toleration of difference is concerned.

Of course, it is tempting to do more than merely draw reassurance from what has been said. The tolerant interactions of the fellow-members of a tradition might be thought attractive as a model for how citizens should rightly relate to those stranger-members of their citizenry who belong to a different tradition. The mere existence of difference in the second case might be reckoned of no greater consequence than its mere existence in the first. Recognition of the tolerance that exists in the first case might be held to legitimate the introduction of greater tolerance into the second. However, this would be to press far beyond anything argued here. Indeed, the present argument can also be extended in the opposite direction. For to stress that difference is ubiquitous provokes the question of what it is, in that case, that keeps traditions distinct and separate notwithstanding, and serves as a reminder that boundaries between traditions are sustained by far more than the differences and similarities in their practices and standards.

---

[13] This is not to deny that much of the sophistry currently being poured forth in actual efforts to secure 'tolerance' does indeed merit just such criticism.

Formally speaking, there may be as much difference in practice and in the evaluation of practices within traditions as there is between them, which means that different traditions cannot be defined simply as sets of different practices and standards. It is necessary to look to the interactive basis of traditions, and to make reference to their carriers, even in describing what they are. Different traditions must be recognised as different sets of members, in differentiated networks, who coordinate their practices separately, around different foci, by reference to each other rather than to non-members. Thus, for example, adjacent conflicting street-corner gangs, or two sets of citizens each disapproving of the presence of the other within their territories, or groups of football fans with their renowned virtuosity in projecting contempt and disdain for each other, may be strikingly similar in the general tenor of their practical moral and ethical judgements, even as they assert cultural difference and distinctiveness. And the function of what little is marked as different and distinctive here seems often to be to display and celebrate distinctiveness itself, so that participants can remain interactively aligned, not with the appropriate set of standards, but with the appropriate set of members, as they coordinate their actions overall. Traditions of this sort may, in the extreme case, differ only in the distinctions and discriminations they make between members and non-members, and tolerance of the other may be a matter, not of a collective moderating its hostility to difference, but of its desisting from continuing to manufacture it.[14]

This brief allusion to the way that traditions are always incarnate in the activities of particular collectives points to a vast number of additional problems, many of which are sadly neglected in theoretical discussions of tolerance. But the allusion is made here, at the very end of this essay, only to make clear the limits of its argument. By considering what is necessarily involved in participation in a cultural tradition, I have sought to show that tolerant interaction, far from derogating from a genuinely moral and ethical life, must actually be constituted into any ideal conception of it, and recognised as a crucial aspect of the essential relations of mutual respect between participants. But this confirmation that tolerance is indeed very much more than a secondary virtue is not a sufficient basis upon which to advocate the extension or broadening of existing patterns of tolerance. Several other problems must be addressed before an argument of that sort can be made. One is the familiar problem of identifying the limits of tolerable behaviour. Another is that of delineating the proper scope and bounds of tolerant interaction. The argument of this essay should make this second problem recognisable as a version of a more familiar one – that of specifying the specific moral agents with whom efforts to engender a good life should be made. But to recognise this is not to solve the problem, and indeed no solution to it is offered here.[15] What is claimed is that if we live in social

---

[14] Indeed, it can be misleading to speak of intolerance in this kind of situation, and it would often be better to analyse what is involved as an aspect of processes of status exclusion. But neither everyday discourse nor the technical literatures are so fastidious, and both will continue to speak, for example, of racial and religious intolerance, when referring to collective exclusionary strategies.

[15] What has been said makes the search for an answer more difficult. For my arguments are premised on the intransitivity of sameness, whilst attempts to extend moral standing to others like to proceed by pointing to those ways in which others are the same as ourselves. (This is true, not just of efforts to

relations with others then we will be tolerant, but of the others with whom we should enter into such relations nothing is said. A different set of arguments is needed to deal with this problem.

universalise across human beings, but also of recent highly visible efforts to secure moral standing for animals.)

CHAPTER 2

MONTAIGNE: THE EMBODIMENT OF IDENTITY AS GROUNDS FOR TOLERATION[*]

Ingrid Creppell

"To give The Flesh its weapons to defeat the Book"
From "Montaigne," Auden, *Collected Poems*

One of the most important and pressing issues facing political thinkers today is the conflict between identity groups that has mushroomed in the last quarter century and accelerated since the fall of communism. Can the concept of toleration provide resources for thinking about how to respond to such a conflict? What does it require that we do and what are the conditions for its realization? If we stick to what many have held as the standard definition—rejection or disapproval of a practice or belief followed by a constraining of oneself from repressing it—then the usefulness of the idea has clear limits. When mobilized communities of people confront one another with charges of injustice, betrayal, heresy or social repression, then the two-step personal morality of disapproval and then allowance cannot adequately account for thinking about how we ought to engage with one another. If we seek to make political and social conditions of toleration among diverse people a stable reality, then we need to flesh out more deeply and widely what that depends upon.

Indeed, if we go back to the history of toleration, it becomes obvious that the essence to which it has been reduced was not its original impulse. In the sixteenth and seventeenth centuries, following the Reformation, when toleration was first constructed as a general political norm, its objective was to create conditions of peaceful collective life among diverse groups of believers. Those arguing for toleration had a double

[*] I would like to thank Andrew Altman, Dario Castiglione, Richard Dees, John Ferejohn, Iain Hampsher-Monk, Jack Knight, Alan Levine, Catriona McKinnon, and Garrath Williams for comments on versions of this essay.

motivation: to allow for differences and to create conditions of political community. Many strands of change went into helping this new political possibility survive in the long run. Would the general public divided into religious camps accept explicit policies of toleration imposed by political rulers in the interest of the state or argued for by religious innovators? Part of what enabled them to do so was a revaluation of values. That is, what people came to perceive as worth killing and dying for changed. Notably, it is not a full-fledged moral principle justifying toleration as an individual virtue that led to toleration as a political and social norm. But change at the level of individual morality had to happen to ground toleration in a more generalizable language. In this essay, I examine one strand of change in moral valuation underpinning political toleration: ideas about the body, time and the self as explored by Michel de Montaigne. I would suggest that we can extract from this historical analysis a way to think about grounding toleration today, when we aim for political and social toleration. One important means to that end is a recognition of the value of our embodied selves.

Montaigne confronted the problem of interminable religious and political conflict in a stark new way. He recognized the need to create a new attitude toward oneself and public obligations, but instead of questioning directly the nature of political bonds, Montaigne performed a profound act of cultural invention by putting himself on display. This was an act not only of diversion but of basic revaluation of what ought to matter, what ought to motivate how to live one's own life. The question of identity is at the center of Montaigne's *Essays*.[1] His perspective set the ground for what would become major keys of modern thinking, the critique of knowledge, self-analysis, and openness to a diverse world of experience.[2] We cannot understand changes in the relation of identity and toleration in the early modern period without a reading of his work. Specifically, I focus on an issue that has not been sufficiently explored in Montaigne studies or in the foundations of toleration—Montaigne's revaluation of the body. In what follows, I begin by briefly noting three prevalent interpretations of his toleration. I then present an alternative interpretation of him, as grounding toleration in an ethical orientation that takes embodied existence as its starting point.

It is generally recognized that Montaigne was one of the most important early defenders of toleration and freedom of religion. Three explanations have been given for his position: scepticism, pragmatism, and individual privacy and self-interest. But each of these, either individually or taken all together, do not go far enough in explaining his

---

[1] M. de Montaigne, *The Complete Essays*, trans. by M.A. Screech (Harmondsworth, England: Penguin, 1991). All references to Montaigne's work are from this edition, and will be given in the main text, between brackets, indicating volume, essay and page number.

[2] Schneewind says of Montaigne that it is he who "opens up the modern era of moral thought" in R. Rorty, J.B. Schneewind, and Q. Skinner, eds., *Philosophy in History* (Cambridge: Cambridge University Press, 1984), p. 174. And more recently, Schneewind writes: "His moral scepticism was the starting point of modern moral philosophy. We have been concerned with Montaigne's questions ever since he asked them" in J.B. Schneewind, *The Invention of Autonomy* (Cambridge: Cambridge University Press, 1998), p. 45.

perspective. In the history of philosophy, Montaigne is primarily known for his defense of scepticism. Yet, as Richard Tuck argues, scepticism is not a self-evident ground for toleration.[3] One may believe that nothing is certain and *therefore* that public order requires protecting a single version of some public truth for the good of the society. Moreover, and perhaps more tellingly, Montaigne's vigorous rejection of persecution throughout his *Essays* cannot be based on scepticism, as if finding secure grounds of truth would in fact make it justifiable to burn people. Second, Montaigne was pragmatic about his politics—he supported the moderate *politique* approach rather than a radical Catholic League position.[4] He did counsel toleration of Protestants given their proliferation before and during the French civil wars. Yet, we do not continue to read Montaigne as a founder of toleration more generally because of his pragmatic attitude: this would not set him apart from many other thinkers of the time. He offers a much deeper justification for the appeal of a world of toleration than can be found in that.

Finally, Montaigne's new approach to the self has been highlighted, a focus that many consider his most important contribution to the history of political thought.[5] "All men gaze ahead at what is confronting them: I turn my gaze inwards, planting it there and keeping it there. Everybody looks before himself: I look inside myself; I am concerned with no one but me; without ceasing I reflect on myself, I watch myself, savour myself…I turn round and round in myself" (II:17, 747). This attitude toward the self is striking when we consider it in the context of his time: the extent to which he explores his "soul," his recording of the infinite movements of body and mind, and his exposition of intimate details to public view, all of which I explore more fully below. But what about Montaigne's conception of the self would ground toleration in general terms? Is it that one is no longer concerned about public issues and therefore political quietism precludes actions that are inherently coercive of others? Or is it that one's predominant desire for private satisfaction leads one to care about securing public conditions only insofar as these serve the purpose of self-interest? In the first instance, toleration is a byproduct of a private reorientation; in the second case, toleration is seen as the necessary condition for the pursuit of self-interest. There are two problems with

---

[3] R. Tuck, "Scepticism and toleration in the seventeenth century" in S. Mendus, ed., *Justifying Toleration*, (Cambridge: Cambridge University Press, 1988), 21-35.

[4] Skinner maintains that "there can be no question…that Montaigne believed very strongly in the necessity of upholding religious uniformity and traditional religious observances," and he refers to "the conservative outlook voiced by Montaigne throughout the *Essays* on the need for religious uniformity and on the rights of the Church authorities" in Q. Skinner, *The Foundations of Modern Political Thought, Volume Two* (Cambridge: Cambridge University Press, 1978) pp. 280-281. Montaigne's pragmatic toleration is rooted in an understanding of the nature of social conflict and change, and is therefore seen as a necessity. However, instead of viewing Montaigne primarily in political terms as a conservative, I would paint him as a pragmatist here and derive his apparent conservatism from this more fundamental predisposition.

[5] Schaefer writes: "If there is one point on which practically all interpreters of the *Essays* can be said to agree, it is the centrality of the 'self' (*moi*) as the object of Montaigne's investigations", in D.L. Schaefer, and D. Lewis, *The Political Philosophy of Montaigne* (Ithaca, NY: Cornell University Press, 1990), p. 312.

the emphasis upon the private individual as the foundation of toleration. First, Montaigne's understanding of the relation between the individual and the public, social world was much more complex than this explanation assumes. Second, toleration cannot be secured only on a basis of individual self-interest but requires a public culture that propagates or at least allows for a certain type of openness. To put it another way: a typical explanation of toleration in general, and of Montaigne's view of it in particular, is that the growing recognition of the value of individual freedom of thought led to toleration. But that way of being a person, or experiencing subjectivity, is fundamentally dependent on a type of social culture in which the body comes to play a prominent normative role. By elevating the individual self and privacy to paramount values, Montaigne is often seen to have denied the importance of the public or collective life,[6] and that regardless of his own commitment to public duty, he rendered social-political life secondary. This judgment mistakes the nature of Montaigne's emphasis on the self and therefore how his work supports toleration. In the long run, toleration requires attention not just to the individual but to the social/political relations between persons and how these create conditions for being an individual.

THE SALIENCE OF THE BODY

The three interpretations of Montaigne's toleration just outlined do not go to the heart of his position, nor do they recognize what is most strikingly new about it. The problem of intolerance pervaded his political and ideological world, and shadows his *Essays*. Scepticism, peace and privacy are direct responses to this problem, and yet they do not go far enough to explain the deep toleration embedded in his perception. Montaigne exemplified what we would call toleration both as a mode of openness and nonjudgment, and as a rejection of coercion. Here is a passage in which he describes his own nonjudgment:[7]

> I do not suffer from that common failing of judging another man by me: I can easily believe
> that others have qualities quite distinct from my own....I can conceive and believe that there

---

[6] This is one of Keohane's and esp. Schaefer's principle critiques of Montaigne, see N.O. Keohane, *Philosophy and the State in France* (Princeton: Princeton University Press, 1980) 98-99, p. 116); and D.L. Schaefer, and D. Lewis, *The Political Philosophy of Montaigne* (Ithaca, NY: Cornell University Press, 1990), p. 395.

[7] Note that the usual definition of toleration includes negative judgment followed by a restraining of oneself from repressing what one judges negatively. Many do not believe that an act can be called toleration if it is not premised upon the initial negative response – otherwise, one describes the allowance or nonrepression as indifference or approval, not toleration. It is certainly true that part of the power of toleration as an ethical concept is that it acknowledges the conflicts and negative judgments that people will always have about one another, and yet it insists upon restraint of the usual outcome. That two-step reasoning or psychological process is part of the intuitive appeal of toleration. But it would be misconceived to dismiss Montaigne as irrelevant for thinking about the sources of toleration because he is already inherently open: what he presents to us is the good of a world that is collectively created when its members do not insist upon uniformity.

are thousands of different ways of living and, contrary to most men, I more readily
acknowledge our differences than our similarities..... (I:37, 257, see also III:8, 1046).

Later he writes: "But the most beautiful of souls are those universal ones which are open
and ready for anything, untaught perhaps but not unteachable" (II:17, 741).

This deeper toleration was not argued for directly as a moral principle itself, but it
was supported directly through the alternative moral psychology that Montaigne's
Essays lay out. In one sense, Montaigne's *Essays* can be read as an exercise in
constructing and practicing a new moral psychology.[8] He withdrew to the solitude of his
tower in Bordeaux but his mind did not withdraw from the world. The decades-long
exercise in essaying himself—testing his limits—was undertaken in a context of
religious, political and cultural upheaval and violence. Writing the *Essays* embodied an
original mode of grappling with this world, filtering it through the many other worlds
that populated his mind. It was not so much a philosophical project as a comprehensive
effort to come to terms with the forces—political, psychological, physical, literary,
cultural, ideological—that shaped him. Montaigne believed that his own personal
odyssey could be a metaphor for others:

> Every man bears the whole Form of the human condition. Authors communicate themselves
> to the public by some peculiar mark foreign to themselves: I – the first ever to do so – by my
> universal being, not as a grammarian, poet or jurisconsult but as Michel de Montaigne (III:2,
> 908).

If we interpret what Montaigne is doing as constructing a new moral psychology, we
can better understand how toleration is central to the book. Montaigne shows the reader
a possible way to live in the world: what sorts of things one ought to pay attention to and
cultivate, alternative modes of feeling, thinking about and responding to stimuli. The
survey of life, history and ideas that he goes through is always interwoven with his
engaged response. In what follows, I will lay out how Montaigne's moral psychology
supports toleration. We can find its source in his basic reorientation of value away from
timeless, abstract truths to immediate, concrete experience.[9] The body in its complex

---

[8] W.G. Moore observes about Montaigne's last essay "On Experience": "Montaigne attacks one of the hardest
problems of morals, the subject of Nature. In none of his essays is this so firmly grasped. The test of living is
not conformity with any model of conduct thought out by men, it is conformity with laws and constitutions of
the creature we call man. This conformity we can each of us find within ourselves, and more surely than by
listening to any outside authority. This is no new note in Montaigne's writing....but we should be at a loss to
account for the frequency of this appeal to nature throughout the essay on Experience were it not plain that for
Montaigne Nature and Experience are, as it were, obverse and reverse of the same medal. In other words, he
writes about experience because he is aiming at a more direct contact with nature than books or systems or the
opinions of others can give him" W.G. Moore, "Montaigne's Notion of Experience" in *The French Mind*
(Oxford:
Clarendon Press, 1952), p. 46.

[9] In *The Machiavellian Moment*, J.G.A. Pocock writes: "the late medieval and Renaissance intellect found the
particular less intelligible and less rational than the universal" (Princeton: Princeton University Press, 1975), p.

relation to the mind and to social existence stands as a limiting point in the endless variability of morality and ideas that Montaigne delights in contemplating. This centrality of the body is clear throughout the *Essays*, a very physical, visceral book. He argues the value of corporeality directly and indirectly via the images and topics that it takes up (animals, death, food, illness, nature, sex, suicide, war). "We are always dealing with Man, whose nature is wondrously corporeal" (III:8, 1054). Or earlier, "We are not bringing up a soul; we are not bringing up a body: we are bringing up a man. We must not split him in two. We must not bring up one without the other." (I:26, 185). Speaking about the body in the very last chapter of the book he writes: "There is no part unworthy of our concern in this gift which God has given to us; we must account for it down to each hair. It is not a merely formal commission to Man to guide himself according to Man's fashioning: it is expressly stated, inborn, most fundamental, and the Creator gave it to us seriously and strictly" (III:13, 1266).[10]

The turn toward the body as a moral orientation did not lead to privatism or hedonism. Rather it gave him a vantage point from which to condemn, in the starkest terms, the intolerance generally accepted at the time concerning three highly public issues: witchcraft persecutions, the use of torture for political purposes, and Spanish colonization of the Americas. During the flare-up of witchcraft persecutions in the sixteenth century, which such thinkers as Bodin supported, Montaigne scathingly criticized those who believed in and killed so-called witches. In one of his concluding chapters "On the lame," Montaigne writes: "To kill people, there must be sharp and brilliant clarity; this life of ours is too real, too fundamental, to be used to guarantee these supernatural and imagined events" (III:11, 1167). And he continues, "After all, it is to put a very high value on your surmises to roast a man alive for them" (1169). In "On conscience" and more elaborately "On cruelty" (II:11), he considers torture and the cruelty that feeds on itself in the civil wars, and denies that we ought to resign ourselves to this bloodshed. Finally, in one of the most moving passages in the *Essays*, Montaigne denounces the chauvinistic horrors of the Spanish Conquistadors' treatment of the Indians in the new world. On these issues, Montaigne has no problem judging those who

---

4. He then goes on to explore the transformation in the understanding and valuation of time and history. I would suggest that a parallel transformation, one indeed linked to it, is that of the significance of the body, of the physicality and particularity of the human being in time.

[10] Others have analyzed the importance Montaigne places on the body – see W.G. Moore, "Montaigne's Notion of Experience" (1952); M.A. Screech, *Montaigne and Melancholy* (Selinsgrove: Susquehanna University Press, 1983); J. Starobinski, *Montaigne in Motion* trans. by A. Goldhammer (Chicago: University of Chicago Press, 1985). Screech, for instance, notes Montaigne's debts to Aristotle and Sebond among others along these lines. Note Sayce's comment about why Montaigne is not usually considered a philosopher: "It is not just that he argues in the abstract the influence of bodily processes on thought, which is what materialists and even perhaps existentialists may be held to do, but that his own thinking is at every point vivified or contaminated (whichever one prefers) by the pressure of sheer physical life" in R.A. Sayce, *The Essays of Montaigne* (Northwestern University Press, 1972), pp. 180-81.

would coerce others. He cuts through the layers of justification and obfuscation of these acts and denounces them as brutal inflictions of bodily suffering, which ought not to be justified in any language or ideology. The body here is not a retreat from the public but a means of engaging and judging it. Montaigne's position asserts the sheer value of life as it exists for any particular human being. In questioning the Stoic's concern with death, Montaigne writes: "Life must be its own objective, its own purpose. Its right concern is to rule itself, govern itself, put up with itself" (III:12, 1191). What exists without doubt is physical life, and the moral logic is that one ought to create and nurture it rather than destroy and tear it apart.

To claim that Montaigne upholds life above all, including goals like salvation or truth, does not directly show us how this position leads to toleration. "Life" is endlessly variable. For humans who live with minds and in societies, not simply as animals with instincts of the body, being alive is always filtered through ideal and particular forms: we believe many different things about the world and we feed ourselves, sleep, procreate, and function through culture. Natural human lives and societies are customized and diversified. How would the moral psychology that Montaigne develops in his book enable persons who are attached to different forms of living to accept those unlike themselves? N answering this question, I begin by looking at two dimensions which affect the possibility of toleration—the individual/social relation and the mind/body relation. I will explore how Montaigne thought we ought to understand the pulls within each of these relations and orient ourselves toward them in such a way as to minimize violent conflict and coercion. First, in regard to the individual/social relation, the individual is, on the one hand, embodied through society/culture, and this makes the particularity deriving from the culture a source of irreducible meaning that must be respected. On the other, the possibility of individual freedom rests in protecting particularities not only of societies but within persons. Thus, particularity is itself a value: Montaigne was a skeptic about any particular value, but he was not a skeptic about the value of particularity. Second, in the mind/body dimension, Montaigne asserts that the fact that we live in a physical body is as important as the fact that we have a mind. The body pushes the person toward valuing life in the present-time, toward immediacy, a perspective that can underscore an attitude of toleration.

INDIVIDUAL/SOCIETY: THE SPECTRUM OF PARTICULARITY

A root distinction in western thought is the individual-society dichotomy. Liberalism is defined in part as the protection of the individual against group or social demands. Along these lines, Montaigne is often seen as a founder of ideals of individual liberty. The following famous quotation would seem to exemplify Montaigne's support for individual freedom:

> We should set aside a room, just for ourselves, at the back of the shop, keeping it entirely free
> and establishing there our true liberty, our principal solitude and asylum (I:39, 270, 272).

But this sharp contrast between the individual and social is misleading for Montaigne's depiction of the person. Montaigne did not reject the social in favor of the individual, but held that the social world and the individual assertion of self against it represented different ways of living that ought to be accepted for their distinctive compulsions. Put simplistically, we might say that in the face of the dichotomy, the social represents the body, the weightedness, limits and embeddedness of one's orientation to the world. The predisposition one ought to cultivate toward it is respect. In contrast, the individual represents the unbounded, creative, limitless possibilities of the self. The predisposition that one ought to cultivate toward this is freedom.

The person that Montaigne describes in such many-sided terms—the creature of individuality—is as much a socially embedded and constrained person as he/she is a holder of individual liberty. A profound theme of the *Essays* is the constant magnetic force of society, custom, law and others in every capacity to hold a person and to make that person who she or he is. This understanding of the person as simultaneously bonding to and retracting from society indicate that we ought not to define his toleration as supporting only one half of this complex relation. For Montaigne we simply cannot be frozen in one or the other of these incarnations. Because we can never escape society, we ought not to try to base a moral psychology on overcoming it. The room at the back of the shop—an "arriere boutique" all one's own—is precisely a protected space, but one that necessarily remains attached to a larger orientation. It cannot be back of anything if there is no social space to give meaning to the noninterference and protectiveness that one finds there.

SOCIETY: INFUSING PARTICULAR BODIES

For Montaigne we have to understand human nature by beginning with the social: humans are always born into a social world which gives them shape and identity as persons, individually and collectively. "There is nothing more unsociable than Man, and nothing more sociable: unsociable by his vice, sociable by his nature" (I:39, 267). Montaigne held that the obligations society places on persons should not be dismissed as morally secondary to the dictates of the self. Here is an eloquent defense:

> To my taste, those men who steal away from common obligations and from that infinity of
> thorny, many-sided conventions which a punctiliously decent man treats as binding when
> living in society spare themselves a great deal, no matter what singular penance they inflict
> upon themselves. That is to die a little so as to flee the pain of a life well lived. They may win
> some other prize, but never, it seems to me, the prize for difficulty; for where hardship is

concerned there is nothing worse than standing upright amid the floods of this pressing world, loyally answering and fulfilling all the duties of one's charge. (II:33, 831-32).[11]

These observations are not made simply to assert that one ought to fulfil one's social duties. They also indicate a way of approaching life: the thick of social involvement demands more of a person than the difficulties of solitude. His explicit moral injunctives indicate that Montaigne did not counsel withdrawal for the individual. More interesting however than Montaigne's traditional demands in this regard are his trenchant observations about how society forms a person and the moral conclusions we can draw from this.

We are by nature constructed to give ourselves a second social nature:

> Whatever the cost, human society remains cobbled and held together. No matter what position you place them in, men will jostle into heaps and arrange themselves in piles, just as odd objects thrust any-old-how into a sack find their own way of fitting together better than art could ever arrange them (III:9, 1083).

Society is functional at one level—ordering a group of persons—but it takes on, at the individual level, a subjective compulsion. Montaigne's description of the existential fact of social embeddedness is sometimes presented in negative terms:

But the principal activity of custom is so to seize us and to grip us in her claws that it is hardly in our power to struggle free and to come back into ourselves....Since we suck them in with our mothers' milk and since the face of the world is presented thus to our infant gaze, it seems to us that we were really born with the property of continuing to act that way. And as for those ideas which we find to be held in common and in high esteem about us, the seeds of which were planted in our souls by our forefathers, they appear to belong to our genus, to be natural. (I: 23, 130)

Custom or habit is "a violent and treacherous schoolmistress" and he elaborates this physically coercive image: "she establishes in us, little by little, stealthily, the foothold of her authority; but having by this mild and humble beginning settled and planted it with the help of time, she soon uncovers to us a furious and tyrannical face against which we no longer have the liberty of even raising our eyes. We can see her at every turn forcing the rules of nature" (I:23, 77). Finally, he concludes: "Nature brought us forth free and unbound: we imprison ourselves in particular confines" (III:9, 1101). The language of constriction that Montaigne uses to describe society's hold would seem to imply that we

---

[11] Another version of this attitude is found here: "Sometimes we must make a loan of ourselves to those we love: even when we should wish to die for ourselves we should break off our plans on their account. It is a sign of greatness of mind to lay hold of life again for the sake of others, as several great and outstanding men have done" (II:35, 849). And in Book III: 10, "he who does not live a little for others hardly lives at all for himself: "*Qui sibi amicus est, scito hunc amicum omnibus esse.*" [Seneca: Know that a man who feels loving friendship for himself does so for all men.] (1138).

should do all we can to escape. Yet, given that that is impossible, how ought we to interpret what he is saying?

Society constructs persons physically through the habits, tastes and customs it imprints upon the body. Like the constraints of physical nature, those erected by society are absorbed by persons so deeply that it is exceedingly difficult to extract oneself from their grip. Particular habits infuse lives with substance, distinctiveness and coherence. Their magnetism is described on one occasion as follows:

> Consider the diversity between the way of life of my farm-labourers and my own. Scythia and the Indies have nothing more foreign to my force or my form. And this I know: I took some boys off begging into my service: soon afterwards they left me, my cuisine and their livery merely to return to their old life. I came across one of them gathering snails from the roadside for his dinner: neither prayer nor menace could drag him away from the sweet savour he found in poverty. Beggars have their distinctions and their pleasures as do rich men, and, so it is said, their own political offices and orders. Such are the effects of Habituation. (III:13, 1229)

One implication of viewing society as a naturalized force which thereby creates meaning for persons is that we ought to give it a prima facie respect. His extensive historical and anthropological interests led Montaigne to dwell on the variability of human customs and rules. He pointedly notes that as political theorists,

> we have to take men already fashioned and bound to particular customs: we are not begetting them anew like Pyrrha and Cadmus. We may have the right to use any means to arrange them and to set them up afresh, but we can hardly ever wrench them out of their acquired bent without destroying everything (III:9, 1083).[12]

If we see custom and society as investing our bodies with ingrained predispositions and particularized types of pleasure and pain, then rejection or denial of another culture is a type of physical harm. Consequently, the importance of preserving various cultures is based not on a "conservative" attitude toward change but rather on his perception that social practices embody persons. The goodness of particular cultures and worlds comes not from being old per se but from constituting the tissue out of which humans have lived life, providing an organic order to a mass of human desires, expectations and demands. Much of his conservative rhetoric in the chapter "On habit: and on never easily changing a traditional law," derives from the observation that the destruction of laws and customs is akin to physical harm and full scale change works only by violence. On this interpretation, Montaigne does not encourage adherence to tradition and laws because of the radical indeterminacy of knowledge of good and bad (the skeptical argument), but rather because he believes that there will be less suffering in the world if we do so. A

---

[12] "A polity is like a building made of diverse pieces interlocked together, joined in such a way that it is impossible to move one without the whole structure feeling it" (I: 23, 134).

recognition that custom is a 'second nature' ought to make anyone reticent to attack another community.

But as always with Montaigne, the matter doesn't rest here. Innovation and criticism are not automatically questionable for him. First, the interlocked entity that we conceive of as a stable society is always in a constant state of change:

> There is no existence that is constant, either of our being or of that of objects. And we, and our judgment, and all mortal things go on flowing and rolling unceasingly. Thus nothing certain can be established about one thing by another, both the judging and the judged being in continual change and motion (II:12, 455).

Furthermore, the whole society at times comes unraveled and Montaigne believed that France was suffering through such an "extraordinary accident." In that case, innovation is inevitable: "When you resist the growth of an innovation that has come to introduce itself by violence, it is a dangerous obligation and a handicap to keep yourself in check and within the rules,...against those who are free as air, to whom everything is permissible" (I: 23 89). Significantly, Montaigne ends his chapter on custom with the same words that end his chapter on freedom of conscience: "it would be better to make the laws will what they can do, since they cannot do what they will" (I: 23, 89).[13] We are not condemned to a total uncertainty about deciding between what is simply different and what is wrong/evil and must therefore not be tolerated. We don't respect cultures because they are old but because they provide viable and life-affirming possibilities for their inhabitants as embodied persons.

Montaigne's cosmopolitism is a desire to experience the world and communicate with those in it. If we wish to do so, then a recognition that all persons are indelibly particular would force us to accept that as a starting point of interaction. Most importantly, not all social embeddedness is justified, for the sheer fact of being either collective or old does not justify it. If it is the body that justifies the power of the collective, then it is also the body that judges the substance and meaning given by a collective. As I noted earlier, practices of torture, witchcraft persecutions and the destruction of the native cultures by Spanish conquests were all condemned in the harshest terms by reference to the body.

INDIVIDUAL: CREATING PARTICULAR MINDS

As one anchor of toleration, then, Montaigne depicted the person as shaped by the particularity of the collective world of which he or she was a part. To repress social particularity is to cause harm nearly equivalent to bodily harm. But from the point of

---

[13] The concluding words of II: 19 are: "And yet I prefer to think, for the reputation of our kings' piety, that having been unable to do what they would, they have pretended to will what they could."

view of the individual living in society, the pressure from the collective may be experienced subjectively as a wholly negative force. Thus, while the view of society as a naturalized source of meaning and substance gives a justification for tolerating social/customary differences, it does not necessarily recognize a demand for individual freedom, of beliefs, ideas or practices against the society or others in it. One point of Montaigne's writing the *Essays* was precisely to push himself beyond the confines of a settled world of convention and appearance. Society may clamp down on our bodies through instilling habits and traditions, but we can hope for a realm of freedom in the mind's capacity to transcend social strictures, standards and beliefs:

> [L]et us disentangle ourselves from those violent traps which pledge us to other things and which distance us from ourselves. We must unknot those bonds and, from this day forth, love this or that but marry nothing but ourselves. That is to say, let the rest be ours, but not so glued and joined to us that it cannot be pulled off without tearing away a piece of ourselves, skin and all. The greatest thing in the world is to know how to live to yourself. (I:39, 271-272).

In passages such as this, we can see how Montaigne finds freedom in release from social embeddedness. But his freedom, the form of release from society is of a particular kind. It is not on the one hand, the liberal impulse to experiment with various forms of living, nor on the other hand is it a Stoic version of freedom, a life of *ataraxia* or imperturbability of the passions, the life of inner tranquillity and outer obedience. Freedom for the individual is primarily found in a building up of the internal self as distinct from society's picture of what that self should be, such that true self-reflection can proceed.

How was that inner voice or eye woven together from the kaleidoscope of pieces that make up the experiences of a person? The search for form is itself part of the exercise of freedom. The mind can lead the person out into wide open pastures or dense forests:

> Just as fallow lands, when rich and fertile, are seen to abound in hundreds and thousands of different kinds of useless weeds...so too with out minds. If we do not keep them busy with some particular subject which can serve as a bridle to reign them in, they charge ungovernably about, ranging to and fro over the wastelands of our thoughts (I:8, 30).

And in concluding this same short chapter, he describes his own motivation for dwelling on his mind:

> [I]t bolted off like a runaway horse, taking far more trouble over itself than it ever did over anyone else; it give birth to so many chimeras and fantastic monstrosities, one after another, without order or fitness, that, so as to contemplate at my ease their oddness and their strangeness, I began to keep a record of them, hoping in time to make my mind ashamed of itself (I:8, 31).

What gives order to this wildness are settled patterns that one can find and that one adopts as right for oneself. A person must give him or herself internal standards, which both absorb and question the outside world and which create a depth to self-reflection. Toleration is related to this type of freedom in two ways: first it protects the possibility of such a freedom by enabling sources of particularity. Second, when one thinks of and experiences oneself in these terms one will be more open to toleration; in other words, a moral psychology of this nature is inherently more open to others.

Montaigne's exploration of the mind is from within and beyond the boundaries set by the particularity of society. Montaigne presents a complex psychology in which the individual's experience of itself is necessarily embedded in social norms but also attempts to break free of these and to give itself its own individual standards.[14] Note this remark: "My one desire is that each of us should each be judged apart and that conclusions about me should not be drawn from routine *exempla*." (I:37, S257). This is a desire for others' judgment of him, not for a life lived in solitary hedonism. His fundamental ethical claim here is that the value and appreciation that the individual has of itself must not collapse into the standards imposed upon it by the outer society.[15] How would we protect the capacity of the individual's mind from sinking into an unreflective acceptance of beliefs and dogma around it?

For Montaigne we are creatures who live in a spectrum of particularities: within the singular person, between individuals, between societies/customs. Within a person, different selves predominate at different times and two (or more) aspects of the self may be balanced or compete simultaneously. There is no permanent resolution of the self. We change constantly and are confronted with particular angles or persona that are surprising: "If my soul could only find a footing I would not be assaying myself but resolving myself. But my soul is ever in its apprenticeship and being tested" (III:2, 908). And later in the same vein he notes:

> in the natures of men, there are hidden parts which cannot be divined, silent characteristics which are never revealed and which are sometimes unknown even to the one who has them but which are awakened and brought out by subsequent events (III:2, 917).

The theme of the self's inconstancy and of its layers and diversity is central to the book, and there are many memorable passages that could be brought to bear. It might be summed up in this: "there is as much difference between us and ourselves as there is between us and other people" (II:1, 380).

How ought we to pay attention to this inward diversity? Does reflection on it lead only to a series of selves or a pastiche of various fragments? For this inner diversity to provide one landing-place in a psychology of toleration, a person—as an agent—would have to appreciate, not fear or avoid, the depths of the self. That is, for a person who acts

---

[14] The extreme complexity of Montaigne's thoughts on this subject is explored in J. Starobinski, *Montaigne in Motion* (1985).

[15] The chapter "On Solitude" in particular elaborates this desire for being able to withdraw self-approval from the standards set by the crowd.

in a world external to the self, this experience of the self's internal particularisms must be a source of positive orientation and not a source of confusion, incoherence and frustration, which might then lead the person to assert a singular dominant and often intolerant public identity. Part of Montaigne's objective is to demonstrate by his own action of self-reflection the intrinsic value of exploring the myriad selves within a person. He brings the reader along on the voyage, as if leading an exploration of a foreign land. Self-knowledge is made less threatening and more familiar. If one motivation for intolerance is the desire to demonstrate unity and simplicity of identity by publicly asserting superiority, then the impulse toward this is undercut if unity and simplicity of identity are consciously recognized as impossibilities, and their opposite is seen as a source of meaning and enrichment. It is true that many people do not want to explore the darker regions of the self. Montaigne's method is to bring these regions into the light of day and make them less terrifying.[16]

We need to pass to the next level—relations between individuals—to see how out of multiplicity the self is made more whole. Here Montaigne highlights the particularities between individuals, which he sets forth in three modes. First, he dwells on the distinctiveness of persons by describing their unique appearance, habits, and traits, ranging from examples such as the peasant thief Pincher in Armagnac (who became rich in his old age and gave back to the heirs of those from whom he had stolen) to the looks, peculiarities, and excellences of Socrates or Alexander. He often contrasts himself to others by giving intimate details of his own features, experiences, desires, etc. throughout the book. Second, Montaigne presents an idea of a person's "master-form":

> Provided that he listen to himself there is no one who does not discover in himself a form entirely his own, a master-form which struggles against his education as well as against the storm of emotions which would gainsay it (III:2, 914).

What this master form might be—given the flux of the individual personality referred to above—is a key question of the *Essays* that I shall not try to answer here. As a fixed, final endpoint, it remains permanently elusive. Yet, the search for individual integrity is essential to human freedom and is an objective that Montaigne believes ought to guide how we live. Third, the individual's distinctiveness or wholeness vis-à-vis others comes out in the various roles and social forms that he or she is called upon to occupy.

> *Mundus universus exercet histrionem.* [Everybody in the entire world is acting a part.] We should play our role properly, but as the role of a character which we have adopted. We must not turn masks and semblances into essential realities, nor adopted qualities into attributes of our self (III:10, 1144).

---

[16] As one of his biographers has noted, Montaigne was "aware that hatred of self is a mortal enemy to love of others", see D. Frame, *Montaigne* (New York: Harcourt, Brace & World, 1965), 320-21.

Previously, he had asserted: "We are nothing but etiquette. We are carried away by it and neglect the substance; we cling to branches and let go of trunk and body" (II:17, 718). Montaigne's chapter attacking glory also contains extensive analysis of the sources of false distinctiveness for the individual, thereby setting up an alternative authentic individuality.

How useful is a notion of an authentic individuality? What is the substance, the "trunk and body" of a distinct person? If Montaigne begins with the transitoriness of our souls, where does the solidification of identity come from? On the one hand, relations between persons can make us lose ourselves in the external presentation of self. This he sees as a loss; yet on the other, relations between persons also give us the contrast by which to constitute ourselves. In the interplay with others, one comes to recognize the substance of what makes each person a different whole. We all have distinctive physical, mental and aesthetic constitutions, which taken as a bundle make a person unique. But while an individual gathers his or her *uniqueness* from being situated in a context of other persons, these other persons do not give the individual his moral *worth*. That intrinsic worth comes from the sheer fact of existing as life. The idea of the intrinsic worth of each person's life, however unheroic and pedestrian, reappears throughout the book. Near the end, he writes:

> What great fools we are! 'He has spent his life in idleness,' we say. 'I haven't done a thing today.' – 'Why! Have you not lived? That is not only the most basic of your employments, it is the most glorious.'… If you have been able to examine and manage your own life you have achieved the greatest task of all. Nature, to display and show her powers, needs no great destiny: she reveals herself equally at any level of life, both behind curtains or without them (III:13, 1258).

Earlier in the chapter on glory he observes "How many beautiful individual deeds are buried in the throng of a battle?" (II: 16, 707). The actions of our lives must be undertaken not with a hope for some external (social or historical) reward and recognition but because they are well-done for their own sakes. The measure by which we ought to judge ourselves must be carried about within us.

Because a cliché about liberal toleration is that it is based on the protection of the individual from the intolerant tendencies of social constraints, I have set out an alternative depiction of the relation between these two that nevertheless demonstrates the centrality of toleration. One may be tempted to describe the two models as either protecting the group or protecting the individual—the tradeoff can't be erased. But that would be wrong: when one perceives social forms as justified through their connection to the body, then it is also the body that puts limits on the allowable social practices. The latter are not justified *sui generis*. On the other hand, the freedom of the individual that Montaigne supports is not at the expense of society or against it, but essentially depends on society for its realization. Montaigne's toleration would therefore protect particularity across the board: between societies and within individuals' depth of self. But confrontation with particularity is inherently charged. It is, after all, collective particularities—of ideas, race, religion, traditions, etc.—that have caused the horrors of human intolerance. In the next section, I look at another root distinction in western thought—that between mind and body. Montaigne's focus on the body in this juxtaposition helps us to find another way in which the threat of particularity can be modified, and toleration made a less provisional part of a cultural world.

MIND/BODY: THE VALUE OF IMMEDIACY

In the traditional evaluation of the mind/body relationship, the mind (or soul) is ranked above the body. The mind is the part of the human that is elevated, beyond and something distinctly other than the body, which links us back to the animal realm. Montaigne accepts that humans are distinguished from animals insofar as they reflect on themselves and use verbal language and thought to construct worlds out of the involuntary basis of the body. "[O]f all the animals, Man alone has freedom to think and such unruly ways of doing so that he can imagine things which are and things which are not, imagine his wishes, or the false and the true!" (II:12, 514). The values of the mind in part lie in the fact that it can conceive of the world and of acting as other than what has existed in the past; it can extract itself from time, create possibilities for a better or different life. It does not only go beyond in abstracting from what is, but can also go deeper and accentuate what does exist at a particular time. And finally, it can create the illusion of holding existence constant by creating memories. These capacities make the mind an extraordinary and distinctive tool for the human moving about in the world.

In the traditional ranking of the mind and body, religious and philosophical thinkers denied the intrinsic value of the body, and considered motivations deriving from it as, for the most part, a negative weight on the soul. Montaigne completely rejects this tradition of philosophy and of the ascetic movements within the Church:

> I who am always down-to-earth in my handling of anything loathe that inhuman wisdom which seeks to render us disdainful and hostile towards the care of our bodies

and later

> I hate being told to have our minds above the clouds while our bodies are at the dinner-table....Aristippus championed only the body, as though we had no soul: Zeno embraced only the soul, as though we had no body. Both were flawed (III:13, 1256, 1257-8).[17]

---

[17] This theme is repeated throughout the book: "I certainly do not have a mind so distended and flatulent that I would go and swap a solid flesh-and-marrow joy like health for some fancied joy all wind and vapour....Health! For God's sake!" (II:37, 887) or later in remarking on his old age "Since it is the privilege of the mind to escape from old age I counsel it to do so with all my might: let it meanwhile sprout green and flourish, if it can, like mistletoe on a dead tree. But it is a traitor, I fear: it is so closely bound in brotherhood to the body that it is constantly deserting me to follow my body in its necessity" (III:5, 951).

Why did this denigration of the body matter to Montaigne? The issue is not a question of style or aesthetic preference. Montaigne believed the mind, when disconnected from the body, had a predisposition to intolerant actions. Dangers are inherent in our mental capacities to abstract from the concreteness of the here and now. In completing his description about what distinguishes humans from animals that I began above, Montaigne observed:

> But he has to pay a high price for this advantage – and he has little cause to boast about it, since it is the chief source of the woes which beset him: sin, sickness, irresolution, confusion and despair (II:12, 514).

The negative aspects of the unfettered mind are noted repeatedly. "Our minds are dangerous tools, rash and prone to go astray: it is hard to reconcile them with order and moderation" (II:12, 629) and "What an outrageous sword the mind is, even for its owner, unless he knows how to arm himself ordinately and with discretion" (II:12, 630). "We are never 'at home'" he said,

> we are always outside ourselves. Fear, desire, hope, impel us towards the future; they rob us of feelings and concern for what now is, in order to spend time over what will be – even when we ourselves shall be no more (I:3, 11).

The mind ignores values of order, moderation and discretion, and propels itself outward and into a chimerical future, toward a world that will likely never exist.

This compulsion to go beyond might be harmless if it were in search of abstract knowledge about nature, or in the use of the imagination for creative, artistic purposes, but people use ungrounded ideas as blueprints to act. What does exist and the persons who actually occupy space in the world are taken to be justifiably dominated, coerced and overridden in the service of making abstract ideas a reality. The mind motivates actions to impose on others and to create the world after its own inventions—to reshape it to fit an abstract image of what ought to be. These images themselves do not come from rational contemplation but are fed by impulses from disparate directions, often motivated by desires to dominate others for one's own aggrandizement. This is the crucial point: for Montaigne, if the mind works without a firm cognizance of the immediacy and concreteness of the body in time, it will fly off in potentially harmful and coercive directions, led as it is to make its constructions a reality.

This detrimental quality of the mind was a prominent feature of the civil wars in the context of which Montaigne wrote. He criticized those who were most led astray by abstract ideas and pure beliefs—the philosophers and religious fanatics on both sides of the confessional wars. Philosophy ought to be denounced because it failed to provide answers about how to live in the world.[18] And religious reformers ought to be denied because they sought to remake society from the top down to conform to their beliefs; possessed by religious fervor they believed that the body must be harnessed to the realization of those beliefs. In one of Montaigne's most groundbreaking chapters "On Some Lines of Virgil" (III:5), where he defends the naturalness and goodness of human sexuality, he depicts this correspondence between philosophers and religious fanatics, specifically in the coercive self-repression which lead them to a righteousness in the repression of others:

> What a monstrosity of an animal, who strikes terror in himself, whose pleasures are a burden to him and who thinks himself a curse....We show our ingenuity only by ill-treating ourselves: that is the real game hunted by the power of our mind – an instrument dangerous in its unruliness....Alas, wretched Man....You are not afraid to infringe her [Nature's] universal and undoubted laws yet preen yourself on your own sectarian and imaginary ones: the more particular, uncertain and controverted they are, the more you devote your efforts to them. The arbitrary laws of your own invention – your own parochial laws (*les regles de ta parroisse*) – engross you and bind you: you are not even touched by the laws of God and this world. (III:5, 994-995)

A mind unfettered by the body is potentially dangerous and coercive. It makes the body secondary, a mere instrument to be used for some greater glory (religious, communal or otherwise).[19] Montaigne fundamentally indicts the logic of this system of value—"are we then not beasts to call the labour which makes us bestial?" (III:5, 993)—a logic that serves as a major source of cruelty, violence and domination.

Given the potential of the mind to construct and justify situations of intolerance, how in contrast does a recognition of the body modify these impulses? One possibility is that an emphasis on the experience of pleasure gives us a perspective by which to come to understand other persons. The *Essays* dwell on the rightfulness of the pleasures that the ordinary person (as opposed to the hero, sage or ascetic saint) experiences. In reflecting on one's own body's sensations, one might be led to recognize in other persons the fact of similar (if not exact) experiences of pleasure and pain. This recognition produces a level of familiarity, more of a natural sympathetic response, in contrast to antagonism that frequently results when encountering others through abstract, alien ideas.[20] And

---

[18] Montaigne calls philosophy "this hollow and fleshless bone" (II:12, 376). He later remarks: "Boast that you have found the bean in the cake, when you consider the clatter of so many philosophical brains!" after listing a string of conflicting interpretations of the nature of God from classical authors (II:12, 383).

[19] Montaigne's critique of glory is another constant theme in the *Essays*, and one that sets him apart from the classical culture that he admired.

[20] The frame of mind that Montaigne emphasizes here – empathizing with others as sentient beings – would seem to reduce us to the level of animals, which raises the question of whether humans must then also approach animals in a similar way. A striking part of the chapter "An Apology for Raymond Sebond" is his lengthy discussion of the capacities of animals to feel and communicate, a comparison he uses to denigrate human arrogance, which believes itself to be superior to other creatures. "I make men feel the emptiness, the vanity, the nothingness of Man, wrenching from their grasp the sickly arms of human reason" (II:12, 500-501). He

importantly, an orientation toward the body and its pleasures would preclude justification of large-scale social intolerance in the name of a higher goal.

Nevertheless, an awareness of one's body does not necessarily lead to empathy or preclude coerciveness. It might lead to using others as instruments for one's own pleasure.[21] Montaigne was also highly aware that some persons derived pleasure from harm done to others, and thereby his emphasis on sentience raised the issue of the formation of our experiences of pleasure and pain. "Pain and pleasure, love and hatred, are the first things a child is aware of" (III:13, 1262) he notes, and he explores the ways in which persons develop and are educated to gain pleasure and pain from diverse sources—these are not brute, uncultivated experiences. Unfortunately, Montaigne observes, many in France at the time gained great pleasure from inflicting pain:

> I live in a season when unbelievable examples of this vice of cruelty flourish because of the licence of our civil wars...If I had not seen it I could hardly have made myself believe that you could find souls so monstrous that they would commit murder for the sheer fun of it; would hack at another man's limbs and lop them off and would cudgel their brains to invent unusual tortures and new forms of murder, not from hatred or for gain but for the one sole purpose of enjoying the pleasant spectacle of the pitiful gestures and twitchings of a man dying in agony, while hearing his screams and groans (II:11, 484).

Pleasure by itself therefore cannot be the measure of value. Pleasure must be life-affirming rather than life-denying, and his directive in the chapter "On educating children" stresses the necessity of gentleness rather than harshness in the education of a person: "Get rid of violence and force; as I see it, nothing so fundamentally stultifies and bastardizes a well-born nature" (I:26, 185). Thus, Montaigne rejects two opposing sources of value: transcendent ideals and brute pleasure.

If the body must be engaged equally with the mind, it is not simply the body as a processor of pleasure. Montaigne's emphasis on embodiment carves out a specific conception of human experience that engages the body and mind in mutually supportive roles, and he acknowledges the distinctive impulses of each. "Let the mind awaken and quicken the heaviness of the body: let the body arrest the lightness of the mind and fix it fast" (III:13, 1266). How should we understand what Montaigne is saying? The mind is

---

continues: "How can he [i.e. man], from the power of his own understanding, know the hidden, inward motivations of animate creatures? What comparison between us and them leads him to conclude that they have the attributes of senseless brutes? When I play with my cat, how do I know that she is not passing time with me rather than I with her?....Why should it be a defect in the beasts not in us which stops all communication between us? We can only guess whose fault it is that we cannot understand each other: for we do not understand them any more than they understand us" (II:12, 505,506). There follows a discussion of nonverbal forms of communication: eyes, hands, head, eyebrows, shoulders, silence, etc. The point is that we come to understand one another and "work purposefully together" because we are able to grasp the meaning of physical movements (II:12, 507). Being animals, our sentience is a profound basis for our communication.

[21] And, there is always the problem of perceiving others' bodies as repositories of impurity and danger, as explored in M. Douglas, *Purity and Danger* (London: Ark Paperbacks, 1989). 1966?

the locus of agency, the active center to which Montaigne's appeals are addressed. We must be able "to put into effect the counsel that each man should know himself" (III:13, 1219), and we can only put this counsel into effect by the volition of the mind. Hence, the value of freedom of mind is essential to his world-view. Yet, while the mind is the source of freedom and agency, it can, as we previously noted, be led astray in this capacity perhaps more easily than it moves toward self-realization. The body weights the mind and keeps it from flying off into diseased acts.[22]

There is another path, however, through which attention to the body contributes to the capacity for toleration. When the mind is wedded to the body, the person becomes highly aware of the body's existence and movement through time. Montaigne emphasized the importance of living each moment cognizant of the irreplaceable value of any particular person's experience in time and the body's embeddedness in it. "Some have lived long and lived little. See to it while you are still here" (I:20, 106). And again: "For, in the end, life is our being and our all" (II:3, 397).

> Go on then, just to see: get that fellow over there to tell you one of these days what notions and musing he stuffs into his head, for the sake of which he diverts his thoughts from a good meal and regrets the time spent eating it. You will find that no dish on your table tastes as insipid as that beautiful pabulum of his soul (III:13, 1267).

And in a key passage about the importance of time:

> Above all now, when I see my span so short, I want to give it more ballast; I want to arrest the swiftness of its passing by the swiftness of my capture, compensating for the speed with which it drains away by the intensity of my enjoyment.....Other folk enjoy all pleasures as they enjoy the pleasure of sleep: with no awareness of them....I deliberate with my self upon any pleasure....Do I find myself in a state of calm? Is there some pleasure which thrills me? I do not allow it to be purloined by my senses: I associate my Soul with it, not so that she will bind herself to it but take joy in it; not losing herself but finding herself in it; her role is to observe herself as mirrored in that happy state, to weight that happiness, gauge it and increase it. (III:13, 1263)

Through stressing the connection of the mind, body and time, Montaigne offers a view of the moral importance of a specific type of experience. When the mind focuses on the body not only does it passively experience the emotions and sensations that occupy the body, it also experiences those emotions and sensations as moving through itself and thereby leaving a sensation of the passage of time. What it may want to hold onto it cannot do so for long, as the person moves through space and time as well as thoughts and emotions.

---

[22] In his chapter "On restraining your will" he writes about how we ought to limit our desires to "accessible and contiguous pleasures": "Any action carried through without such a return on itself – and I mean a quick and genuine one – is wayward and diseased: such are those of covetous and ambitious men and of so many others who dash towards a goal, careering ever on and on" (III:10, 1143).

This passage of time can be a painful and regretted state, and the mind creates memories to retrieve and restore the desired lost time. We seek to keep what we value the same, and a reminder of the passage of all into nothing would seem to foster nihilism more than a valuation of that very present time which will not last. But while the body makes us conscious of the passage of time, in this realization there may also be a recognition of the absolute value of each moment that one lives. Each moment is irreplaceable and brings the person closer to death. Knowing that all will pass into oblivion, if one seeks value at all, one must accept and live as fully as one can in the immediacy of life:

> I who boast that I so sedulously and so individually welcome the pleasures of this life find virtually nothing but wind in them when I examine them in detail. But then we too are nothing but wind. And the wind (more wise than we are) delights in its rustling and blowing, and is content with its own role without yearning for qualities which are nothing to do with it such as immovability or density. (III:13, 1256-57)[23]

Living in the immediacy of life does not mean instant gratification or mindless sensualism. An approach to living this way induces an attitude toward others that is not instrumental or coercive. How would this psychology work? Remember that for Montaigne all humans (healthy ones at least) are basically constructed to want life and to avoid death.[24] When one lives in the present, one's way of interacting with the surrounding world is not to take a static picture and apply it to reshape an "outside" world. To do so would be to assume a value separate from the present. Rather, it is to engage with the persons, places, and events in the midst of which one finds oneself without enforcing a set script or static picture. If one is truly open to the immediacy of experience, one is struck much more by diversity of forms of life than by sameness: "no quality is so universal as diversity and variety" (III:13, 1207). The self that is cognizant

---

[23] Starobinski describes Montaigne's valuation of the present in this way: "In many places in the *Essays* Montaigne speaks of the present as the slimmest of moments, sustained solely by the evidence of its instantaneity and receiving no support at all from the past. And when he discovers that the present – his own and society's – is subject to the general decline that affects all things, his only recourse, paradoxically, is to turn his mind exclusively to the here and now, to everything that coexists with him in this moment of time" J. Starobinski, *Montaigne in Motion* (1985), p. 283.

[24] And yet remembering that death is always around the corner. Death also sits in the shadow and often is brought out into broad daylight in the *Essays*. I will merely note that at the beginning of his writing, Montaigne took a more classical Stoic attitude toward death "To practice death is to practice freedom" where the mind's overcoming fear of death taught it how to live detached from the concerns of the world and thereby free itself (I:20,96). But at the end of the *Essays* he pretty much rejects this earlier position: "If we have not known how to live, it is not right to teach us how to die, making the form of the end incongruous with the whole. If we have known how to live steadfastly and calmly we shall know how to die the same way. They may bluster as much as they like, saying that '*tota philosoforum vita commentatio mortis est* (the entire life of philosophers is a preparation for death); but my opinion is that death is indeed the ending of life, but not therefore its End; it puts an end to it; it is its ultimate point; but it is not its objective. Life must be its own objective, its own purpose" (III:12, 1190-1191).

of the concreteness of everything around inoculates itself against the fear of what is different. The point of living in immediacy is precisely to be open to contact with the world around you, a contact that generates unforeseen thoughts, emotions and sensations. We can see here how valuing immediacy is a path to toleration. The practice of living in the present precludes the value of forcing others to "believe like me" or to "be like me" because such a rigid picture dissolves into a meaningless replica of value in the face of the openendedness of experience itself. There is a porousness between the self and others which prevents defining oneself and persons one encounters in unchanging categories.

The deep toleration that Montaigne supported then is grounded in a certain way in which the mind moves about the world—attuned to the body in the here and now. On the one hand the mind is a machine, a calculator and a trap: it classifies, systematizes, ranks, compares and makes judgments. On the other hand, the mind is an explorer, adventurer, and artist:

> It makes sorties which go beyond what it can achieve: it is only half-alive if it is not advancing, pressing forward, getting driven into a corner and coming to blows; its inquiries are shapeless and without limits; its nourishment consist in amazement, the hunt and uncertainty (III:13, 1211).

Without the body, the mind is diminished, dry, and inherently prone to intolerance. Thus, it is the experience of the mind as rooted in the body and the body as illuminated by the mind that provides a foundation for toleration. A reorientation of thought away from values internal to thought itself, and toward the experiences of the body (its necessities, beauties, peculiarities, sensations) can begin to undercut the motivations toward "diseased" and intolerant actions. The mind firmly cognizant of the body will not shoot off into a bodiless future, and if the mind's rule-making is filtered through the body, it will not reduce the body to a mere instrument to be used for an abstract glory.

CONCLUSION

In conclusion, I return to the question of how we ought to locate Montaigne's importance in both the history of toleration and its grounding today. Montaigne did not articulate a direct defense of an individual moral principle of toleration *per se*. Yet the whole thrust of his work was to create an attitude toward oneself, others, and the nature of existence that would make toleration the condition of living in the midst of diversity and multiplicity. Norberto Bobbio presents the virtue *mitezza*—a notion of active meekness, a "refusal to exercise violence against anyone"[25] letting the other be himself,

---

[25] N. Bobbio, "In Praise of La Mitezza" in P. Ricoeur, ed., *Tolerance between Intolerance and the Intolerable* (Providence, RI: Berghahn Books, 1996), p. 17.

not out of passivity but as a positive stance. Much of what Montaigne supports is evocative of this notion. Yet, Bobbio holds up *mitezza* as "a nonpolitical virtue," the "antithesis of politics" (17). Montaigne offers something other than a counsel to withdraw from politics and its potential violence, because there is no alternative to coming to terms with politics.

In an age of political violence, how should that coming to terms proceed? Ethical thinking about politics must not ignore the inherently violent potential of humanity. The question should be what resources can be found for conceiving human attachment and duty that do not inherently justify categorical condemnation and domination of those who fall outside the perameters of one's particular attachment and duty. Some thinkers (Montaigne's contemporary Bodin, for example) focused on juridical, institutional measures as a means to counteract and harness divisive attachments. We might understand one inspiration of Montaigne's work as a awareness that strictly formal measures are not enough to counteract particularity—another center of gravity has to be constructed. Embodiment is part of that redirection. Montaigne does not suggest that we can or would want to loose the construction of boundaries and enter a world of postpolitics. Rather, he provides the deep ethical appeal of the embodied nature of human life, and thereby also substantive reasons for why we ought to protect this. I have tried to extract the most powerful and innovative aspects of his moral reorientation in this regard. Recognizing our embodied nature involves an attitude toward mind and body: embodiment emphasizes virtues of attentiveness to the body, to nature and to the particularity of ways of living and of each human life. This is a way of perceiving value that has potentially universal appeal, but it is different from an appeal to an abstract humanity. The need for substantive differences is rooted in our bodies and minds. A recognition of this could give political ethics a logic to both protect those differences and also acknowledge a universal perspective.

CHAPTER 3

DO WE NEED TOLERATION AS A MORAL VIRTUE?

Anna Elisabetta Galeotti

INTRODUCTION

The paradoxical nature of the moral value of toleration has been widely discussed in recent philosophical analyses.[1] The outcome of this discussion can be summarised in a *moral model* of tolerance, which specifies what kind of attitude or disposition tolerance is; the circumstances in which the attitude of toleration is the proper response; the moral basis for this attitude beyond mere prudence; and, finally, the limits of tolerance as a moral virtue.[2] This model aims, on the one hand, to accommodate the positive value generally accorded to toleration, with the negative connotation that comes from the idea of 'putting up with' something either disliked or disapproved; and, on the other, to provide the moral grounds for both the social practice and the political principle of toleration beyond a mere *modus vivendi*.

In this essay I will argue that the virtue of tolerance as proposed by the *moral model* cannot constitute the micro-foundation for the corresponding social and political principles and practice. If the model were generally adopted, it would engender an intolerant and sclerotic society.[3] And yet, if we assume that the liberal society needs some political principle of toleration to guarantee civil co-existence in

---

[1] In the literature on toleration, I have found no clear distinction between tolerance and toleration; it seems to me that there is a general tendency to use tolerance for the interpersonal attitude and toleration for the social and political principle. In this essay I tend to follow this usage.

[2] The problem of toleration as a moral virtue is addressed in many contributions to the volumes produced by the Morrell Toleration Project. For example, see S. Mendus and J Horton, eds., *Aspects of Toleration* (London: Methuen, 1985); S. Mendus and D. Edwards, eds., *On Toleration* (Oxford: Clarendon Press, 1987); S. Mendus, ed., *Justifying Toleration* (Cambridge: Cambridge University Press, 1988); S. Mendus, *Toleration and the Limits of Liberalism* (London: Macmillan, 1989); J. Horton and P. Nicholson, eds., *Toleration: Theory and Practice* (Aldershot: Avebury, 1992); J. Horton, ed., *Toleration, Identity and Difference* (London: Macmillan, 1999); S. Mendus, ed., *The Politics of Toleration* (Edinburgh: Edinburgh University Press, 1999). Other recent collections on the *moral model* of toleration comprise: D. Heyd, ed., *Toleration: An Elusive Virtue* (Princeton, N.J.: Princeton University Press, 1996); and *Ratio Juris*, special issue on toleration, Vol. 10, 1997.

[3] A sketchy outline of the political principle of toleration for contemporary pluralism can be found in A.E. Galeotti, "Contemporary Pluralism and Toleration", *Ratio Juris,* 10 (1997), 223-233.

conditions of pluralism, the moral virtue of tolerance may have an important role in bridging private and public reasons for toleration. Tolerance can provide the individual with moral reasons not to act upon her personal convictions in order to fulfil the political requirements of neutrality and impartiality. The gap between public and private morality, between the citizen and the private individual, can thus be filled by the moral virtue of toleration. In this way, tolerance works to support Rawls's overlapping consensus, in so far as it makes up for the discontinuity between morality and politics as advocated by deontological liberalism.[4]

THE MORAL MODEL OF TOLERANCE

Tolerance is the disposition to refrain from exercising one's power of interference on others' disliked actions and behaviours, which are considered important for both the tolerator and the tolerated. If good moral reasons can be provided for suspending one's convictions and for not interfering with what one dislikes or disapproves of, then tolerance appears to be a special value, since it implies sacrificing one's moral beliefs for the sake of a higher principle. The tolerator overcomes a moral conflict, and the more important her sacrifice, the more valuable is the choice for tolerance. A person tolerating out of the weakness of her moral convictions cannot properly be regarded as tolerant, but indifferent, as it will be argued below. The moral merit of tolerance lies in the effort that one makes in setting aside one's convictions in favour of a higher principle, assuming that what is being tolerated belongs to the grey area of things that can be regarded as morally objectionable, and not to things on which there seems to be a general agreement on their being universally condemned, such as killing or doing wanton harm. Indeed, tolerance is a virtue only when supported by a higher moral principle, which a theory of toleration must, in its turn, be able to provide. In any case, tolerance is valuable only within the limits of the harm principle, beyond which it becomes indulgence, and hence from a virtue turns into a vice.

In order to be defined as a virtue, tolerance must be clearly distinguished from two attitudes, which are very similar in their practical consequences, yet very different from a moral point of view, namely, indifference and acquiescence. The distinction between tolerance and indifference[5] is grounded on the notion of *important, relevant* differences as a precondition for toleration.[6] If the notion of important differences allows toleration to be distinguished from indifference, it nevertheless raises some difficulty in the model of toleration as a moral virtue. If a difference is important and it is disliked for reasons that the potential tolerator takes to be significant, then accepting the difference becomes an important matter for the tolerator. Overcoming dislike or disapproval for a higher value or principle which gives good moral reasons for accepting a disliked difference is what gives toleration

---

[4] John Rawls, *Political Liberalism* (New York: Columbia University Press, 1993).
[5] Such a distinction has been stressed by B. Crick, "Toleration and Tolerance in Theory and Practice", *Government and Opposition*, 6 (1971), 144-171. It has been further analysed by P. King, *Toleration* (London: Allen & Unwin Ltd, 1976).
[6] See especially P. Nicholson, "Toleration as a Moral Ideal", S. Mendus and J Horton, eds., *Aspects of Toleration*, 158-173.

the tolerated person is completely powerless, makes tolerance a genuine alternative to repression. But if being tolerated were just better than being persecuted, then toleration would at most be a second best, a device for a *modus vivendi* instead of a just principle for civil coexistence. In sum, the potential tolerator's standpoint characterizes a moral perspective concerned with good rather than just dispositions, which is why the moral virtue of tolerance cannot provide the philosophical foundations for the political principle of toleration.

The *moral model* considers tolerance as a strictly negative attitude of non-interference, which contrasts with the acceptance with which toleration is often equated in common usage. The virtue of tolerance consists in the effort of overcoming one's disapproval or dislike for stronger moral reasons, for example, reasons of respect due to other persons. Therefore tolerance cannot mean acceptance: on the one hand, acceptance seems to imply no effort, and on the other, it is inconsistent with the dislike or disapproval that tolerance overcomes. Only if the proper object of tolerance is not the difference itself, but the person with the difference, can tolerance acquire the positive meaning of acceptance. This is indeed the position recently endorsed by David Heyd, who holds that tolerance only applies to people, who are worth respect whatever their ideas, habits and behaviour.[10] However, this position is not widely shared, and for good reasons. If persons rather than their ideas and behaviour are tolerated, this implies that the latter are *not* tolerated. Hence, such disliked ideas and behaviour should be censored and suppressed, even though one may be prepared to accept the 'sinner', so to speak. (This, incidentally, corresponds to the position that the Catholic Church holds about homosexuals: homosexuality is regarded as a sin and a moral wrong and as such execrated, but homosexuals, as all other sinners, are welcome in the Church's fold with open arms). Such an attitude is hardly one of tolerance, since tolerance minimally implies that ideas, habits and behaviour which harm no other should not be interfered with, let alone suppressed. It would therefore seem that ideas, attitudes and behaviour qualify as the proper objects of tolerance, understood as non-interference rather than acceptance. Although the respect we owe to persons, even to those whose opinions and values we either dislike or disapprove of, provides the moral grounds for tolerance, such respect is not the same as tolerance. In brief, according to the *moral model*, tolerance consists in non-interference, whilst the proper objects of tolerance, as distinct from the objects of respect, are the disliked differences: it is because I accept you as a moral (actual or potential) partner that I put up with the values and lifestyle to which I object.

CRITICAL DIFFERENCES

Before going on to discuss the moral justification of tolerance, something should be said about the differences that provide the proper circumstances for tolerance.

---

[10] See Heyd, "Introduction".

the tolerated person is completely powerless, makes tolerance a genuine alternative to repression. But if being tolerated were just better than being persecuted, then toleration would at most be a second best, a device for a *modus vivendi* instead of a just principle for civil coexistence. In sum, the potential tolerator's standpoint characterizes a moral perspective concerned with good rather than just dispositions, which is why the moral virtue of tolerance cannot provide the philosophical foundations for the political principle of toleration.

The *moral model* considers tolerance as a strictly negative attitude of non-interference, which contrasts with the acceptance with which toleration is often equated in common usage. The virtue of tolerance consists in the effort of overcoming one's disapproval or dislike for stronger moral reasons, for example, reasons of respect due to other persons. Therefore tolerance cannot mean acceptance: on the one hand, acceptance seems to imply no effort, and on the other, it is inconsistent with the dislike or disapproval that tolerance overcomes. Only if the proper object of tolerance is not the difference itself, but the person with the difference, can tolerance acquire the positive meaning of acceptance. This is indeed the position recently endorsed by David Heyd, who holds that tolerance only applies to people, who are worth respect whatever their ideas, habits and behaviour.[10] However, this position is not widely shared, and for good reasons. If persons rather than their ideas and behaviour are tolerated, this implies that the latter are *not* tolerated. Hence, such disliked ideas and behaviour should be censored and suppressed, even though one may be prepared to accept the 'sinner', so to speak. (This, incidentally, corresponds to the position that the Catholic Church holds about homosexuals: homosexuality is regarded as a sin and a moral wrong and as such execrated, but homosexuals, as all other sinners, are welcome in the Church's fold with open arms). Such an attitude is hardly one of tolerance, since tolerance minimally implies that ideas, habits and behaviour which harm no other should not be interfered with, let alone suppressed. It would therefore seem that ideas, attitudes and behaviour qualify as the proper objects of tolerance, understood as non-interference rather than acceptance. Although the respect we owe to persons, even to those whose opinions and values we either dislike or disapprove of, provides the moral grounds for tolerance, such respect is not the same as tolerance. In brief, according to the *moral model*, tolerance consists in non-interference, whilst the proper objects of tolerance, as distinct from the objects of respect, are the disliked differences: it is because I accept you as a moral (actual or potential) partner that I put up with the values and lifestyle to which I object.

CRITICAL DIFFERENCES

Before going on to discuss the moral justification of tolerance, something should be said about the differences that provide the proper circumstances for tolerance.

---

[10] See Heyd, "Introduction".

Indeed, do only moral differences qualify for toleration? If not, should we both consider non-moral differences that are both elective and ascriptive? I contend that, according to the *moral model*, only chosen and revisable differences should count. This may require some explanation, for most contemporary issues of toleration have to do with unchosen or ascriptive differences, such as sex and race.

In the recent literature, the question of whether the differences providing the proper conditions for tolerance should be the subject of disapproval *only*, or whether they can *also* be the subject of dislike, is debated. This is not a merely academic issue, since the scope of toleration varies according to different answers to this question.[11] If only disapproved of differences are held to be conditions for toleration, this circumscribes toleration to behaviour, practices and traits, which are liable to moral assessment. If disliked differences are also included as conditions for toleration, the scope of the latter will encompass tastes and personal preferences as well, and maybe also ascriptive differences. Those who hold that moral disapproval is a condition for toleration are keen to emphasize the specific *moral* quality of toleration. It is because the tolerator morally disapproves of something that she needs to make a special effort to overcome her feelings by appealing to a stronger moral reason.[12] If disliked behaviour, including taste differences, were to be regarded as a condition for tolerance, then the moral effort of toleration would be less remarkable, and its moral quality less compelling, which creates the risk that it is, in fact, no more than indifference.[13]

This strict position on tolerance presupposes the distinction, commonly held by economists, between values and tastes, external and internal preferences. Yet the divide between values and tastes is neither clear-cut nor self-evident, as shown by the fact that disagreement over matter of taste is the object of widespread discussion and arguments.[14] The effort that is often required to overcome one's distaste in the name of respect for others is sometimes as morally valuable as that required to control one's disapproval.[15] Without wanting to enter into this other discussion, one may notice that further conditions have been recently added in the literature for differences to provide the conditions of tolerance. On the one hand, attitudes or behaviour should be morally disapproved of, yet not universally condemned:[16] attitudes such as racism and practices such as slavery or torture, which are

---

[11] This issue is raised by D.D. Raphael, "The Intolerable", in Mendus, ed., *Justifying Toleration*, 137-153. Raphael maintains that the subject of toleration can only be morally disapproved of behaviour or practices. In turn, that implies that the grounds for toleration be respect for persons, and, in his view this accounts for the apparent contradiction between toleration and disapproval: "Acts of which we disapprove, but which do not infringe rights may be tolerated despite our belief that they are wrong, and should be tolerated if those who do the acts have deliberately chosen to do them", p. 147. In his argument, then, choice becomes a necessary condition for an act to be tolerated. Mary Warnock, on the other hand, argues that toleration may also be directed to what is merely disliked. See M. Warnock, "The Limits to Toleration", Mendus and Edwards, eds., *On Toleration*, 123-139. In *Toleration and the Limits of Liberalism* (pp. 8ff), Susan Mendus focuses on this problem, which she views as one of the various contradictory aspects of the liberal theory of toleration: she argues that only a socialist foundation of toleration can account for its moral character.
[12] Cf. Raphael, "The Intolerable".
[13] S. Mendus, "Introduction", in Mendus, ed., *Justifying Toleration*, 1-20.
[14] See on this point, A. Hirschman, "Against Parsimony", *Economics and Philosophy*, 1 (1985), 1-15.
[15] Cf. Warnock, "The Limits to Toleration".
[16] See J. Horton, "Toleration as a Virtue", in Heyd, ed., *Toleration: An Elusive Virtue*, 28-43.

universally acknowledged to be morally wrong and unjust, cannot be a condition for the virtue of toleration. Being tolerant with reference to these practices is definitely not a virtue, but a moral wrong. In other words, to qualify as tolerable the disapproved behaviour or practice should belong to the area of the morally controversial objects, such as contraception, divorce and sexual promiscuity. Concerning these practices, which some find questionable, but which are by no means universally condemned because they do not infringe any right, a virtuous Catholic, for example, can rightfully be said to be tolerant. On the other hand, it is only if disapproval, and perhaps dislike, are neither arbitrary nor clearly unjust, that tolerance can be said to be a virtue. For example, if Mike tolerates something in John, which he dislikes just out of prejudice, bias and so on, his attitude is not morally praiseworthy. In other words, disapproval and dislike should be founded on some reasons – albeit not universally shared reasons – for the moral attitude of tolerance to apply.[17] In the absence of such reasons, respect for others requires us to stop disapproving of them altogether.

The problem with this strict and rigorous position on tolerance is that if disliked differences are excluded from the conditions of tolerance, then tolerance would be very limited in scope, excluding much of what is commonly identified as tolerance.[18] Those who maintain that dislike may also be a condition for tolerance conceive it as a less rigorous virtue, but one closer to common practice. However, whether one takes dislike as a proper object for toleration, ascriptive differences cannot really be included in the *moral model*, even under the category of 'disliked differences'. Such differences are excluded by the fact that tolerance is defined as the suspension of the power of either interference or suppression of disapproved or disliked differences; but this power cannot be exercised if the differences in question are not modifiable, at least in principle. Hence, unchosen and unmodifiable differences such as race, ethnicity and sex cannot be considered proper conditions for tolerance. Therefore, whether or not the differences that qualify for tolerance are restricted to the outcome of *moral* choices, they are still confined to the outcome of *choices*, moral or otherwise.[19]

This exclusion is rather troublesome given the reality of contemporary pluralism, where the most relevant and divisive differences are those related to race, ethnicity, sex and nationality. For this reason, some supporters of the *moral model* have tried to incorporate those unchosen and crucial differences into the conditions of toleration, hence changing the definition of toleration itself. When considering unchosen differences, or so it is argued, the power involved is not that of interfering or suppressing them, but of penalising the bearers of the disliked differences.[20] But by accepting such a modification, the *moral model* itself risks being put into

---

[17] See Williams, "Toleration: A Political or Moral Question", p. 37.

[18] M. Warnock, "The Limits to Toleration"; Mendus, *Toleration and the Limits of Liberalism*. Indeed Bernard Williams comes to the conclusion that the practice of tolerance does not need the attitude of tolerance and requires a different, merely political, foundation, cf. his "Toleration: A Political or Moral Question?".

[19] Raphael, "The Intolerable", p. 147.

[20] See Preston King, "It is not a tolerance which allows the identity to persist (usually the tolerator has no power over this), but which does not penalize the bearer of an identity as a consequence of his identity", King, *Toleration*, p. 64.

jeopardy. The very philosophical analysis aimed at understanding in what sense tolerance is a *moral* virtue, even though the tolerator refrains from acting against what she regards as being morally wrong, would count for nothing. For, when we consider ascriptive differences, disapproval and dislike are not in order. It would therefore seem that tolerance does not apply, because there is no first order moral stance to be overcome. There is no merit in refraining from racist attack, because it is wrong to have racist attitudes in the first place. Respect for others requires the suppression of racist hatred rather than the toleration of people whose skin is of a different colour. From this perspective, moral tolerance is not an attitude that applies to ascriptive differences.

One obvious way out is simply to state that ascriptive differences do not belong to the field of tolerance, but rather to the special domain of anti-discrimination, which does not concern modifiable behaviour or opinions, but identity.[21] However, this amounts to a declaration of failure: it is an admission that the moral theory of toleration cannot cope with the most relevant and divisive differences characterising contemporary pluralism. It does not even accommodate common language usage, where tolerance and intolerance refer to racial, sexual and ethnic differences as much as, if not more often than, differences in moral, political, aesthetic values. In conclusion, the *moral model* cannot be adapted to ascriptive differences by simply adding an extra qualification such as refraining from penalising other people.

JUSTIFICATION

For the *moral model* of toleration, the issue of justification is a crucial one. Why indeed one should allow something that one morally disapproves of, and that one things there are good reasons – reasons open to public discussion, and not mere idiosyncratic preferences – to stop?[22] Put this way, toleration looks paradoxical.[23] So much so that it cannot be expressed as a general principle in the form of: "Everyone ought to do what s/he thinks s/he ought to do". Moreover, its application has been shown to be self-destructive when applied to the intolerant. The tolerator seems torn between two contradictory duties, one urging him or her to intervene in order to prevent some wrongdoing and the other to let others do what they regard as right. The conflict can be solved if tolerance is acknowledged to follow from a higher order principle than our first-order moral judgements. Even so, toleration cannot be framed in terms of the above general principle and understood as a general duty because tolerance is morally good only with reference to a certain kind of behaviour – that which is disapproved of with good reason, yet not universally condemned. In this way, toleration is a moral virtue in the sense of being a medium between two extremes: indifference and repression. It can be practised in the restricted area

[21] This is the position maintained by N. Bobbio, "Le ragioni della tolleranza", *Mondoperaio*, November 1986, 42-47. Cf. also N. Bobbio, "Tolleranza e verità", *Lettera Internazionale*, 15 (1988), 16-18.
[22] Cf. Raphael, "The Intolerable".
[23] See B. Cohen, "An Ethical Paradox", *Mind*, 76 (1967), 250-259; G. Harrison, "Relativism and Tolerance", P. Laslett and J. Fishkin, eds., *Philosophy, Politics, Society* (Oxford: Blackwell, 1979), 273-290.

between two prohibitions: that of permitting harm, and that of interfering with the disliked but harmless behaviour of other people.

Three candidates are usually listed for providing reasons to practice toleration which extend beyond personal morality. The first is a sceptical argument, according to which moral disapproval, being a purely subjective matter, cannot justify repression. The second refers to the distinction between opinions and actions, according to which holding a belief and acting upon it are quite different matters; so that believing something wrong does not *ipso facto* justify repression of, or interference with, that thing. The third is an argument in terms of respect for other people.[24] When supported by the first two arguments, tolerance turns out to be at most a derivative value, whose character is more pragmatic or epistemological than moral. Moreover, as Richard Tuck has convincingly argued, the link between toleration and scepticism is historically contingent, since scepticism can likewise lead to the acceptance of dominant opinions for prudential reasons.[25] In the current literature, conceptions of tolerance as either a rational ideal or as the prudential alternative to repression are often rejected as weak forms of justification,[26] which do not account for the special moral quality of tolerance. By contrast, the third type of justification provides strong moral reasons for accepting what is disliked or disapproved of.

As already argued, in dealing with toleration, respect is an attitude towards persons, and not towards the differences of which one disapproves of. This implies that one can morally separate the person from the difference in question, and, in turn, this suggests that the difference itself is the product of choice, since in this case there is a well-established distinction between the moral value of the agent and that of the act.[27] Naturally, the distinction between a person and her chosen acts can be questioned,[28] but it seems more easily acceptable than distinguishing a person from her attributes such as sex, race and nationality. The moral value of the agent, beyond her acts, is what the virtue of toleration is supposed to recognize. But such a moral value can be understood in two different ways: either the agent is recognized to act in good faith and to mean well, despite the wrongness of her acts; or her capacity for free choice is recognized as valuable in itself. In other words, the values backing respect are either integrity or autonomy, or both. Yet, I would argue that integrity

---

[24] Cf. Mendus, "Introduction" of *Justifying Toleration*.

[25] R. Tuck, "Scepticism and Toleration in the Seventeenth Century", in Mendus, ed., *Justifying Toleration.*, 21-35.

[26] See J. Waldron, "Toleration and the Rationality of Persecution", in Mendus, ed., *Justifying Toleration*, 61-86. Waldron's reconstruction of Locke's argument for toleration shows the limits of the purely rational argument in favour of toleration.

[27] "The moral ideal of toleration does not require the tolerator to acknowledge any merit in the opinions of which he disapproves; but he must respect the personality of the holders of those opinions, and treat them as rational moral agents whose views can be discussed and disputed, and who are also capable of changing their minds on rational ground", Nicholson, "Toleration as a Moral Ideal", pp. 165-166.

[28] The communitarian critique of the liberal self, for example, is that the deontological conception of the agent is as separate from and prior to his/her aims, ends and projects: the agent is an empty chooser. For communitarians, in order to choose rationally, we must know who we are, and since our identity is defined by our attachments as well as by our ends and projects, the agent cannot be conceived of independently from his aims. See, for example, M. Sandel, *Liberalism and the Limits of Justice* (Cambridge: Cambridge University Press, 1982), pp. 15-54.

without autonomy is only of limited value. When someone acts out of ignorance, lack of technical ability, irrational use of information, or blind trust in another person, being in good faith and having good intentions are likely to be considered poor excuses, rather than command proper respect. The moral quality of the agent vanishes if he is not recognized as a free chooser. Thus, the capacity for free choice turns out to be the real ground for respect, even when the chosen actions, attitudes and beliefs may be objectionable. The value of free choice, independently of what is chosen, is autonomy: so, in so far as the differences to be tolerated are the result of free choices, autonomy turns out to be the ultimate value on which to ground tolerance.

AUTONOMY

Although in liberal democratic ethics autonomy is the ultimate value on which respect for those we tolerate ultimately rests, grounding toleration on autonomy has its drawbacks. As it will be argued below, this may result in either the disappearance of the moral character itself of tolerance, or in the virtue of tolerance being regarded as socially problematic and ultimately undesirable.

We might conceive of autonomy as a quality we attribute to others in order for us to both regard them and interact with them as persons. In this vaguely Kantian sense, autonomy is equivalent to agency, and as such rather than providing the basis for respect of others, it is an aspect of it: other people, as agents, are always moral partners to be respected, whatever they do. But, if it is this sense of autonomy that justifies tolerance, a difficulty immediately arises. When so conceived, autonomy makes the very disapproval of what others freely choose to do illegittimate, which calls into question the moral nature of the act of disapproving itself; for showing disapproval of others' behaviour is already an infringement of their autonomy. This is indeed the conclusion at which Bernard Williams arrives when he suggests that the practice of toleration should be founded on political reasons independently of the moral value of autonomy.[29] Moreover, understanding autonomy and respect in this very general sense – as a necessary assumption for morality in the Kantian tradition – does not help to grasp the specific, intuitive, and more substantive, sense of tolerance expressed in familiar sentences such as: "I totally disapprove of his line of conduct, but I am tolerant of it because I respect his choice. He is in earnest, responsible, and has shown courage, strength of character and independence, so I won't interfere with his plans, even though, unfortunately, we disagree very deeply". Here, the disapproval understandably co-exists with the acceptance of the other as an adversary to be morally respected, and because respect is substantively motivated by the specific moral qualities of the agent, tolerance bears no trace of condescension and makes the tolerated person a moral partner with the tolerator. Hence, if autonomy is to be the ultimate foundation for tolerance, it must be understood as something more specific than a general attribute of human beings. In order to sustain tolerance, autonomy needs to be conceived as a valuable human capability whose exercise is to be critically assessed.

---

[29] Cf. Williams, "Toleration: A Political or a Moral Question?"

Even in this sense, autonomy admits of a variety of interpretations.[30] For some, autonomy corresponds to rational choice in the standard economic sense: in this case, non-autonomous behaviour is basically irrational, stemming from ignorance, impulsiveness or imprudence.[31] For others, autonomy must also refer to the agent's preferences:[32] not only should an autonomous agent's actions be rational, but they should also derive from autonomous preferences, that is, those which are not adaptive and have undergone a process of critical reflection so that they contribute to a character-planning project and to the well-being of the agent. In this sense, autonomy is more a characteristic of the chooser than of the choice. On this account, an autonomous *person* can still sometimes choose irrationally, make mistakes, and fall prey to weakness of the will or self-deception, and thus act in a non-autonomous way. Furthermore, although some people conceive of autonomy in a purely formal and procedural way, others conceive of it in terms of some substantive value, such as prudence, detachment from material and sensual goods, non-conformism, and the fulfilment of one's potential.[33] The distinction between these alternative values is rarely clear-cut. Both Kant and Mill, who in the liberal tradition represent the spokesmen of the value of autonomy, endorsed a conception which is at the same time formal and perfectionist: for Kant, despite the formality of his conception, someone who simply follows his inclination is not an autonomous moral agent; for Mill, beyond the procedural character of his notion, people who act blindly according to the views and values of the moral majority have not developed an autonomous individuality.

What is relevant here is that few of the various interpretations of the concept of autonomy make it possible to settle from the outside which desires, volitions and actions count as autonomous and which do not. There are no clear independent criteria for an external observer to judge whether others' actions are autonomous. If tolerance is grounded on respect, and this in its turn on autonomy, then judging others to be autonomous is crucial for adopting attitudes of tolerance. But if it is difficult to judge whether or not others' actions and volitions are autonomous, then

---

[30] For a discussion of autonomy as the grounds for toleration see Mendus, *Toleration and the Limits of Liberalism*, pp. 57-65.

[31] This idea is prominent in the following. J. Feinberg *Harm to Self* (Oxford: Oxford University Press, 1986); D. VanDeVeer, *Paternalistic Intervention* (Princeton, N.J.: Princeton University Press, 1986). For a comment see D.W. Brock "Paternalism and Autonomy", *Ethics*, 98 (1988), 550-565.

[32] On this point see H. Frankfurt, "Freedom of the Will and the Concept of Person", *Journal of Philosophy*, 68 (1971), 829-39; A. Sen, "Rational Fools: A Critique of the Behavioural Foundation of Economic Theory", *Philosophy and Public Affairs*, 6 (1977), 317-344; J. Elster, *Sour Grapes* (Cambridge: Cambridge University Press, 1983); G. Dworkin, *The Theory and the Practice of Autonomy* (Cambridge: Cambridge University Press, 1988); J. Christman, "Constructing the Inner Citadel: Recent Work on the Concept of Autonomy", *Ethics*, 99 (1988), 109-124.

[33] Typically, liberal theory has conceived of autonomy as independence from one's background and traditions. Yet, in the present debate, autonomy has also been connected with one's traditional culture, which is seen as the necessary condition for autonomous and meaningful choice. See, for example, W. Kymlicka, *Liberalism, Community and Culture* (Oxford: Oxford University Press, 1989); J. Raz, " Multiculturalism: A Liberal Perspective", *Dissent* (Winter, 1994), 67-79; A. Margalit and J. Raz, "National Self-Determination", *The Journal of Philosophy,* 87 (1990), 439-461. Culture is necessary not only as a basket of options, and as a network of meanings, but also because it sorts autonomous actions from whimsical choices. The paradoxical consequences of this extreme position is that non-conformist and heterodox actions are judged as non-autonomous.

– given the principle *in dubio, pro reo* [in doubt, absolve] – any action should count as autonomous in the absence of sufficient contrary evidence. In these cases, the value of autonomy turns out to be weak, and so does that of tolerance: the latter comes down to a negative form of prohibition of interference with others' choices, for lack of sufficient reasons. On the one hand, this conception of autonomy seems too weak to ground the respect for person that moral tolerance requires (at most, it can ground a form of 'non-disrespect'); on the other hand, it is too broad to account for the limits of toleration. This makes tolerance hardly distinguishable from indifference. To be more precise, tolerance becomes a sort of processor for transforming dislike into indifference.

However, assuming that it is possible to make external judgements about the autonomy of others, we need a strong conception of autonomy to provide the proper basis for the moral value of tolerance, such as that provided by perfectionist accounts. Although such accounts are controversial – it has been argued, for example, that Kant's and Mill's conceptions of autonomy are culture-dependent, hence inapplicable outside Western liberalism – it is possible to imagine that the value of autonomy, in a perfectionist sense, may offer some ground to respect agents whose actions we may either dislike or disapprove of. On this account, respect means the recognition of others as moral equals, as potential or actual moral partners. But this conception is not problem free either. Let us suppose that we are confronted, in Dworkin's expression, with a 'couch potato', who spends his time watching junk television while eating junk food.[34] Such a lifestyle looks closer to addictive, unreflexive behaviour than to any autonomously chosen life plan (assuming that the latter can be given a clear definition). If respect is founded on autonomy, then we have no reason to respect someone living this way. He may be a potential moral partner, but he is not making use of his capacity for autonomy. In this case, tolerance would not be considered a moral virtue but mere indulgence. Does this imply that we have a reason for repressing the couch-potato lifestyle, assuming we have the power to do so? Suppose I own the apartment where such a person lives. Am I justified to threaten him with eviction, unless he changes his lifestyle? Most of us would agree, I think, that this is too harsh a way of treating people, besides being too demanding a condition for smooth and regular social interactions.

Even from a perfectionist conception of autonomy, it is far from clear whether interference with non-autonomous behaviour is always justified. Kant and Mill, for example, hold anti-paternalism as a rule: people cannot be coerced to be free. Although interference with another's behaviour to improve their welfare can sometimes be justified, this does not imply paternalism as a general policy. Parents can educate their children against their will; but, according to Kant, this is justified by their duty as parents to provide their offspring with the opportunity to become free and independent adults. According to Mill, the state can force parents to educate their children, but this is because society has a right of self-defence against

---

[34] The example of the 'couch potato' comes from R. Dworkin, "Fondamenti filosofici della neutralità liberale", in *L'idea di giustizia. La filosofia politica americana contemporanea*, Sebastiano Maffettone, ed.,(Napoli: Guida, 1993), 57-72.

the burden of supporting uneducated, dependent people, who cannot earn their own living.

Even those who believe that paternalism can be justified in some circumstances, do not justify paternalistic intervention by simply arguing that behaviour in question is non autonomous.[35] Danny Scoccia, who has argued for a purely formal, but quite well specified conception of autonomy (in terms of desires and preferences rather than single choices), favours limited paternalism when one of the following three conditions holds: (a) the person has highly autonomous desires, but the choice made does not accurately express those desires, and the person would consent to the interference if he were fully rational; or (b) the person has low autonomy desires, he lacks the capacity to form highly autonomous desires, and the interference is necessary to preserve his potential to develop later; [or] (c) the person has low autonomy desires, the interference would increase the autonomy of his desires, and the person would not object to the interference if he were rational and had highly autonomous desires[36].

The conditions specified here are highly detailed, but allow interference only in very clear-cut cases. For instance, the case of an autonomous person who, in a state of drunkness, risks falling from a balcony (condition a); or a child who is playing with fire (condition b). However, condition (c) is hardly ever applicable: how can one be sure that the proposed intervention will turn out to be successful? There is no way of predicting what a non-autonomous person would do once he or she embraced an autonomous lifestyle. (What lifestyle would Dworkin's 'couch-potato' eventually embrace?). Recognition of these practical difficulties, for example, account for someone like Alan Ryan, who defends both perfectionism and paternalism, but nonetheless believes that there is little room for successful interference in real life.[37]

Even if a strong conception of autonomy underlies respect – and thus, indirectly, tolerance – this does not imply that all behaviour and preferences subject to dislike or disapproval, and judged non-autonomous, should not be tolerated. As we have seen, only very special cases justify paternalistic intervention. But what happens in cases where persons neither deserve respect because they lack autonomy, nor fall within those instances where paternalistic intervention is fully justified? They would be tolerated by default, so to speak. In conclusion, the moral quality of tolerance makes it an almost "impossible virtue", as Bernard Williams has remarked, for only comparatively few cases are entitled to tolerance on the basis of real respect. If the analysis of tolerance as a distinctive moral virtue is intended to provide a sound philosophical basis for the corresponding social practice, it has clearly failed: in

---

[35] This position is shared by G. Dworkin, "Paternalism", in P. Laslett and J. Fishkin, eds, *Philosophy, Politics and Society* (Oxford: Blackwell, 1979), 78-96; D. Brock, "Paternalism and Promoting the Good", in R. Sartorius, ed., *Paternalism* (Minneapolis: University of Minnesota Press, 1983); D. Scoccia, "Paternalism and Respect for Autonomy", *Ethics*, 100 (1990), 318-334. These positions contrast with J. Glover, *Causing Death and Saving Life* (New York: Penguin, 1977), D. Van deVeer, *Paternalistic Intervention*; J. Feinberg, *Harm to Self*; and R.J.Arneson, "Mill *vs.* Paternalism", *Ethics*, 90 (1980), 470-480.

[36] Cf. Scoccia, "Paternalism and Respect for Autonomy", pp. 330-31.

[37] Alan Ryan, "Can We Coerce People To Be Free?", (Princeton, 1992), *mimeo*.

most instances, social practice does not satisfy the requirements of tolerance as a moral virtue.

THE HARM PRINCIPLE

An implication of the theoretical difficulties surrounding a strong and discriminative conception of autonomy, as just outlined, is that no clear limit to tolerance can be derived from it. Since the *moral model* seems to imply that, in order to be a virtue, tolerance must be practised within limits, we are left with the harm principle as the last resort. No one questions the idea that causing harm to other people is a good reason for interfering with the person who causes the harm, but the harm principle often turns out to be too vague and indefinite to provide a clear justification for interference with others' behaviour, and thereby to offer a reliable defence against tolerating what should not be tolerated. For example, it is open to debate whether harm consists only of physical injuries and concrete damages to property, or whether it can also be construed as psychological and moral offences, or threats causing distress and fear.[38] Mill claimed that the harm principle applied only to actions and not to opinions, because the offence that might be caused by a person's opinions is not as serious as the harm done to the society as a whole if that person is silenced. However, expressing an opinion is a kind of act.[39] These are all issues in the controversial debate over free speech in the contemporary literature. Another difficulty in establishing the harm principle concerns the distinction between self-regarding and other-regarding actions. Mill indeed maintained that, in order to insure the maximum of individual liberty, the harm principle should apply only to other-regarding actions; but the distinction is far from being self-evident, since any action, whether self or other-regarding, may have side-effects and consequences for others.[40]

Appeals to the harm principle seem trapped in a dilemma: either to consider a limited class of harms, thus extending the scope of toleration and freedom, but limiting the protection from harm; or, conversely, including all possible classes of harm, thus widening protection, but drastically limiting the scope of personal freedom and toleration. Even from the sketchy way in which the harm principle has been here discussed, it should nonetheless be clear that such a principle is of little help in settling hard cases – cases in which toleration's limits are invoked on the basis of a wide range of offences, such as moral and cultural damages, or the worsening of people's sets of opportunities.

ASSESSING THE MODEL

---

[38] See, for example, the discussion of the concept of harm in J. Feinberg, *Social Philosophy* (Prentice Hall, 1973), ch. 3.

[39] On this point see, for example, T.M. Scanlon, "A Theory of Freedom of Expression", *Philosophy and Public Affairs*, 1 (1971), 204-226.

[40] Cf. J. Horton, "Toleration, Morality and Harm", in Mendus and Horton, eds, *Aspects of Toleration*, 113-135.

As discussed here, the model of toleration as a moral virtue focuses on the kind of value tolerance represents. This approach aims to investigate the peculiarity of a virtue that allows wrong-doings without necessarily appealing to either prudential or epistemological reasons. The model combines the negative meaning of toleration, as 'putting up with', with the positive sense of acceptance: tolerance is the disposition to put up with disapproved behaviour for the sake of accepting other people as moral partners.

The analysis supporting the *moral model* is often developed at a high level of generality, abstracting from the social and political dimensions, and is meant to provide a general interpretation of the virtue of tolerance which can constitute the philosophical basis for the crucial corresponding practice. However, focusing exclusively on individual dispositions to tolerance, it also limits its possible application at the social and political levels: for example, the virtue of moral toleration cannot be predicated of political authority in a liberal democracy, for it cannot disapprove of any behaviour which stays within the limits of the law.[41] The critical analysis of the model has revealed a particular difficulty. Although the classical paradox of toleration seems to be resolved by adopting this model, it is doubtful whether the resulting virtue can provide the philosophical grounds for strengthening the correspondent practice of toleration, thereby enhancing a tolerant, liberal and pluralist society. First, only chosen differences are the appropriate candidates for tolerance. But this means that therefore the scope of tolerance cannot extend to include the most relevant and divisive issues of contemporary pluralism, namely, race, sex, and ethnicity. Secondly, even within the range of chosen differences, only those which can be clearly ascribed to autonomous choice are properly entitled to moral tolerance, understood as grounded on respect. All other differences appear to be either tolerated by default, or to be indifferently received. In other words, the moral virtue of tolerance applies only to a very restricted area of what is usually tolerated. In this respect, its link with the crucial practice of toleration is tenuous. If the *moral model* is intended as a solid philosophical basis for toleration, both as a practice and as a social and political ideal, then it turns out to be flawed, for the moral virtue of tolerance does not work as a micro-foundation for social and political theory.

There is more. If tolerance were generally practised as a strict moral virtue, the corresponding society would risk becoming intolerant. The virtue of tolerance, as distinct from indifference and acquiescence, would engender rigidity and moralism, preventing the development of any real sympathy between tolerators and tolerated. Instead of being a principle of civil coexistence, it would turn into a source of resentment of the tolerated against the moral condescension of the tolerators. Even if it is grounded on respect for others' autonomy, tolerance could not be easily accepted by the tolerated because, based on a social asymmetry of power, it suggests a moral asymmetry between the 'virtuous' tolerators and the 'powerless' recipients. When applied within the social and political domains, the moral virtue of tolerance becomes a problematic social attitude, undermining reciprocity and mutual respect. One may conclude that it is fortunate that the moral virtue of tolerance should be

---

[41] On the applicability of toleration to democratic authorities, cf. both Glen Newey's and Saladin Meckled-Garcia's contributions in this volume.

restricted within the realm of personal relationships, for this offsets its perverse effects at the social level.[42] It would therefore seem that those who draw social and political implications from the *moral model* of tolerance are either mistaken or misleading in their conclusions.

THE VIRTUE OF TOLERANCE AND
THE POLITICAL PRINCIPLE OF TOLERATION

Should we conclude, from what argued so far, that the socially valuable practice of toleration is no more than a pragmatic compromise? Can we not make sense of the political ideal of toleration in ethical terms? Is a tolerant society founded on nothing more than indifference and acquiescence in order to guarantee co-existence? The response to these questions is to be found in the discontinuity between moral philosophy and political theory which characterizes an influential stream of liberal thought, presently best exemplified by John Rawls's political liberalism. If the political domain is presented as freestanding, in no need of metaphysical or moral depth, then the same relationship holds for the virtue of tolerance and the ideal of toleration; though the relevant and pertinent reasons vary and are independent in the two cases. As a political ideal, toleration must not be conceived as a mere *modus vivendi*. Like any political principle, it can and should be grounded on impersonal public reason and principles of justice. As such, its ethical force is independent from non-political moral convictions. The political ideal of toleration overcomes the moral asymmetry implied by the virtue of tolerance, and can be practised in ways that neither undermine reciprocity nor suggest condescension. The discontinuity between moral and metaphysical views, on the one hand, and the political conception, on the other, has its own difficulties. It implies some kind of division in people's beliefs and in the self; a division between the private individual and the citizen. In a sense, Rawls' s notion of the overlapping consensus is an attempt to escape from such criticisms; the virtue of tolerance can work in a similar way.

Although the argument here developed has shown that the *moral model* cannot constitute the foundation either of the practice or the political ideal of toleration; there is no reason to discard the possibility that the moral virtue of toleration can prove helpful in bridging the gap between moral integrity and the political obligation we have to tolerate disapproved behaviour and practices that are within the law. Suppose, for instance, that someone, from the impersonal viewpoint of citizenship, endorses the political principle of toleration, acknowledging that it constitutes the best and most fair kind of protection for religious and moral convictions.[43] Suppose further that this person finds herself in a public position, and hence under the obligation of being tolerant of practices which she strongly disapproves of. In these circumstances, the person experiences an internal conflict between public duty and personal obligation to her own moral code. In such a conflict, toleration can easily appear as the necessary pragmatic solution, in which

---

[42] This conclusion is implicitly embraced by Williams when, at the end of his analysis in "Toleration: An Impossible Virtue", he states that in our society we probably need more indifference than tolerance.
[43] The justification of toleration as a political principle can be found in J. Rawls *A Theory of Justice* (Cambridge, M.A.: Harvard University Press, 1971) ch. 4 §33-34-35, pp. 205-221.

case the person sacrifices her moral imperatives. But such a pragmatic conclusion would not satisfy the true believer, who would feel that the political obligation reveals intolerance of her convictions. However, the internal conflict can better be overcome with reference to the virtue of tolerance which, as we have seen, is intended to provide moral reasons in favour of toleration, moral reasons which are stronger than the moral motive for interference or suppression of the disapproved behaviour.[44] In this way, a bridge can be built between the impersonal reasons for political toleration and non-political moral convictions. However, it is a bridge that will stand only for those people whose moral views include the principle of respect for others' autonomy as a crucial value and a higher order principle.

---

[44] I have developed this argument while discussing the case of Catholic doctors refusing to prescribe contraceptives to their patients on the basis of their religious doctrine. See A.E. Galeotti, *Multiculturalismo* (Napoli: Liguori, Napoli 1999), ch. 4.

PART II

TOLERATION AND NEUTRALITY

CHAPTER 4

NEUTRALITY AND THE VIRTUE OF TOLERATION

Robert Paul Churchill

INTRODUCTION

Toleration has a very special place in the liberal tradition. Liberals identify themselves as valuing autonomy and the toleration necessary for pluralism. John Rawls identifies the Reformation and religious toleration following in its aftermath as the historical origins of political liberalism.[1] Both Rawls and Joseph Raz argue that toleration is a moral virtue for a liberal constitutional order.[2] Moreover, they claim that a politically liberal state may promote toleration without compromising its neutrality. In recent years some philosophers studying toleration as a virtue have made progress in analyzing it apart from its traditional place in the 'lens' or 'frame' of political liberalism.[3] These analyses suggest some difficulties for political liberalism. In particular, when properly understood as a truly *moral* virtue, toleration is not at all the same as Rawls's and Raz's political notions of toleration as a virtue. Moreover, far from being neutral, 'liberal toleration' may paradoxically endorse hostility ('intolerance') towards the persons, values, and beliefs others are said to be tolerating.

THESIS

In this paper I explicate the differences between toleration as a moral virtue and other conceptions of toleration, including toleration as a 'political virtue' in liberalism. I maintain that there is no simple connection between neutrality and toleration as a moral virtue. Moreover, misguided efforts to promote toleration may

---

[1] *Political Liberalism* (New York: Columbia University, 1996), xxiv-xxx
[2] Rawls, 190-195; Raz, *Morality of Freedom* (Oxford: Clarendon , 1986), 401-407
[3] P. Nicholson, "Toleration as a Moral Ideal", S. Mendus and J. Horton, eds., *Aspects of Toleration* (London: Methuen, 1985), 158-73; J. Horton, "Toleration as a Virtue", D. Heyd, ed., *Toleration: An Elusive Virtue* (Princeton: Princeton University, 1996), 28-43; R. Churchill, "On the Difference between Non-Moral and Moral Conceptions of Toleration: The Case for Toleration as an Individual Virtue" in M. Razavi and D. Ambuel, eds., *Philosophy, Religion, and the Question of Intolerance*, (Albany: State University of New York, Press 1997), 189-211

lead to illiberal results. More specifically, my objectives are the following: (1) I extend an argument begun elsewhere[4] for a plurality thesis according to which there is no univocal meaning of 'toleration' or 'tolerance'.[5] (2) I explicate a conception of toleration as a moral virtue and maintain that it ought not to be confused with toleration thought of as indifference, permissiveness, and endurance. (3) Focusing on *Political Liberalism*, I argue that Rawls fails in his efforts to connect toleration as a virtue with neutrality. If political toleration is a genuinely moral virtue as analyzed here, then Rawls cannot maintain that it is neutral since such a conception of toleration is not a political idea independent of particular conceptions of the good. On the other hand, if political toleration is genuinely neutral in aim, as Rawls believes, then although individuals may be politically tolerant, they may still fail to be morally virtuous or morally commendable.[6]

A PLURALITY OF CONCEPTIONS

Various uses of 'tolerance' and 'toleration' make claims to legitimacy in ordinary language, although they signify quite disparate conceptions. Reflection about examples should persuade us to adopt a 'plurality thesis' according to which there is no unified concept of toleration.[7] As I have discussed these distinctions between 'types' of toleration at length elsewhere, I shall make only some brief observations here.[8]

Indifference as Toleration

It might be claimed that a person could not be tolerant if she is indifferent.[9] But this is not necessarily the case. First, it is helpful to distinguish between *reasons* and *motives* with respect to toleration and intolerance. A person is completely indifferent if she lacks both reasons and motives for toleration. But such a person is

---

[4] Churchill, "On the Difference between Non-Moral and Moral Conceptions of Toleration"

[5] There is some question over the proper distinction between 'tolerance' and 'toleration' and the majority practice seems to be to treat them as synonyms. In this discussion I try to use 'tolerance' when the primary subject of discussion is the complex of beliefs, feelings, motives, and attitudes leading to the actions usually 'behind' actions. I will use 'toleration' to refer to actions (usually of forbearance) and the (largely political) conditions in which tolerant attitudes and motives are manifest publicly. I am grateful to Stephen Barker for clarifying this distinction.

[6] I shall not attempt to answer the question 'why should we cultivate toleration as a moral virtue?' Rather, I assume that toleration as a virtue is good and desirable. In addition, here I do not attempt to defend the logical coherence of the concept of toleration as a virtue from a paradox some believe to be unavoidable. See D. D. Raphael, "The Intolerable", Mendus, ed., *Justifying Toleration*, p. 139 for a formulation of the paradox and Churchill, p. 206 for my response.

[7] J. Jordan adapts this term for use in discussions of toleration in "Concerning Moral Toleration", Razavi and Ambuel, eds., *Question of Intolerance*, at 216. Those preferring something similar to a unitary thesis include Mendus, *Toleration and the Limits of Liberalism* (London: Macmillan, 1989), 18-21; and Nicholson, "Toleration as a Moral Ideal", 158-173.

[8] "On the Differences between Non-Moral and Moral Conceptions of Toleration"

[9] Mendus, *Toleration and the Limits of Liberalism*, 8. B. Williams says of indifference that it negates toleration [tolerance] as an attitude but that it is a type of toleration in political action. See "Toleration: An Impossible Virtue", Heyd, ed., *Toleration*, p. 20.

not wholly indifferent if she disapproves very strongly yet lacks the motivation to interfere. Second, our thinking tends to be influenced by 'positive' examples (or hypothetical cases) of toleration. The tolerant person is thought of as forbearing and restraining herself. But the action or object tolerated may be morally neutral or may possess some degree(s) of good- or bad-making qualities. One can tolerate what is bad or wrong, or ought to be prevented or resisted by failing to speak out or to act in ways open to one. For example, many a bystander tolerates unfortunate or wrongful things that happen to others although they could render assistance with no harm to themselves and at little inconvenience.[10] In such cases, bystanders may deplore the wrong committed (e.g., child abuse) but nevertheless tolerate it because they fail to muster the motivation to respond.[11]

Permissiveness as Toleration

In contrast with those tolerant out of indifference, the permissive believe their toleration is based on principle. They embrace some version of skepticism, relativism, or subjectivism, however inchoate it may be in expression. The permissive also differ from the indifferent because of their positive attitudes toward toleration. In this group are two types. Some individuals, though they personally would not choose or advocate what they tolerate, attempt to be as expansive and nonchalant as possible. They refuse to pass judgments and may believe they ought to be able to adopt the adage 'nothing human is foreign to me' as their motto. Others who are permissive believe that they are unable to avoid or to ignore what they find disagreeable or offensive and therefore ought to opt for a 'live and let live' outlook.

Endurance as Toleration

When being tolerant and especially the forbearance it necessitates are experienced in themselves as disagreeable or onerous (in addition to the offensiveness of what is tolerated) then toleration is to be understood as endurance.[12] If the forbearance is attained with real difficulty, then the tolerant person has a certain fortitude in being able to put up with and endure what she finds highly disagreeable, repugnant, and even condemnable. When she endures certain beliefs or practices she could suppress, then these are indulged as a matter of sufferance, not of right. In either case, she is unlike the indifferent, for she does not lack motives for change, and she is unlike the permissive person with the latter's 'anything goes' optimism or 'live and let live' outlook. Reasons for endurance are usually found in calculations of the

---

[10] B. Latane and J. Darley, *The Unresponsive Bystander* (New York: Appleton, Crofts, 1970); D. Jones, *Moral Responsibility in the Holocaust*, (Lanham: Rowman & Littlefield), 199-226

[11] Clarity would be well served in discussing such cases by the consistent replacement of 'toleration' with 'moral indifference', but conceptual confusion will persist, I fear, just because 'toleration' is available as a euphemism. and the morally indifferent will prefer to mask their failure of concern behind the more positive connotations of 'toleration'.

[12] I have been greatly aided in making the distinctions between permissiveness and endurance by T. Hearns, Jr., "On Tolerance", *Southern Journal of Philosophy*, 8 (1970)

benefits of putting up with something or the costs of interfering.

It might be assumed that one is intolerant if, given sufficient power, she would stop what she endures.[13] Probably many cases of endurance involve an absence of power to change the situation. But not all are like this. With fortitude one may tolerantly endure what is extremely disagreeable (e.g., an arranged marriage) for the sake of others (e.g., one's parents) even if one is able to effect change. Likewise, although now in a position of dominance, one may prefer some 'give and take' with opponents, given the instability of political or social arrangements.

A CORE CONCEPTION?

In the last two decades, Susan Mendus, Peter Nicholson, and John Horton have clarified what might be considered conditions for the 'core meaning' of toleration.[14] These conditions are as follows:

1.   Toleration arises 'in circumstances of diversity', i.e., when people are aware of salient differences existing among them.
2.   Toleration is a matter of leaving others alone or refraining from persecuting them, either through the law or by means of what John Stuart Mill called the 'tyranny of public opinion'.
3.   Toleration requires voluntary forbearance or voluntarily leaving others alone when the diversity itself gives rise to forms of offense such as disapproval, dislike, or disgust.
4.   The tolerant person may not have the power to interfere, but it must be the case that if she has the ability to suppress, disrupt, or censure the offending speech, behavior, or person, she refrains from doing so.[15]

As a proposed definition, conditions 1-4 do capture a common core of many cases of toleration. Consequently, it adds much conceptual clarity for discussants wishing to refer to deliberate, or at least intentional, forbearance when a person believes there is sufficient offense to consider the desirability of intervention. But the definition is unsuited for other 'pluralistic' ways in which we speak of toleration. The definition rules out instances of indifference in which the tolerant lack motivation to respond to offense. The definition also rules out cases of permissiveness by restricting toleration to situations in which a tolerant person must restrain herself from interfering, granted the ability. The major limitation of the 'core meaning' definition, however, is its lack of a moral quality we associate with many acts of toleration.

Consider two hypothetical cases of toleration each satisfying the four conditions necessary for the proposed definition. In the first, a tolerant majority views a minority as having behaved in a manner inappropriate in the community or having

---

[13] Horton, "Toleration as a Virtue", p. 29
[14] Mendus, *Toleration*, p. 8; Nicholson, "Toleration as a Moral Ideal", pp. 158-173; Horton, "Toleration as a Virtue", pp. 28-41.
[15] Horton, p. 29

failed to live up to standards expected of citizens.   Despite strong disapproval, members of the majority are tolerant, believing that, all things considered, it is better that the minority's transgressions should be overlooked, excused, or grudgingly allowed.   Toleration in this case is based on some combination of compromise, social efficiency (e.g., avoiding social strife), fear, indulgence, and concession to human weakness or pity.   As such, toleration is compatible with disrespect, even contempt, for those tolerated.

In the second case, a tolerant majority believes that respect for persons as morally autonomous requires that they give equal consideration to others' beliefs, interests, and choices as manifestations of their conceptions of the good life.   Equal consideration does not entail approval in the sense that tolerant persons believe that the beliefs or behavior they tolerate are right or appropriate.   Nor does it require that the tolerant majority believe that there is no way to determine what is true or right (as some cultural and ethical relativists might believe).   Members of the majority accept that what they should tolerate may occupy a crucial place in others' life plans, even though they may regard what others embrace as quite (regrettably) false or wrong.   But they concede that what they tolerate may occupy a place as central for the minority as the place occupied by the cherished beliefs and practices that animate the tolerant persons' own plans for the good life.   Unlike the first case, toleration manifests respect in the second sort of case.   In the latter situation the tolerant have the capacity to see themselves in the place of the others.   And although they do not approve of certain beliefs and practices of the other group, nevertheless, the tolerant appreciate that these beliefs and practices are deeply 'anchored' in the lives of the others in a manner analogous to the commitments for which the tolerant themselves demand respect.

TOLERATION AS A MORAL CONCEPT

Just because toleration as a manifestation of virtue seems to imply respect for persons, toleration understood in this special, 'respect laden' and moral sense also appears to be logically incompatible with indifference, permissiveness, and endurance.   A start at articulating the conditions for describing toleration as genuinely *moral* can be made by reviewing the conditions in the core meaning. Condition (1) and (2) are satisfactory, but condition (3) needs to be reformulated.

If those who are tolerant are to be morally commended for their toleration then, at a minimum, they forbear from interference even though they *believe* that what they tolerate is morally wrong.   Moral toleration (henceforth interchangeable with toleration as a moral virtue) is to be explained and justified in terms of beliefs, attitudes, and motives subject to guidance and modification through moral reflection.   In other words, moral toleration pertains to what an individual morally disapproves of based on reasons rather than on dislikes, negative feelings, or biases alone.   Such reflection shows that original condition (3) requires reformulation as (3a) for moral toleration.

3a.   Toleration requires voluntary forbearance from interference when diversity itself gives rise to moral disapproval, that is, on disapproval based on morally relevant reasons rather than on simple dislikes, negative feelings, or biases.

Thus when we approve morally of a person's toleration, we approve not just of her voluntary forbearance but of the exercise of this forbearance in the face of behavior we believe the tolerant person disapproves of on morally relevant grounds, and therefore, might have felt justified in trying to suppress. One's toleration is truly moral then only when one can present relevant and weighty reasons for feeling justified in disapproving of the tolerated behavior.[16]

Just as further reflection about the tolerant person has led us to condition (3a), reasoning about the 'objects' of toleration justifies the addition of a new condition. Can the objects of toleration be persons as well as expressions, beliefs, behaviors, and practices the tolerant find offensive? If toleration is to be a moral concept, and (from the moral viewpoint) we are to be able to rule out an expression such as 'tolerant racist' or 'tolerant sexist' as an oxymoron, then we must agree that persons themselves cannot be the objects of toleration.

The argument for this claim is straightforward. Condition 3(a) establishes the rational basis for toleration as a moral virtue. One tolerates what one disapproves of on the basis of reason. Moral disapproval signifies belief in the responsibility of others for the behavior tolerated. It follows, therefore, that one can tolerate morally only what one can regard as subject to change or alteration. It would hardly be rational to tolerate (morally) what cannot be altered or what is beyond anyone's control. (Of course, we do speak of tolerating such things as the frailties of old age, the ravages of storms, and incurable diseases, but only in slipping back to the notion of toleration as endurance.) To speak of tolerating another person, in the moral sense, implies that it is to her discredit that she does not change that feature of herself that is the object of toleration.[17]

When something is unalterable, no praise or blame may properly accrue. This is a simple application of the principle that 'ought' implies 'can.' And thus only those things subject to alteration by agents are the legitimate objects of toleration: individual behavior certainly (whether speech or action), and beliefs and practices (to the extent that they are not resistant to individual's efforts to change them). But such ascriptive characteristics as eye or skin color, sex, genetic inheritance, or origin of birth are beyond individuals' control. It is absurd to imagine that one's sex or race is malleable like preferences for affiliation or life style. It follows, therefore, that no one can be held responsible for such characteristics as sex or race, and that it is incoherent to select them as the grounds for moral disapproval. But the racist and sexist want to disapprove of persons just because they are of a particular race or sex. And this is why, from the moral point of view, it is incoherent to describe one as a 'tolerant racist' or a 'tolerant sexist'. Thus the following condition also is necessary for moral toleration (stated as a new fifth condition):

5.   The objects of toleration, as the expression of a moral virtue, are not

---

[16] Nicholson, "Toleration as a Moral Ideal", pp. 160-161
[17] Mendus, *Toleration,* pp. 16-17 and pp. 149-150

persons per se, but beliefs, attitudes, behavior (including verbal), and practices subject to change or alteration by the persons who hold these beliefs and attitudes or exhibit or participate in the behaviors or practices in question.

Further reflection about the distinction between persons and their 'deeds' reveals a final condition necessary for toleration as a moral concept. This last condition addresses directly the relationship between toleration and respect for persons mentioned earlier. The condition can be stated as follows:

6. Toleration is a manifestation of respect for persons; more precisely, it is the manifestation of the disposition to subject one's moral disapproval of another's beliefs, attitudes, behaviors, or practices to one's respect for the other's attachment to the beliefs, attitudes, behaviors or practices in question.

Given moral disapproval of the objects of toleration, there must be sufficient grounds for voluntary forbearance. The distinction between the doer and the deed, identified in condition (5) points toward the only appropriate grounds for forbearance that can be chosen morally; namely, the relative priority the tolerant person assigns to conflicting moral principles and sensibilities. For, as condition (6) indicates, moral toleration involves a tension between one's moral disapproval of some object, and appreciation (perhaps even approval) for the importance that the other assigns to this object. Respect, especially when understood as respect for the autonomy of the other, supplies the ground for the tolerant person's decision to assign greater weight to the other's attachment to the belief or behavior in question than the weight one assigns to one's disapproval of it.

The necessary conditions so far identified can be briefly summarized as involving all of the following: 1. Awareness of diversity; 2. Voluntary forbearance; 3. Moral disapproval; 4. Self-restraint even if one has power to suppress, interfere, or censure; 5. Taking as objects of toleration alterable beliefs, attitudes, behaviors, etc.; 6. Giving priority to respect for persons over disapproval of their beliefs, attitudes, behaviors, etc. These six conditions are also, as far as I can discern, jointly sufficient for the concept of moral toleration.

MORAL TOLERATION AND NEUTRALITY

There is some disagreement in liberal theory over what neutrality means.[18] Rawls distinguishes between procedural neutrality, neutrality of effect or influence (or

---

[18] C. Larmore, *Patterns of Moral Complexity* (Cambridge: Cambridge University, 1987), pp. 53-59; Raz, *Morality of Freedom*, pp. 114ff.

outcome), and neutrality of aim.[19] Rawls endorses neutrality of aim in the sense that basic institutions and public policy are not to be designed to favour any particular conception of the good life.[20] (The substantive principles of justice as fairness rule out procedural neutrality while neutrality of influence or effect must be abandoned as impracticable.)

There should be no confusion over the differences between neutrality and moral toleration.[21] Moral toleration concerns morally commendable individual behavior whereas neutrality concerns public policy: restraints on governmental and institutional actions. Obviously one can exist without the other. Individuals can be tolerant and virtuously tolerant even under illiberal, repressive governments; likewise, neutrality may regulate public institutions and public policy even in the absence of moral toleration. Third, and most important, neutrality logically cannot be toleration as a moral concept, for if neutrality means anything, then it means that the government must not interfere because it cannot disapprove. A liberal government cannot justify its actions as promoting or protecting some comprehensive doctrines or as disadvantaging others. Moral toleration, by contrast, requires both that persons believe something is immoral and believe that forbearance is proper.

Despite their differences, the connection between neutrality and moral toleration is held to be important for political liberalism. Both Raz and Rawls give a central place to 'moral toleration' as necessary for moral pluralism or political stability in a constitutional regime. Rawls asserts that political liberalism can be neutral in aim but still "affirm the superiority of certain forms of moral character and encourage certain moral virtues..."[22] For instance, a neutral constitutional regime may take steps "to strengthen the virtues of toleration and mutual trust, say by discouraging various kinds of religious and racial discrimination..."[23] Thus, justice as fairness includes an account of certain moral virtues—civility, reasonableness, and the sense of fairness, along with tolerance—as 'political ideas' and 'political virtues'.[24] Rawls characterizes as 'reasonable comprehensive doctrines' the diverse views persons hold about what constitutes a meaningful life and what qualifies as a worthwhile life project. Because the political virtues, including toleration, can be endorsed by citizens generally, they "do not depend on any comprehensive doctrine".[25] Moreover, it is perfectly reasonable for a liberal state to strengthen feelings and beliefs that "sustain fair social cooperation between its citizens regarded as free and equal".[26]

Supposing the political virtue of toleration to be a moral virtue, can government policies be neutral in aim while affirming the superiority of toleration as a moral virtue? They cannot be neutral with respect to any conception of the good life that

---

[19] *Political Liberalism*, pp. 191-194.
[20] Rawls, p. 194.
[21] T. Scanlon appears to disregard these differences in "The Difficulty of Tolerance", Heyd, ed., *Toleration*, pp. 227-228
[22] Rawls, p. 194
[23] ibid, p. 195
[24] ibid, p. 194
[25] ibid, p. 191
[26] ibid, p. 191

regards toleration as a secondary value, especially when this vision advocates intolerance towards other life plans. Nor can the government be neutral towards any comprehensive doctrine that discounts respect for persons. Rawls does assert that duties of neutrality pertain only to citizens who advance 'permissible' conceptions—i.e., those who respect the principles of justice.[27] But the definition of 'permissible' is certainly contestable and even some groups appealing to conscience—absolute pacifists, radical environmentalists, anti-vivisectionists, among others—might be said to find some practices intolerable just because these groups are so scrupulous and inclusive in their efforts to apply just principles.

The more serious question concerns the consistency of toleration as a 'political virtue' with moral toleration as understood here. Given the requirement that it be acceptable to citizens generally, is it plausible to believe that such a political virtue is really a moral virtue? It is not. Any form of toleration that can be justified as politically neutral will be inadequate from a moral point of view, because it will be based only on the recognition of the need for some kind of accommodation. Citizens might accede to mutual toleration for various reasons including perceptions that the costs of interference are too high or because it contributes to something else valued. Exercising forbearance on the basis of such reasons may be prudent, politically expedient, or self-interested, but it can hardly be morally commendable.

In overcoming overt intolerance, people do not automatically become morally tolerant. Because of the plurality thesis, intolerance and toleration are not logically related in such a way that the absence of intolerance guarantees the presence of a specific kind of toleration. In fact, political toleration is entirely compatible with indifference, permissiveness, or endurance. With the end of violent and institutional intolerance there may begin a negative peace or a tense truce, but nothing that fosters or promotes moral toleration. Consequently, political toleration is compatible with condescension, disrespect, and contempt—both for persons and their beliefs and practices.[28]

Can Rawls plausibly derive moral toleration from fundamental and neutral principles of justice? If so, Rawls could claim to have shown that moral toleration is neutral among competing conceptions of the good. In *Political Liberalism* Rawls does attempt to derive the virtue of toleration from the demands of reasonableness characterized as the 'burdens of judgment'. One burden of judgement concerns our fallibility—our inability to know or to be sure we know the answers to ultimate questions. Given this fallibility, another burden of judgment concerns the limits of what we can justify to others. Now, one important consequence of these burdens of judgment is that not all reasonable persons will affirm just one comprehensive doctrine. Moreover, as Rawls says, "they also *recognize* that all persons alike, including themselves, are subject to these burdens, and so many reasonable comprehensive doctrines are affirmed, not all of which can be true (indeed none of which may be true)".[29] Rawls adds, "We *recognize* that our own doctrine has, and can have, for people generally, no special claims on them beyond their own view of

---

[27] ibid, p. 192
[28] See A. Altman, "Toleration as a Form of Bias", *Philosophy, Religion, and the Question of Intolerance*, pp. 230-245
[29] *Political Liberalism*, p. 60 [emphasis added]

its merits. Others who affirm doctrines different from ours are, we grant, reasonable also, and certainly not unreasonable"[30]

The critical issue of course is what exactly reasonableness entails. 'Recognize' in the quoted passages is extremely vague. As a consequence of the burdens of judgment, we may 'recognize' that toleration is the best policy (i.e., perceive the need to avoid conflict), without thereby 'recognizing' (i.e., appreciating) that others merit or deserve toleration or that our toleration is due as a matter of respect for them. For example, certainly we can recognize the need for a 'you leave me alone and I'll leave you alone' accommodation without abandoning faith in the absolute truth of our comprehensive doctrine or giving up faith in its ultimate victory.

If Rawls believes that moral toleration results merely from our cognizance of the burdens of judgment, then this may be because he has already assumed moral toleration as part of an account to be given of what we recognize, or comprehend. If we do recognize, or comprehend, that the different views of others are reasonable comprehensive doctrines and therefore that others are worthy of respect *because they hold these doctrines as reasonable persons*, is not this because we are already capable of moral toleration? Likewise, with Rawls's claim that our own doctrines can make no special claim on others. That is, moral toleration is presupposed by our ability to recognize, or apprehend, that although we may disapprove of the beliefs of others, we nevertheless can view others as *unreasonable in abandoning their own doctrines unless ours prove more reasonable for them*. Insofar as moral toleration is presupposed in the argument, obviously it is not derived from fundamental principles of political liberalism. Contrary to Rawls's assumption, toleration as a moral virtue is not a special political virtue of political liberalism.

Most defenses of toleration as a political virtue independent of any thick theory of the right or good end up relying on arguments that toleration is justified as a pragmatic compromise, a 'Hobbesian equilibrium', and a *modus vivendi*.[31] Pragmatic justifications make toleration wholly contingent on transient social conditions. Hence it is not surprising to find liberals referring to a time when toleration will have superceded itself.[32] This suggests unwarranted optimism about the future. It is assumed without sufficient argument that somehow tense and unstable compromises will 'evolve' into more indifferent and permissive societies, ignoring cases in which exactly the opposite has occurred (e.g., the former Yugoslavia, Afghanistan, Iran, Zimbabwe, and Argentina).

The move towards pragmatic justification raises additional difficulties. For one, as long as toleration is seen as an expedient, then liberals will have a hard time responding to arguments that on occasion intolerance is more effective at promoting

---

[30] Rawls, p. 60 [emphasis added]

[31] Altman, "Toleration as a Form of Bias"; R. Dees, "The Justification of Toleration", *Question of Intolerance*, pp. 134-156; Jordan, "Concerning Moral Toleration"; J. Schneewind, "Bayle, Locke, and the Concept of Toleration", *Question of Intolerance*, pp. 3-15; B. Williams, "Toleration: An Impossible Virtue?", pp. 18-27. Rawls himself sometimes thinks of the value of toleration resulting from a contractual process. See, for example, *Political Liberalism*, p. 62, note 17.

[32] Heyd suggests that "toleration might prove in the future to have been 'an interim value'..." See *Toleration*, p. 5.

pluralism.[33]   Second, such justifications can be expected to reinforce the critical view that liberalism itself fails to be neutral. Critics believe that liberalism must "construe the toleration of non-autonomy valuing sub-groups as a necessary evil, not a genuine good".[34]   Hence, they view liberals as adopting toleration as "a temporary expedient against the day when all are autonomous".[35] Third, pragmatic justifications seem to concede a major divergence between political liberalism and the civic culture needed to sustain it. Liberal institutions and policies that succeed in promoting non-moral forms of toleration may increase publicly tolerant behavior without thereby affecting attitudes of tolerance. Risks of this are high if group members themselves feel oppressed when they are required to put up with beliefs or practices they could effectively suppress. They may even feel contempt for the 'wrongful' behaviors of others. Thus, by insisting on a stand off when divisions are very deep, liberalism permits and may perpetuate attitudes and perspectives that are inconsistent with the conditions for a reasonable and moral justification of toleration.[36] Unfortunately, by insisting on the equal toleration of all permissible comprehensive doctrines, including intolerant doctrines, liberalism may intensify hostilities and rigidify biases.

CONCLUSION

If correct, the reasoning in this paper leads to conclusions most uncongenial for political liberalism. I have considered several ways in which toleration may be understood. Although neutrality of aim is logically consistent with each of these conceptions, only toleration as a moral virtue entails respect for persons as autonomous. But just because the forbearance of moral toleration is justified by respect, moral toleration cannot be a political virtue all citizens could equally endorse. Paradoxically, moral toleration presupposes one comprehensive doctrine among others, namely, a comprehensive liberalism in which autonomy is given pride of place in the pantheon of values. Moral toleration presupposes both the value of autonomy and a ranking of values such that respect for autonomy is given priority over other values expressed by moral disapproval of certain objects of toleration. Consequently, and contrary to Rawls' notion of toleration as a political virtue, because moral toleration is not independent of a particular comprehensive doctrine, a neutral constitutional regime cannot make special efforts to promote it. Assuming that efforts to use state power to promote toleration really can be both neutral in aim and successful, such efforts may promote accommodations and forbearances, but as conditions falling short of the reflection and disposition involved in moral toleration. Moreover, a truce or expedient accommodation is neither sufficient nor necessary for moral toleration. It is not sufficient, since as noted above, an expedient arrangement may make it more difficult to be morally tolerant. Nor is it necessary because, when toleration is genuinely based on respect

---

[33] R. Wolff, "Beyond Tolerance", R. Wolff, B. Moore, Jr., and H. Marcuse, *A Critique of Pure Tolerance*, (Boston: Beacon, 1965), pp. 3-52
[34] Mendus, *Toleration*, p. 144
[35] Mendus, p. 108
[36] B. Herman, "Pluralism and the Community of Moral Judgment", Heyd, ed., *Toleration*, p. 62

for persons, then despite moral disapproval, one has sufficient reason for forbearance, whether or not the forbearance or respect is reciprocated.

The relationships between moral toleration, neutrality, and liberalism need to be re-examined. This is a very large task indeed, and I shall close by making just a few suggestions for the directions it might take. A first need is for liberal theorists to adopt the plurality thesis and to observe the distinctions that more correctly reflect our thinking about concepts of toleration. Many controversies—for example, that too much 'hate speech' is 'tolerated'—might most reasonably be interpreted as controversies over justifiable limits to what ought to be permitted, endured (put up with), or what we ought not to regard with indifference. Controversies of this kind may or may not also involve moral toleration. And, when they do not, they might be best settled without invoking the relative merits, or virtuousness, of parties on either side of the issue.

In the second place, liberals should be clearer and more specific about the 'public good' a policy or institutional procedure seeks to achieve. Sometimes toleration as permissiveness, endurance, or indifference is sufficient and appropriate. In other cases, toleration of these types may be inimical to processes or social conditions conducive to value pluralism.

Finally, as the previous suggestions indicate, political liberals need to reconcile the objectives of neutrality and moral toleration. Neutrality concerns collective will and public power as represented in institutional structures and processes. Moreover, within republican and democratic governments, the ideal of neutrality is one of constraints that the people impose on themselves. By contrast, toleration as a virtue involves individual discretion and choice. This choice concerns matters over which there is no settled moral consensus and political agreement regarding what must be endured, or permitted, or about which one may be indifferent. Again, by contrast, the ideal of neutrality specifies that, whatever their substantive content, comprehensive doctrines ought not to be regarded by citizens as properly subject to the question: 'Should I tolerate this or not?'

Thus the place of moral toleration in political liberalism may be quite different from what it was previously thought to be. The need for moral toleration is greatest before neutral policies have identified beliefs and activities as properly beyond the bounds of toleration and intolerance. Moreover, moral toleration always remains important in a politically liberal society because boundary line problems can never be completely solved. Although political liberalism bids us respect competing comprehensive doctrines, it cannot—according to its own principles and except in limiting cases—specify what belongs 'in' a conception of the good life.

CHAPTER 5

TOLERATION AND NEUTRALITY: INCOMPATIBLE IDEALS?

Saladin Meckled-Garcia

INTRODUCTION

Toleration and neutrality have often featured as interchangeable terms in commentaries on liberal political morality.[1] In this vein influential thinkers, such as John Rawls, speak of liberal neutrality as if it were an extension of the principle of toleration.[2] In what follows I aim to show not only that these concepts are fundamentally different, but also that tolerant and neutralist principles are not even mutually supporting. The concepts clearly have many things in common, especially when we are talking about their relationship to political justification and action, and both appear to capture the aims of liberal political morality. In fact they seem to represent two aspects of one project, taking on different burdens in a moral division of labour: one a virtue of institutions and the other a virtue of citizens. However, the overlap is deceptive and misleading in terms of what liberals should consider themselves committed to. Separating them will clarify their values for liberal political morality. So, my second aim, after distinguishing the concepts, is to consider whether toleration is necessary in a neutralist society. I argue against this view. I then consider whether toleration might not be independently valuable, perhaps as a competitor, to neutrality, an approach which, I also argue, has decisive reasons against it.

---

[1] E.g., neither C. Larmore, *Patterns of Moral Complexity* (Cambridge: Cambridge University Press, 1987), pp. 75-6 and p. 130, nor T. Nagel, *Equality and Partiality* (New York and Oxford: Oxford University Press, 1991), pp. 154 ff., distinguish the concepts.
[2] "political liberalism applies the principle of toleration to philosophy itself." J. Rawls, *Political Liberalism* (New York: Columbia University Press, 1993), p. 10.

By the political morality of liberalism I mean something quite specific. Toleration and neutrality are traditionally offered as responses to the problem of pluralism. This is the problem of finding the appropriate attitude for citizens and state in the context of a variety of widely differing and often conflicting conceptions of the good life.[3] Clearly one response to that problem is unacceptable: to respond to pluralism with enforcement and coercion aimed at producing consensus, or advancing one of the views in the plurality. Rejection of this response is one defining feature of liberal views. In other words, liberals do not demand citizens give up their differences. Nevertheless, another element within this liberal perspective, important in both defining and evaluating toleration and neutrality, is the idea of acceptance: there must be some degree to which citizens accept each other, if they are to live together in a political society.[4] There must be a reason why we are together in political community, rather than mere accommodation, and that reason should reflect appropriate attitudes towards each other. Difference and conflict in a liberal state must go hand in hand with unity and acceptance to some degree. In fact, it would seem that more unity and acceptance in the context of accepted differences, is better than less. Nor can this acceptance be abstract, or arbitrary, but must speak in some way to citizens self-value, and must be reciprocal. The central problem of pluralism is, then, how we can have citizens with different conceptions of the good life accept each other, in a way that they themselves find acceptable.

In the second section of what follows I set out the area to which my discussion is restricted (moral, and more specifically political, toleration and neutrality) and offer definitions for these concepts. On the basis of these definitions I show that the two concepts are fundamentally distinct, and prima facie in conflict. In the third section I consider possible ways that political toleration might be justified as a complement to, or supportive of, neutrality. I show why this option is not available. The fourth section considers whether toleration might not be considered an independent value that has to be accommodated, together with neutrality, or even at the expense of neutrality. I conclude that political neutrality, and not toleration, is necessary as both an institutional value and an attitude of citizens if liberalism is to have even a partially adequate response to the problem of pluralism: one which accommodates both the existence of difference and disagreement, and which incorporates some degree of mutual acceptance.

DEFINING TOLERATION AND NEUTRALITY

---

[3] Thus Rawls, *Political Liberalism*, p. xvi ff., shares this aim with J. Raz, *The Morality of Freedom*, (Oxford: Clarendon, 1986), p. 133. They just differ on the definition of what constitutes an appropriate pluralism.
[4] One extreme of this is a *modus vivendi* where acceptance is at a minimum, but constrained by considerations of prudence.

Given this understanding of the aims of toleration and neutrality in liberal political morality, I can somewhat restrict the scope of my offered definitions of these concepts. I am not considering toleration in respect of any sphere, nor neutrality in respect of any (and every) sphere. In fact the idea of an absolute neutrality is arguably incoherent.[5] One's neutrality between competing views A and B, in a particular sphere, does not imply, or require, neutrality between B and C, or between A and B in every sphere. This is because one is neutral in relation to a range of competing positions, and to a sphere in which they compete. I can be neutral over the result of a race between my sister and her friend without being neutral as to which one does better in life, or whether they both beat a third person in the race. Absolute neutrality, on the other hand, would presume one had no standards or standpoint from which to approach a particular dispute. But, one is always neutral across a range of positions, R, by taking up a position which is not in that range. This, however, implies taking up a position.

I shall limit discussion to moral neutrality and moral toleration. That is, both the limits of what is tolerated and the justification of toleration are to be decided on moral grounds. Similarly the range of what we treat neutrally and the justification for this neutrality. I am interested in moral conflict and moral conciliation, hence this stipulation. The discussion is further restricted to political questions. Thus I focus on political neutrality and toleration, by which I mean attitudes towards the use of state power. A wider notion of toleration where we would consider, say, the moral merits of 'putting up with' a friend's bad table manners or marital infidelity for the sake of friendship will not concern me here. The same is true for neutrality in running races.

A further idea which will become relevant to this issue in the discussion which follows, is the distinction between state political toleration and personal political toleration (and the corresponding notions of neutrality). The distinction centres around who the agent of toleration and neutrality is, rather than the recipient. Its importance will become clear below. So, having imposed these restrictions, I can present my definitions. Toleration of the kind that I am interested in is where:

T: the relevant agent, A, has i) a first order moral reason to repress a view or practice, S, ii) has the power to seek such repression and iii) acts on an appropriate (sufficient) second order reason not to repress views or practices falling into range R, of which S is a member.

I have stated things this way (using 'range R', and second order reasons) to avoid traditional problems or paradoxes of toleration. A standard paradox is how one can have a moral reason to repress, and a moral reason not to repress, a view/practice, on the basis

[5] Raz, *The Morality of Freedom*, p. 117 ff.; Larmore, *Patterns of Moral Complexity*, p. 44 ff.; J. Waldron, "Legislation and Moral Neutrality", in his *Liberal Rights: Collected Papers 1981-91*, (Cambridge: Cambridge University Press, 1993), 143-167, p. 147; Rawls, *Political Liberalism*, pp. 191-4.

of considerations about the contents of that view/practice alone.[6] Using the concept of a relevant range allows the introduction of second order reasons which are not directly focused on the contents of the view, S. A first order moral reason is a moral reason to act or not to act in a given circumstance. A second order moral reason is a moral reason to act, or not to act, on that reason. Thus, a promise is a reason to do what one has promised.[7] But I may have another reason, helping an accident victim, which is incompatible with acting on my first order reason, and the fact that helping an accident victim is more important that keeping a promise to go to the cinema is a reason not to act on my first order reason (the promise). This does not cancel out the initial reason to go to the cinema (my promise still stands), it just overrides it.[8] Conversely, the fact that not acting on the promise will lead to a human catastrophe, say, may give me a second order reason to act on that reason (the importance of avoiding human catastrophe). Consider a relevant example: I may have a moral reason to repress views and practices which involve animal cruelty. How can I also have a moral reason not to repress these views and their associated practices, if I see them as so bad as to morally require repression? The range consideration is helpful here. I may consider these views to be part of a range of non-human-harming, freely chosen, ways of life. Repression of any of these may set a bad example in a society where I would prefer to encourage people to make free choices in their way of life. I consider membership of the latter group an important, and sufficient, second order reason not to act on my first order reason to prevent animal cruelty. I may still argue with people holding those views, and perhaps seek to make other ways of life more available and attractive to newer generations, or even provide positive incentives to abandon these activities. I will not, however, seek to repress them (make their way of life impossible or too costly to be pursued). Note that toleration is about avoiding purely negative action such as repression. It does not imply I refrain from positive political, non-repressive, action which gives advantage to my favoured views and, in a non-repressive way, disadvantages those views I do not see as morally favourable.

---

[6] See, for example, B. Williams, "Toleration: An Impossible Ideal?", in D. Heyd, ed., *Toleration: an Elusive Virtue*, (Princeton: Princeton University Press, 1996), pp. 18-27.

[7] The notion of first order and second order reasons is introduced by J. Raz in his discussion of 'secondary reasons' in *Practical Reason and Norms*, (Princeton: Princeton University Press, 1990).

[8] The matter is rather more complicated than explained here. The fact that a reason, A, may not be cancelled out by another reason, B (whilst we may feel we have to act on B) is not sufficient for B being a second order reason. That just makes it a non-cancelling, but overriding, reason. Thus the possible kinds of reasons relevant to our case are: 1) cancelling and non-cancelling reasons, 2) overriding and non-overriding reasons, and 3) reasons for acting or not acting on other reasons, and combinations of these. A second order reason is a non-cancelling reason to act (or not act) on another reason, which may or may not override that other reason. I may have a reason not to act on a reason to repress Johnny, but that may not override the original reason to repress Johnny, it may just be in competition with it.

There are four things worth noting about this conception of toleration. Firstly, it requires reference to the relevant agent, A's, moral reasons which explain and identify what is to be tolerated: that which A would seek to repress. This may be disputed, and it will form part of an important discussion later. For now I will leave it open which reasons should be used in deciding why A has a first order reason to repress any of those views in R.[9] Secondly, some kind of public conception of second order moral reasons is needed to explain why these views and practices should be tolerated (legitimately).[10] This is because we are interested in political toleration. A public justification must be available on which we base the toleration of different and conflicting views in society, and which we use to justify restraining the repressive apparatus of the state. Thirdly, although the definition may not capture all the nuances of the common concept of toleration,[11] it captures the central idea that toleration requires us to both believe that we have reasons for repressing a view and that we have reasons not to act on those reasons. That is, we need to avoid identifying toleration with simple acceptance and indifference.[12] Fourthly, the definition refers to what it is appropriate to tolerate, range R. This is done in a purely negative way. That is, we decide the limits of what we are willing to tolerate in each other, and everything outside of those limits, outside of R, is not up for toleration, but rather for repression.[13] There may be other reasons for not actually repressing something falling outside of R, such as that it may be difficult or costly to do so, but in principle that which falls outside of R is open to being repressed.

Neutrality, by contrast, is a view about what intentions the relevant agent is to act on when framing either negative *or positive* policy for the state.[14] The view says that A is being neutral when:

N: policies or legislation which distribute benefits and burdens are framed and pursued by the relevant agent, A, which are not motivated by a preference or priority ordering of any of the comprehensive moral views (or conceptions of the good life) of its citizens.[15]

---

[9] See G. Graham, "Tolerance, Pluralism and Relativism", and B. Herman, "Pluralism and the Community of Moral Judgement", both in Heyd, ed., *Toleration: an Elusive Virtue*, pp. 44-59, pp. 60-80, respectively.

[10] J. Horton, "Toleration as a Virtue", in Heyd, ed., *Toleration: an Elusive Virtue*, pp. 28-43, pp. 31-2.

[11] The definition does not, for example, accommodate an understanding of toleration that associates it with open-mindedness or distanced, stoical, forbearance.

[12] See G. P. Fletcher, "The Instability of Tolerance", in Heyd, ed., pp. 158-72, p. 159

[13] It is worth noting that not everything outside of R is up for repression. Some views we will plainly endorse, or be indifferent towards. Thus, these will not be inside R, but they will not be in the class of repressible views either.

[14] By intention I mean sincere justification. The state could appear to be acting neutrally if it justified its policies on grounds that do not make reference to competing comprehensive views. But if successive policy decisions were clearly directed at benefiting some one conception, whatever the justification offered, the state's neutrality would be in question.

[15] This is neutrality of intention rather than effect, Larmore, *Patterns of Moral Complexity*, p. 44; Waldron, *Liberal Rights*, pp. 149 ff.; Rawls, *Political Liberalism*, pp. 191 ff.

This needs qualification. The views or conceptions in questions must fall in a range (R). That range will be those views which are minimally acceptable by some criterion of acceptability.[16] For it would not make sense to say that there are no views or practices that we do not want to hinder. One way of doing this is to make the criterion of membership of R a belief in the inappropriateness of using state power, coercive or otherwise, to advance one's view against others who also believe it is inappropriate to use state power in this way.[17] A further reason for restriction to R is the condition on coherence noted earlier. Neutrality is always relative to a range, and the neutral party must be acting on reasons for being neutral across that range which are not themselves neutral in an absolute sense. Further, an agent can be neutral in two ways. The state can demonstrate neutrality either by acting on reasons not held by any of those in range R or by acting on reasons which are held by all persons in R. So, if A seeks legislation that we should all do one day's voluntary work a week, and this is justified by a Christian belief in charity, shared by only a subset of those views in R, then A is not being neutral. On the other hand, if A is motivated by a desire to see an improvement in the capacity of all citizens within R to equally pursue their conception of the good life, then, so long as all in R share this view, or none do, A acts neutrally. Neutrality thus aims at procedural even-handedness, across different, minimally acceptable views, held by citizens, when it comes to deciding on state policies that may help or hinder those views.

Of two interpretations of neutrality which are logically possible, one where the neutral justification is part of all the views in R and one where it is part of none, a modern liberal conception of neutrality would have to opt for the former. This is because adopted policies will have to be justifiable to people holding views in R, for political society to be properly seen as an association rather than as a bureaucratic machine, imposing alien, albeit neutral, policies on citizens. Participation and transparency are values that liberals would not relinquish easily, and which require the shared version of neutrality.[18] On a more practical level, it would be impossible for citizens to propose and defend neutralist policies if the motivation behind proposing and sustaining those policies was not some conception of just institutions held in common. This holding in common does not necessarily mean the neutralist standpoint is explicitly held in

---

[16] Rawls' notion of 'reasonableness', for example, J. Rawls, *Political Liberalism*, pp. 49 ff.

[17] This echoes ideas from J. Rawls and T.M. Scanlon concerning reasonableness, reasonable rejection, and reciprocity. See T.M. Scanlon, 'Contractualism and Utilitarianism', in *Utilitarianism and Beyond*, A. Sen and B. Williams, eds., (Cambridge: Cambridge University Press, 1982), pp. 103-128, also 'The Structure of Contractualism', in his *What We Owe Each Other* (Cambridge, Mass.: Harvard University Press, 1998), pp. 189-247. Rawls distinguishes these ideas as applied to politics, vs. morality in general, Rawls, *Political Liberalism*, p. 90, n. 1.

[18] Rawls even demands conditions of minimal transparency from non-liberal societies under a 'law of peoples'. The latter peacefully regulates international relations amongst both liberal and non-liberal, but well-ordered, states. J. Rawls, "The Law of Peoples", in S. Shute and S. Hurley, eds., *On Human Rights* (New York: Basic Books, 1993), pp. 41-82, p. 61.

common, so long as those holding views in R can, and do, employ the neutralist standpoint in their reasoned attitudes to the state, without giving up their views. Political neutrality thus goes hand in hand with the idea of a shared mode of reasoning about institutions.[19]

Consider the alternative: a state with neutralist institutions in which citizens do not support those institutions for neutralist reasons. The alternative kinds of reasons for doing so would be considerations of prudence, such as the thought that we would not want the sate used non-neutrally against our view, or principled reasons such as the thought that the consequences of non-neutrality, excessive uses of state power, are morally unacceptable. It would not be because we thought it was wrong to repress others' views (within an appropriate range) simply on the basis that we disagree with them, which is the neutralist view. In other words, we would have a modus vivendi, or something close to it, in which the terms of co-operation include a neutralist state. We would not have a society which accepts that recourse to state power is not an appropriate response to disagreement. This basis for neutrality seems inherently unstable. Should the balance of power change, or the conditions arise in which prudence, or principle no longer counselled putting up with neutrality, then the neutral institutions would no longer be acceptable, and supported. This might never get as far as making repression a recourse, but it could very well put differential treatment on the cards, giving advantages to some views over others, as those who are merely tolerant are disposed to do. There is also a consideration from the point of view of the proposal of policies. Neutrality of the kind I am discussing is neutrality of intention, not outcome. That is, the fact that a given policy has the result of benefiting one kind of view over another is not sufficient to make it non-neutral, so long as the policy is initiated for neutralist reason. However, it is quite possible for individuals to hide their non-neutralist reasons for initiating policy behind neutralist justifications. Which presents us with another reason for desiring that citizens in a well ordered society display the virtue of neutrality. So, while it is commonly thought that neutrality is purely a virtue of institutions, if one values neutrality for non-instrumental reasons (say because one is reasonable) then neutrality as a virtue of citizenship seems to be necessary for sustaining a well-ordered neutral polity.

So we have introduced an important distinction. That is between personal political toleration and state political toleration; personal political neutrality and state political neutrality. The state can aim to act in such a way as to satisfy T above, but so can individuals in their attitudes to state power. In the case of individual tolerance we might speak of the disposition of a person to act on T. Which can be understood as possession of the virtue of political toleration. In both cases, what makes acting on T toleration, and not something merely resembling toleration, is that condition (iii) demands we act on *reasons* not to repress views and practices in range R. These reasons must be appropriate

---

[19] What Rawls calls 'public reason', *Political Liberalism*, pp. 212 ff.

moral reasons. So, if my second order reasons to refrain from repression are that, say, I can see my opponents tripping themselves up, then I am not being tolerant although my actions and stance could be perceived as tolerant. I am just patient and clever. There is parallel with neutrality. The state can aim to implement legislation backed by considerations and justifications that do not make reference to the superiority of any view in R. That will need to be a demonstrable aim on the part of the state for it to claim that it is acting neutrally. At the same time, those members of the state involved in making political decisions (and this will extend to voting) will be expected not to seek policies that fail to conform with N. For any individual member of the state there will be the additional requirement that they genuinely do not seek policy motivated by an aim to favour a conception. That is, private and public justification must come together. Willingness, and in fact commitment, to this kind of policy discussion defines membership of R. Otherwise one could have putatively neutral policies, presented on neutral grounds, but nevertheless serving non-neutral ends.

One way that neutrality and toleration may be seen to overlap is in sharing the range of appropriate objects of the attitude, R. I have been using range R, the same range, for both political toleration and political neutrality, but this needs justification. I will discuss possible objections to this below. In the meantime let us say that what makes it plausible that R in political toleration and neutrality are coextensive is that in both there is a non-repressive attitude towards that which is itself not repressive. It seems unlikely that even a perfectionist will want to resort to repression, rather than incentives, for views that are not harmful or themselves intolerant. It is only those views that are actively harmful and/or not self-restraining in the use of coercion against fellow citizens which will be prime candidates for repression, rather less drastic political measures.[20]

The above discussion shows how toleration and neutrality–from persons and state–are fundamentally different. The key difference in practice is that toleration is not by itself sufficient to justify quite as much as neutrality. They share the negative characteristic of not sanctioning repression of views within a range on the basis of disagreement. Toleration, however, has no inherent commitment to refrain from using the state in positive ways. For example, there is no inherent intolerance in using the state

---

[20] It is worth noting that the use of state power, and even the use of coercion, do not by themselves amount to repression. There are various degrees of coercion and other methods the state can use in relation to a view a perfectionist state does not favour. J. Raz is keen to claim that coercion is not the first resort of a perfectionist state in relation to chosen styles of life: 'Furthermore, not all perfectionist action is a coercive imposition of a style of life. Much of it could be encouraging and facilitating action of the desired kind, or discouraging undesired modes of behaviour.' *The Morality of Freedom*, p. 161. He uses the example taxation incentives and disincentives as a non repressive method. On the range of methods a state can use, which would not necessarily add up to repression, but which neutralists would not accept see, G. Sher, "Liberal Neutrality and the Value of Autonomy", in E. F. Paul, F. D. Miller and J. Paul, eds., *Contemporary Political and Social Philosophy*, (Cambridge: Cambridge University Press, 1995), pp. 136-159, p. 150.

to encourage or aid conceptions of the good one overtly morally favours. Neutrality precisely bars the state from doing this.

This distinction should be of little surprise to anyone. After all, perfectionists clash with anti-perfectionist neutralists on just this point: whether the state can not only be used to prevent certain harmful activities, but whether it can be used to promote some activities over others, or even 'gently' aim to make some activities extinct over time. Perfectionists think that the state can be used in these positive ways, and, consequently, toleration but not neutrality is a value and virtue that perfectionists try to accommodate.[21] The distinction has also been alluded to in the past.[22]

The two concepts, however, most essentially come apart in their respective structures of reasoning. With political toleration, the second order reasons to refrain from repression (or seeking repression) must not cancel out the first order reasons. If they did then we would not have a second order reason not to act on the first order one. Rather, we would have a new first order reason; the conclusion of a piece of practical reasoning. Keeping one's first order reasons, whilst not acting on them, is just what it means to tolerate a view rather than accept it entirely or even be indifferent towards it. In the case of neutrality, however, our acceptance of the justified neutrality of the state means that our felt disagreement with others in R is not felt at the level of seeking repression. Even if that may originally have been our reaction or tendency, neutrality gives us a first order reason not to repress or seek repression as well as not to seek favours from the state. We do not, in the first place, see the content of our own view, or someone holding a conflicting view to ours, as a good reason to take political action for our view or against theirs. Which is different from saying we have a reason, but we also have a reason not to act on that reason. More concretely, I refrain from seeking state repression of your religion or advancement of mine. I do not so refrain because of some overriding reason not to act on a valid initial reason to repress. Rather, I see it as unreasonable to treat religious views (or their holders) within R as subject to state intervention–positive or negative–in relation to others in R. I see it as unreasonable because I only see it as reasonable, say, to resolve or at least engage such questions at the level of un-coerced discussion.[23]

Making this distinction contrasts with Rawls, for example, who is a neutralist, but nevertheless calls his version of our appropriate attitude to the state the 'democratic idea of toleration'. He also talks of his theory of justice as requiring the political virtue of

---

[21] See Raz, *The Morality of Freedom*, p. 404 ff., and S. Wall, *Liberalism, Perfectionism and Restraint*, (Cambridge: Cambridge University Press, 1998).

[22] See Wall, *Liberalism, Perfectionism and Restraint*, p. 67, and Horton, "Toleration as a Virtue".

[23] It is interesting that Locke argues we should tolerate religious views because religion requires conscience, and coercive power cannot be efficacious in the sphere of conscience. This argument could support either a tolerant stance or neutralist measures. J. Locke, *A Letter Concerning Toleration*, (Indianapolis: Bobbs-Merrill, 1955).

toleration from good citizens.[24] As I mentioned in a footnote above, political liberalism, in fact, is seen as an extension of the principle of toleration: 'political liberalism applies the principle of toleration to philosophy itself.'[25] The motivation for associating neutrality with toleration seems straightforward enough. Liberalism is the view that has historically defended political toleration. This began with religious toleration. It was extended to other kinds of toleration, such as those ranging over sexual orientation, and finally encompasses controversial philosophical divisions over the correct vision of a flourishing human life. Yet calling these developments 'toleration' is too simplistic. It may be that tolerance based reasoning was behind several liberal programmes. But some of these were motivated by perfectionist values, such as in Mill, whilst others associated with toleration argued for the removal of religious questions from the functions of the state—i.e., a neutralist move.[26] The final move, to remove substantive moral of philosophical conceptions (within R) from consideration by the state as a grounds for action is also a neutralist move. Calling this 'toleration', however qualified, only obscures matters and confuses commentators.[27]

Conceptual distinctions notwithstanding, perhaps this misses some of the complexity of traditional liberal views. There are two possibilities that I must consider. Firstly, that toleration at the personal level may be a necessary condition for, or at least lend support to, neutrality at the state level. This would explain their correlation in liberal thought. Alternatively, toleration may be valuable in itself, such that liberals need to accommodate it in their political theories. It is these two arguments that I will consider for what remains of this essay.

TOLERATION AT THE SERVICE OF NEUTRALITY

The first way of bringing toleration and neutrality together is by proposing a moral division of labour in which a virtue of the state is supported by or complemented by a different virtue on the part of individuals. Toleration requires and explains coercive restraint on the part of the good citizen. Neutrality requires coercive restraint, as well as other kinds of restraint. No citizen can be entirely neutral in their daily practices and

---

[24] Rawls, *Political Liberalism*, p. 194.

[25] Supported wholeheartedly in this by those who want to exclude philosophical questions from the justification of policy. E.g., R. Rorty. See his 'The Priority of Democracy to Philosophy', in A. Malachowski, ed., *Reading Rorty*, (Oxford: Basil Blackwell, 1990), pp. 279-302, especially p. 283 ff.

[26] This is a move supported, for example, by Jefferson, see R. Rorty, "The Priority of Democracy to Philosophy", in Malachowski, ed., *Reading Rorty*, p. 280. J. Locke too argues in a neutralist tone: 'The business of laws is not to provide for the truth of opinions, but for the safety and security of the commonwealth, and of every particular man's goods and person.', *A Letter Concerning Toleration*, p. 45.

[27] For example, S. Wall (after distinguishing toleration from neutrality) gets a lot of mileage out of criticising Rawls' view of toleration compared with his own understanding of the concept. Wall, *Liberalism, Perfectionism and Restraint*, pp. 71 ff.

exchanges, they can, however, be tolerant. Thus it benefits the neutral state for citizens to be tolerant. This allows coexistence under neutral institutions. So, toleration is a complement, perhaps a necessary complement, to neutrality.

As attractive as it may seem the distinguishing features of toleration and neutrality identified above are sufficient to discourage this scheme. Citizens of a neutralist state can be neutralist without giving up, or seeking that others give up, their conceptions of the good life, because neutrality purely concerns an attitude to the state. But if they are tolerant citizens, then their toleration will conflict with their neutrality. They cannot both be tolerant and see the state as justifiably neutral given that toleration implies these citizens hold on to reasons for repressing each other which are not cancelled out by better reasons not to act on these, repressive, reasons. They (the tolerant) maintain they have a reason to repress scurrilous views, but simply have other, overriding, reasons besides. That is, they have a valid (but inactive) reason to repress, as well as a reason not to repress. A neutralist, by contrast, will not think state repression is ever an appropriate course of action in disagreements between reasonable people. So there is a deep conflict between the two attitudes which makes it rationally impossible to hold both in relation to the same views.

Nor could we be happy with the view that citizens support neutral institutions as a consequence of their tolerant attitudes. For neutral institutions go too far for those who are exercising mere tolerance. The injunction not to even use institutions in a positive, non-repressive, way to support one conception of the good over others cannot be sustained on tolerance-based considerations alone. Citizens exercising political toleration could only accept neutral institutions for instrumental reasons, given that their attitudes conflict conceptually with a neutralist standpoint. They, after all, think it is legitimate under certain conditions to use the state to further their views, in non-repressive ways, and would only defer from doing so in conditions where this is unattainable or inadvisable. But the institutions of a well ordered society should be justifiable to its citizens on the basis of the justice of these institutions. The justice of neutralist institutions does not lie in their serving the temporary or prudential interests of non-neutralist citizens, but rather in the reciprocal respect demonstrated by upholding such institutions. This evaluation of those institutions fundamentally conflicts with their evaluation from the point of view of tolerance. Thus, it would seem that, to be justified to those they govern, neutral institutions require politically neutralist citizens in a well ordered society. It is not rationally available to citizens to be tolerant, once they accept the appropriate justification of neutralist institutions.

But there are other possibilities. It might be claimed that neutrality is too demanding a stance for citizens to take, whilst toleration is more in keeping with their differences. If citizens are to live their conceptions of the good, from within which they see other conceptions as wrong and misguided, it is psychologically difficult for them to see things neutrally. In which case toleration can serve as a convenient crutch. But it is unclear why citizens might find it harder to be neutral than tolerant in their every day lives. Both require a reflective stance: considerations of reasons for not seeking state action. If citizens cannot adopt the reflective stance of neutrality, then that is an argument against neutrality, not an argument for state neutrality backed up by personal toleration. On the other hand, if citizens can adopt the neutralist stance with respect to the state, then they will already have accepted the neutralist structure of reasoning, and this will conflict with their being tolerant (rather than neutralist).

My argument that tolerant citizens cannot be neutral citizens may be too quick. I have ignored the possibility that the range of views over which the neutral citizen is neutral is not identical with the range of views over which the tolerant citizen is tolerant. That is, the extension of R might not be the same for neutrality as for toleration. Are there any circumstances in which we would not include a view in the range we would be neutral over, but where we would nevertheless feel it valuable to tolerate that view? Here the question is not about how we define the content of R (for clearly neutrality and toleration have different ways of identifying their objects). Rather, what interests us is what is left outside of R: what is a cnadidate for repression and/or disadvantageous treatment? I have been assuming that what gets left out in both toleration and neutrality is the same.

If there are views that we would not be neutral towards, but could be tolerant towards, then the value of toleration would be in its 'mopping up', as it were, the troubles that neutrality does not deal with. The range of views neutrality is exercised over in a properly neutralist state is the range of reasonable or minimally acceptable views and practices. That is, R, in a neutral state, exhausts the views and practices that we would feel any obligation to refrain from exercising state power over. This is because range R properly describes views which can come together in what has been called a well ordered society, that is, views that do not seek to use state power against each other.[28] Who would neutral citizens exercise tolerance towards, rather than neutrality? Consider any view that does not satisfy the minimal acceptance criterion for neutral treatment. This would be a view that held it to be acceptable to use coercion, rather than un-coerced discussion, to obtain agreement or participation. Neutrality does not demand that we take such a view into account when formulating neutral policy. Intending that the state either suppresses the practices associated with the view, or seeks to make the view extinct through positive measures such as incentives, is perfectly consistent with neutrality. Neutralist citizens would seem to have no reason to tolerate such views rather than accept, and demand, the state acts against them. However, what if members of society exist who hold the view, but who are not pressed to act on it in contravention of neutralist policy? Would tolerance make sense here?

This helps us see an important aspect of political toleration. It is ideally suited to those who are forced to live together under some accommodation and who therefore

---

[28] Rawls, *Political Liberalism*, p. 35 ff.

have reasons to keep from seeking to repress each other. If one is forced to enter into transactions with people who's conception of the good one would otherwise repress, without repressing them, then it seems that one had better be tolerant. What I am describing is, of course, a *modus vivendi*.[29] It is precisely as a *modus vivendi* that those who are not members of R would exist in relation to those who made up a society that was otherwise well-ordered and neutral.[30] Given that these individuals might exist in a predominantly neutral society, what attitude would we need to exercise towards them?[31] Surely here, an unwillingness to repress them given their (perhaps temporary) political inactivity, paired with a willingness to employ the state to positively discourage and change these views, we have toleration? Consider the non-neutral (and intolerant) religious political militant who preaches and writes against the neutral state. Should she be silenced, or do the neutralists restrict use of repressive power to limiting any unconstitutional action on her part? If she is not silenced, but we must put up with her, then there appears to be a place for toleration in a neutral state. Neutralist citizens would have to live side by side with those holding these views, and yet refrain from seeking repressive restrictions. This would involve putting up with their speeches, meetings, and literature. Accordingly they would have to exercise a virtuous restraint.[32]

This view strikes me as wrong. It is true that citizens of a neutral state would refrain, in some instances, from exercising coercive power on inactive religious political militants. But the motivations for this do not have to come from toleration. They can just as well come from commitment to neutralist principles. Having decided the appropriate principles for political justice on neutral grounds, across R, citizens then apply those principles even towards citizens whose views are not in R. Their motivations are then that the principles are appropriately–neutrally–derived principles. They need not make any reference to toleration. It is not that neutralist citizens have an initial reason to repress these views which is overridden by another reason, although they will act when such views are actively unconstitutional. Rather they are considered to be wrong but not up for repression in the context of neutrally derived principles. Consider a principle that

---

[29] I do not mean to imply that tolerance is an accommodation resulting from self-interest. My reasons for tolerating another might come from my moral convictions. So, the objection that to be tolerant, it must be in one's power to repress or obtain repression, does not show that toleration proper is not involved in all *modus vivendi* type accommodations, only those based on sheer prudence.

[30] One could argue that toleration, being a moral value, cannot issue in a *modus vivendi*, because political toleration requires public reasons to tolerate, whereas in a *modus vivendi* we all have our own reasons for accommodating. But the public reasons could be shared without giving up the idea of a *modus vivendi*. We could all be united by moral disapproval of social unrest and war: what has been called the social peace argument. See B. Barry, *Liberty and Justice* (Oxford: Clarendon Press, 1991), p. 26.

[31] Cf. J. Rawls, *A Theory of Justice* (Oxford: Oxford University Press, 1973), pp. 218-9.

[32] It is interesting in this context that C. Larmore identifies the neutralist state with a *modus vivendi*. Larmore, *Patterns of Moral Complexity*, p. 75 and p.130. Cf. also, Waldron, 'Rushdie and Religion', in his *Liberal Rights*, 134-142, p. 137.

ascribes liberty rights, for example, the right to speak one's mind.[33] One would extend this to all citizens, on the basis of neutralist considerations. It would therefore be equally extended to the religious political militant. It is only when the militant's actions threaten or violate the neutrally arrived at principles that repression becomes a consideration. But here toleration too would have reached its limits. The neutralist would seek to repress the unreasonable and active militants, and at least disadvantage unreasonable inactive views. The tolerant citizen would seek to repress those citizens whose views were both scurrilous *and* threatening. Assuming that active unreasonable views, and scurrilous and threatening views, require the same coercive means for their repression, toleration does not extend beyond neutrality in this respect.

TOLERATION BEYOND NEUTRALITY

This brings me to the other way that one could present toleration as relevant to good citizens within a neutralist state. It might be conceded that neutrality does not require toleration from its citizens nor from the state. Nevertheless, toleration might be seen as a value in its own right.[34] This is a difficult case to make, for the discussion so far seems to indicate that neutrality has occupied all the justificatory space that toleration could have occupied. Why see toleration as a value if it does not add anything to neutralist concerns, and is in fact ruled out of the practical reasoning of neutralist citizens? Perhaps the point is deeper. If toleration is an independent value then citizens may have a reason to tolerate views that a neutralist conception would repress. Consider those views and practices outside R, which will be repressed in a purely neutral state. Is there any toleration-based, rather than neutrality-based, reason not to repress those views? Here again what we are considering is whether the limits of toleration might be different, reaching further, than the limits of neutrality. We also have to ask, in cases where the limits will be in this way different, whether there are any reasons to accept the tolerant stance rather than the neutralist.

What, then, might lead one to give an independent justification of liberal toleration that goes beyond neutrality? It seems that all the available options are inadequate. Consider the standard move of trying to ground toleration on considerations of

---

[33] I am aware there is a wide literature on freedom of expression, and that there are arguments that this has its limits. But liberalism is committed to the idea that what sets the limits can in principle be distinguished from value judgements of the content of the views expressed. Mill's harm principle is one attempt to articulate this distinction. See S. Mendus, *Toleration and the Limits of Liberalism* (Basingstoke: Macmillan, 1989). Also see, for example, T.M. Scanlon, "A Theory of Freedom of Expression", *Philosophy and Public Affairs*, 1 (1972), 204-226; J. Cohen, "Freedom of Expression", *Philosophy and Public Affairs*, 22 (1993), 207-263; R. Langton, "Speech Acts and Unspeakable Acts", *Philosophy and Public Affairs*, 22 (1993), 293-330; J. Feinberg, "Limits to the Free Expression of Opinion", *Freedom and Fulfilment*, (Princeton: Princeton University Press, 1992), pp. 124-152.

[34] Rawls identifies toleration as a political virtue amongst others, Rawls, *Political Liberalism*, p. 194.

epistemological restraint, such as fallibility, or perhaps acceptance of the nature and burdens of human reason.[35] The problem here is that what we will have to show coercive restraint towards is what the neutralist will require us to show restraint towards, and that which we will have to repress, for not showing epistemological restraint, will be what the neutralist will seek to repress because it violates neutralist principles.[36] The baseline of acceptability of liberal neutrality is the same as that for liberal toleration.

This leaves one option: that political tolerance is to be preferred as a personal value over political neutrality. This would justify employing toleration rather than neutrality in our daily dealings with each other. It would not be incompatible with having a neutralist state, just because neutrality of the state might be instrumental in furthering toleration. Those aiming at toleration in the past have often sought to achieve it through the removal of certain concerns from the hands of the state, such as the question of religion. Thus toleration has been sought through neutralist measures. [37]

Do we have any reason to think toleration is a better value than neutrality for citizens of a liberal polity to endorse? There is at least one reason for thinking the opposite is true. It has been previously noticed that the idea of toleration, with its acceptance that citizens have reasons to repress each other, albeit reasons they do not think they should act on, is intrinsically problematical for political community.[38] A way of seeing the problem is by considering those things that people might be asked to tolerate. A certain kind of religious view that sees homosexuality as wrong might be asked to tolerate homosexuality because of a belief that repression breeds a culture of forced choices, or civil discord. In such a case, however, there seems something intrinsically disturbing in proclaiming that citizens should tolerate homosexuality. What is disturbing is best understood from the point of view of the person who adopts that way of life. People who are gay do not want to be tolerated, they want to be accepted. That does not mean, furthermore, that they want to be accepted as people while having their homosexuality tolerated. If our political views are such that we do not care about citizens attitudes to each other's ways of life, then of course toleration makes sense. And here again the affinity of toleration for a *modus vivendi* is evident. However, it is a valuable aim that citizens accept each other's ways of life. Tolerating each other does not represent political community, but a compromise. If the choice is whether we are tolerated or accepted, where 'we' includes our life choices, then we would prefer to be accepted.

---

[35] See B. Barry, *Liberty and Justice*, pp. 24-5, and *Justice as Impartiality* (Oxford: Clarendon, 1995), for the former, and Rawls, *Political Liberalism*, pp. 58-62, for the latter. See also Wall, *Liberalism, Perfectionism and Restraint*, pp. 93 ff.

[36] For a discussion of the faults of using epistemological restraint in supporting neutrality, see J. Raz, "Facing Diversity: The Case for Epistemic Abstinence", *Philosophy and Public Affairs*, 19 (1990), 3-46.

[37] See footnote on Jefferson and Locke, above, and Rawls' account of the history of toleration, Rawls, *Political Liberalism*, p. xxiv ff.

[38] See Horton, "Toleration as a Virtue", p. 36. Also, Fletcher, "The Instability of Tolerance".

This might be thought to be a red herring. After all, toleration as I have defined it leaves it open whether our first order reasons for wanting repression need or need not be moral reasons; need or need not be legitimate in some public moral sense. If we fill this in by making it a necessary condition that the reasons one has to repress have to be appropriate moral reasons, then we can accommodate the above point.[39] Of course it is not appropriate to say that we *tolerate* people who are gay: we should have no compulsion to repress homosexuality in the first place. At the same time, there are things that it might be morally appropriate to seek to repress, and it is to some subclass of these that tolerance may be relevant.

I do not think that this move can be used to defend the kind of toleration we are interested in. If we recall, what concerns us is political toleration: toleration with respect to the exercise of political repression. The concern motivating liberals in seeking this kind of toleration is the existence of differing and sometimes conflicting views of the good life amongst citizens of a state. *Political* toleration is brought in to reconcile these views within range R in a political society without basing 'reconciliation' on differential claims about the moral value of these views.

If this is true, then toleration would have to walk a thin line between explaining how one can accept condemnation and (initial) tendencies to repress, at the same time as holding that the views, and their holders, are to be *accepted*. The latter implies more than not *actually* seeking to repress those views.

How can we ask for toleration itself as a primary value of a liberal political community, if that value implies that individuals in living their ways of life, are not accepted by others at some significant level (which is, after all, what toleration implies). Bringing in a discriminating moral criterion for what is appropriately tolerated, on the merits of the content of views and lifestyles, either undermines the point of trying to introduce toleration, or simply rubs salt in the wounds. It is like saying 'We are justified in tolerating you because it is morally acceptable to want to repress you.' A public account of why those within range R should be tolerated may be appropriate to political toleration. But a public account of who amongst our fellow citizens should and shouldn't be considered worthy of repression in the first place, based on the content of their views and lifestyles, seems out of place in liberal political morality.

Understanding the notion of appropriateness I am employing here will clarify the point. There are reasons we can use in deciding what is justifiably excluded from range R, and therefore open to repression. This can be done without reference to the truth or falsity of those views, but rather, on the basis of their effects in practice. On the other hand, we can consider a view as worthy of repression on first order considerations with respect to the content of that view, and therefore available for tolerance, if second order

---

[39] Horton, for example, forcibly argues that one cannot be considered tolerant if one's first order reasons are morally inappropriate. The example he uses is that of whether a racist can be called tolerant for not seeking to repress other races. "Toleration as a Virtue", pp. 31ff.

reasons can be found to not act on the first order ones. Any view falling inside R will be one of these views. So, a public conception of what appropriately belongs in R, and is a candidate for toleration, will also be a public conception of what it is appropriate to repress on first order considerations referring to the nature of the views within R: a public moral judgement of those views as worthy of repression in the first instance. It is from this last implication of a public conception of what is worthy of toleration that the liberal will recoil.[40]

A toleration theorist can do one of two things in response to this impasse. The first is to bite the bullet and deny that mutual acceptance of people's choices, to any degree, is a necessary condition for a well ordered political community. We do not accept each other's lives and life styles, but do tolerate each other because of some second order reasons. For example, in accepting that people have a right to private choices, we may not accept that Christianity is a legitimate choice. But we would rather not interfere with that choice for fear of setting a bad example for the rest, or because we believe the exercise of choice is more valuable than the exercise of the right choice, under certain circumstances. The other option is to look at the foundations for the values we think a state should embody, perhaps taking on the perfectionist view that toleration has a limited role to play. For the perfectionist, R is the range of views that are versions or ways of living a flourishing, valuable, life. We do not tolerate views in R, we accept them as valuable forms of living the good life. We do not tolerate views outside of R, but repress them, or work to make them extinct. We only tolerate those character traits or features of persons which are necessary components of, or necessarily associated with, living one of the versions of the good life in R. They, in turn, cannot feel a lack of acceptance on such meagre grounds.

Neither option does justice to the problem we are trying to solve. The first just concedes that in a political society we do not accept each other as the beings we are, with the particular identities we have. If that was all that was on offer then it would make sense to compromise on it. If, on the other hand, we can have even a degree of acceptance, with our disagreement, then that seems a preferable option. Meanwhile, the perfectionist view is not open to all of us. It is strange to have to be committed to perfectionism because of a failure of toleration in solving the liberal problem. Neutrality is still an option: why not just give up toleration?

But does neutrality fare any better on this score. After all, it too must deal with moral dispute and differences, and it too must reconcile this with some public basis for employment of state power, which is not substantially the same as any one of the disputed views. If there is dispute and yet we believe the state can be used, then there must be a degree of non-acceptance of the views of others to the degree that we want to exclude them from being used to decide questions of public policy. Thus, the gay person

---

[40] A similar point is made by E. Galeotti, in this volume.

under a neutralist system can equally complain that her way of life is merely being 'put up with' by neutralist citizens rather than accepted.

This is an inaccurate portrayal of the well ordered neutralist state. Although neutralist citizens do not necessarily agree with each other about substantive life choices, they do agree about when it is and is not appropriate to make public judgements about each other, including those that could potentially lead to the exercise of coercion. There are no initial reasons exercised by neutralists citizens which play the role of the first order reasons in T (the initial and persisting reason tolerant citizens have to repress the views they tolerate). Even if there were, these will be revised in the light of neutralist considerations. Thus neutrality does not bring with it a built in reference to repressive tendencies towards each other. There is some lack of acceptance of each other's views and choices. Firstly, we do not accept holding any particular view within R as sufficient to confer the right to use state instruments or coercion to further that view, and secondly, that we may simply disagree with those views within R. Nevertheless, and at the same time, acceptance is built into the idea that we take views within R not to be subject to repression of any kind, but open to adoption, discussion and reassessment by individuals. That consideration is built into all the views in R, as a condition for their membership of R. It is also partly in recognition of that consideration being part of our fellow views in R that we see them as worthy of the attitude of acceptance. That is, the attitude of neutralist citizens towards each other contains a degree of reciprocal acceptance. There is thus a degree of acceptance, under neutralist terms, which is not present in the case of toleration.

It is important to note here that 'acceptance', in the way I have been using the term, should not be taken to mean agreement. It is possible to think of a view that (a) I disagree with morally (think it is wrong), (b) my disagreement is not sufficient to warrant repression of it, or any view, taken as a view simpliciter, and (c) my disagreement with the view does not have any coercive bearing on my attitude towards a holder of the view. [41] I may find the ideas or the lifestyle of the devout evangelising Christian, the glutton, the snob, or the dedicated hunter to be morally reprehensible, and yet my moral disagreement is not sufficient to warrant repression of these views even at an initial, first order level. They can be members of R, and I would not take it to be the case that merely making such choices warranted any coercive attitude towards the holder. In sum, this form of acceptance is the attitude that says 'I disagree with you, and yet accept that this is under no circumstances a sufficient basis for coercion.'

There is then a way of avoiding the negative, repression centred, connotations that toleration brings with it whilst addressing the problem of pluralism. This is in itself a positive move in the direction of acceptance. Citizens might find this unsatisfactory.

---

[41] Note that perfectionists would deny (c) by saying that if we allow someone to hold wrong views we are clearly showing moral disrespect towards her, e.g., Raz, *The Morality of Freedom*, p. 157.

After all, it is not true or full acceptance, in the sense of convergence, or mutual endorsement. It is still possible on this view for someone not to like the fact that I pursue an atheist or gay lifestyle, and not to like me for it. Whereas I, like many others, would prefer they wished me well, and saw my lifestyle as an achievement. But here we have reached the limits of acceptance and community within the bounds of liberalism.

CHAPTER 6

TOLERATION AND NEUTRALITY: COMPATIBLE IDEALS?

Peter Jones *

The relationship between toleration and liberalism has not been one of mutual entailment. Historically, many who have favoured toleration have not been liberals. The liberal who does not favour toleration has been a rarer specimen. Given societies as we know them, most liberals have regarded some form of toleration as both necessary and desirable. That would seem as true of present as of past liberal theorists and no less true of those contemporary liberal theorists who are commonly identified as 'neutralists'. John Rawls is a clear example. For Rawls, religious toleration is one of the 'settled convictions' from which he develops his political liberalism; it constitutes a 'fixed point' that "any reasonable conception must account for"[1] His political liberalism generalises that settled conviction by applying "the principle of toleration to philosophy itself".[2] One of his principal concerns is to establish the grounds of toleration in modern democratic societies[3] and toleration figures in a pivotal way in the political conception of justice that he goes on to construct. Accordingly, he ranks tolerance as one of the 'great political virtues' that a well-ordered society should cultivate amongst its citizens.[4] The theories developed by other neutralist liberals, such as Nagel, Larmore, and Barry, would seem equally hospitable to the idea of toleration.[5]

---

* I am grateful to Derek Bell for his helpful comments on an earlier draft of this chapter.

[1] John Rawls, *Political Liberalism* (New York: Columbia University Press, 1993), p.8.

[2] *Political Liberalism*, p.10.

[3] *Political Liberalism*, pp.4, 47.

[4] *Political Liberalism*, pp.122-3, 157, 194-5.

[5] Thomas Nagel, *Equality and Partiality* (Oxford: Oxford University Press, 1991); Charles Larmore, *Patterns of Moral Complexity* (Cambridge: Cambridge University Press, 1987), and *The Morals of Modernity* (Cambridge: Cambridge University Press, 1996); Brian Barry, *Justice as Impartiality* (Oxford: Clarendon, 1995). Barry and Larmore make scant use of the language of toleration but it is clear that they, no less than Rawls and Nagel, conceive mutual toleration as a central feature of a liberal society. All four thinkers provide reasons why people, who have different and conflicting conceptions of the good, should refrain from using political power to suppress or disadvantage conceptions with which they disagree - reasons that do not require them to forfeit their belief that those conceptions are wrong. It is not only the proponents of neutralism that associate toleration with political neutrality. Michael Sandel criticises neutralism because it fails to deliver a better quality of respect for diverse forms of life than mere

Yet, despite this ready association of toleration with neutrality, a number of writers, most notably Saladin Meckled-Garcia in this volume, have challenged the compatibility of neutrality and toleration. In this chapter, I shall try to meet that challenge. I shall argue that the ideals of neutrality and toleration are indeed compatible, by which I mean that both can figure coherently in a single political theory.

I do not claim either that toleration must entail neutrality or that neutrality must entail toleration. Clearly a political system may be tolerant of beliefs and practices without being neutral amongst them. Historically, a religiously tolerant state has commonly been one that has *not* been 'neutral' in that it has been officially committed to a particular religion; it has nevertheless been 'tolerant' in that it has permitted the practice of more than just its officially approved religion. More generally, a state may be tolerant without being neutral in that it may appraise and treat some conceptions of the good more favourably than others but still permit the pursuit of those conceptions it disfavours. Toleration does not have to be even-handed.

Equally, a political system can be neutral without being tolerant. Imagine a society whose members wish to live different forms of life but each of whom regards the different forms pursued by others as reflecting no more than their different preferences. People's preferred forms of life are diverse, but that diversity neither reflects nor generates disagreement. No-one finds reason to object to anyone else's chosen form. In such a society there could still be a place for neutrality: it might be thought right that political power should not be used to advantage or disadvantage some people's preferred ways of life. But there would be no place for toleration, for there would be nothing objectionable for anyone to tolerate.

My claim will not be, therefore, that neutrality and toleration *must* go together. Rather it will be that neutrality and toleration *can* be compatible ideals and that they *are* compatible in the political liberalism of John Rawls.

TOLERATION AND NEUTRALITY: MUTUAL EXCLUSION?

One way in which toleration and neutrality may be thought mutually exclusive is implicit in what I have already said. Toleration entails not preventing something of which we disapprove. Now if a state adopts a position of neutrality with respect to different conceptions of the good, it remains officially agnostic on the relative merit of those conceptions: it neither approves of some, nor disapproves of others. But if there are no conceptions of the good of which it disapproves, there is none that it can tolerate. Neutrality therefore precludes toleration.[6]

---

toleration: *Democracy's Discontent: America in Search of a Public Philosophy* (Cambridge, Mass.: Belknap, 1996), p.107. Kok-Chor Tan and Will Kymlicka both criticise Rawls for giving an unduly fundamental role to the value of toleration in his political liberalism: Tan, *Toleration, Diversity and Global Justice* (Pennsylvania: Pennsylvania University Press, 2000); Kymlicka, *Multicultural Citizenship* (Oxford: Clarendon, 1995), pp.152-63.
[6]Glen Newey observes, "Toleration demands that the policy-makers have a particular motive, namely disapproval of the practice that they tolerate. But to the extent that they are thus motivated, the policy-makers contravene neutrality"; *Virtue, Reason and Toleration* (Edinburgh: Edinburgh University Press, 1999), p.124. Similarly, John Horton remarks, "... if we take neutrality toward competing conceptions of

The answer to this claim is easily made. To observe that a state cannot act at once neutrally and tolerantly is to look at the relationship between neutrality and toleration in the wrong way. The ideals of neutrality and toleration do not function on the same plane. Toleration comes first and neutrality second: the members of a liberal state have reason to tolerate one another's different and conflicting conceptions of the good and the establishment of a neutral state is the outcome of their commitment to toleration.[7] So we should look for toleration not in the immediate functioning of a neutral state but in the reasons for that state's functioning in a way that is neutral amongst conceptions of the good. It is because we have reason to tolerate one another's different and conflicting conceptions of the good that we should establish political arrangements that are neutral in respect of those conceptions.

It is specifically on the score of *reasons*, however, that Meckled-Garcia argues that the attempt to combine neutrality and toleration must fail. The neutralist ideal, Meckled-Garcia points out, must encompass citizens as well as institutions. In a neutralist society, neutrality is a virtue required of citizens as well as institutions.[8] But if citizens, or other decision-makers, approach and resolve political issues in accordance with a principle of neutrality, they cannot simultaneously engage in toleration.

More specifically Meckled-Garcia's argument runs as follows. He defines toleration such that it entails having both a first-order reason to repress a view or practice and a second-order reason not to repress that view or practice.[9] This combination of first- and second-order reasons he sees as essential to toleration since, if we are to be properly described as 'tolerating' x, it is essential that we continue to find x objectionable even though we refrain from preventing it. If our reasons for allowing x were such as to cancel its objectionable character, we would no longer be tolerating x. Thus, "toleration requires us to believe both that we have reasons for repressing a view and that we have reasons not to act on those reasons".[10]

Meckled-Garcia seeks to prise apart neutrality and toleration at the level of citizenship by insisting that the reasons that citizens must act upon *qua* citizens of a neutral state are incompatible with the reasons they would need to act upon if they were to be tolerant.[11] As we have seen, if our reason for refraining from repressing x were such as to cancel the reason we had to repress x, we should be left with nothing to tolerate. That, according to Meckled-Garcia, is what happens when we move to a neutralist position. Rather than recognising two sorts of reason - a first-order reason

---

the good as central to liberalism, then it might reasonably be asked whether liberalism is properly described as *tolerant* even toward those conceptions it permits? Here the thought is not the familiar one that complete neutrality, however it is interpreted, is either incoherent or impossible, but simply that because liberalism professes to be neutral toward a range of conceptions of the good - that it has no objection to them - it cannot therefore be tolerant of them"; "Toleration as a virtue", in David Heyd (ed.), *Toleration: An Elusive Virtue* (Princeton: Princeton University Press, 1996), 28-43, at p.36.

[7] Thus Newey, in denying the possibility of a "neutralist justification of toleration", is looking at things the wrong way round; *Virtue, Reason and Toleration*, p.130.

[8] Saladin Meckled-Garcia, "Toleration and Neutrality: Incompatible Ideals?", this volume.

[9] "Toleration and Neutrality", p.[296].

[10] "Toleration and Neutrality", pp.[297-8].

[11] "Toleration and Neutrality", pp.[302-4].

to repress and a second-order reason not to repress - neutralism presents us only with a first-order reason not to repress: "neutrality gives us a first-order reason not to repress or seek repression as well as not to seek favours from the state".[12] What is missing from the neutralist's account is any reason for repression over which that neutralist reason prevails. So, for example, if I am a consistent neutralist, I refrain from repressing your religion not because I have a second-order reason that prevails over an initial first-order reason I possess for repressing your religion. I have no reason, initial or otherwise, to repress your religion. I regard it as simply unreasonable to use state power to repress or favour religious views.

In what follows I take issue with Meckled-Garcia on three counts. First, I question his claim that toleration requires a combination of first- and second-order reasons. Certainly, our tolerating x requires that we have both reason to disapprove of x and reason not to repress x but those reasons, I shall argue, can be merely competing first-order reasons. Secondly, I argue that the members of a Rawlsian society do have reason to repress one another's views as well as countervailing reason not to engage in that repression. In other words, I argue that Rawlsian individuals can possess the duality of reasons that toleration requires. Thirdly, although I show that a tolerant position does not have to be one that combines first- and second-order reasons, I argue that toleration as it figures in Rawls's political liberalism conforms closely to the combination of first- and second-order reasons set out in Meckled-Garcia's model of toleration.

FIRST- AND SECOND-ORDER REASONS

The distinction between first- and second-order reasons derives from the work of Joseph Raz.[13] Raz distinguishes two ways in which reasons can conflict. First, two conflicting reasons may be of the same order. How then do we decide which should prevail? Reasons are not always of equal importance; some matter more than others. Thus we attribute weight or strength to reasons and, when two or more reasons conflict, we assess their relative strengths and allow the stronger to override the weaker. For example, I may have reason to help Jim and reason to help John, but I cannot help both of them. So I assess the relative weights of these reasons and find that I have greater reason to help Jim than to help John. My reason to help Jim therefore outweighs and overrides my reason to help John. This does not mean that I cease to have reason to help John; whatever reason I have to help him remains.[14] It means simply that I should not act on that reason because it is overridden by my reason to help Jim.

Raz describes the reasons at issue here as conflicting first-order reasons since they operate on the same level; one reason simply outweighs and overrides the other. In other cases, however, conflicting reasons can be of a different order. Raz characterises a second-order reason as a "reason to act for a reason or to refrain from

---

[12] "Toleration and Neutrality", p.[302].

[13] Joseph Raz, *Practical Reason and Norms* (London: Hutchinson, 1975).

[14] Cf. Raz: "a reason is a reason even if outweighed by other conflicting reasons"; *Practical Reason and Norms*, p.25.

acting for a reason".[15] As this definition indicates, second-order reasons can be either positive (reasons to act for a reason) or negative (reasons not to act for a reason).[16] We can disregard here the case of positive second-order reasons, since it is negative second-order reasons that are significant for the analysis of toleration.[17]

Raz describes negative second-order reasons as 'exclusionary' reasons since they function by excluding rather than by merely overriding conflicting first-order reasons. Suppose, for example, that I promise to mow your lawn at regular intervals while you are away. Having made that promise, I have an exclusionary reason to do what I have promised. My promise is not just one more first-order reason that should weigh along with other first-order reasons in determining whether I should or should not mow your lawn. Promising gives me a reason of a special kind, a reason that excludes or pre-empts reasons that would otherwise figure in an on-balance calculation of whether I should mow your lawn. In particular, the reasons for keeping a promise are not reducible to the reasons for making it in the first place. Or consider what is involved in being subject to authority. A superior officer commands a soldier to fire on an enemy position. If the soldier responds to this command as an authoritative command, he will not assess the intrinsic merits of what he has been told to do and respond accordingly. The mere fact that he has received a command will provide him with a reason for doing what he has been ordered to do and a reason which excludes reasons that would otherwise determine whether he should or should not fire on the enemy position. Exclusionary reasons are not limited to promises and authoritative instructions; they are also an essential feature of mandatory norms, rules of thumb, and decisions, as well as of some non-mandatory norms and all prescriptions that are not norms.[18]

In some cases, a reason's being an exclusionary reason will make no difference to what I should do; that is, what I should do once I have an exclusionary reason, may be no different from what I would have had overriding reason to do without that exclusionary reason. Having promised to do x, I have an exclusionary reason to do x; but, even without that promise, the balance of reasons may still have dictated that x was the right thing for me to do. In other cases, however, the introduction of an exclusionary reason will alter not only my reasons but also what I should do. Having promised to do x, I have an exclusionary reason to do x; but, if I were to disregard the exclusionary character of the promise and engage in a simple on-balance calculation of the best thing to do, I may discover that the balance of reasons favours my not doing x. Hence we sometimes find that keeping a promise or complying with an authoritative command or abiding by a rule requires that we do something other than what, on the balance of first-order reasons, would seem the best thing to do.[19] One well-known manifestation of this point is the inability of simple consequentialism to do justice to the way in which promises, authority, rules,

---

[15] *Practical Reason and Norms*, p.39.

[16] Raz, *The Authority of Law* (Oxford: Clarendon, 1979), p.17.

[17] For discussions of positive second order reasons, see Raz, *Authority of Law*, pp.16-17, and *The Morality of Freedom* (Oxford: Clarendon, 1986) pp.32-5.

[18] Raz, *Practical Reason and Norms*, pp.47-106.

[19] Raz, *Practical Reason and Norms*, pp.41-5, 74-5; "Promises and obligations", in P.M.S. Hacker and J. Raz, eds, *Law, Morality and Society* (Oxford: Oxford University Press, 1977), 210-28, at pp.220-3; *Authority of Law*, pp.14-16, 21-5; *Morality of Freedom*, pp.41-2, 47-8, 58-62.

rights, and the like, figure in our practical reasoning.

There are two further features of exclusionary reasons that we should note. First, a promise or authoritative instruction or mandatory norm provides us with a first-order reason as well as an exclusionary reason. Thus, having promised to do x, I have both a first-order reason to do x and a second-order reason that excludes reasons that would otherwise weigh for or against my doing x. Similarly, if I am ordered to do x by someone who has authority over me, that order constitutes both a first-order reason for my doing x and a second-order reason that excludes reasons that would otherwise determine whether I should or should not do x. In these cases I have exclusive reason to act on a particular first-order reason. Raz describes first-order reasons that are immured by exclusionary reasons variously as 'protected' or 'peremptory' or 'pre-emptive' reasons.[20]

Secondly, exclusionary reasons need not be unlimited in scope. Rather than excluding all other reasons, they may exclude only some. Thus, while a promise must have the exclusionary or pre-emptive character that I described above, there may be some countervailing considerations that it does not exclude. The exclusionary scope of my promise to do x may stop short of excluding a conflicting reason that I have to do y; that conflicting reason may then outweigh and override my reason to do what I have promised. That is how it can sometimes be right to break a promise. Likewise, an order from someone who has authority over me constitutes an exclusionary reason but not necessarily a reason that excludes every possible other reason that bears upon what I am ordered to do. It may not exclude, for example, concerns about human rights such that I can have reason to defy an order commanding me to violate another person's human rights.[21]

TOLERATION AND ORDERS OF REASON

How then does all this apply to toleration? Meckled-Garcia claims that the logical structure of a tolerant position is one in which the tolerant person has a first-order reason to repress x but a second-order reason (an exclusionary reason) not to act on that first-order reason. But does our reason for being tolerant have to be of that exclusionary kind? Cannot toleration be required simply by a first-order reason that overrides whatever first-order reason we have for repression? Suppose I am disposed to repress all but (what I believe to be) the one true religion. Consider the following reasons that I might be presented with to persuade me not to act on that repressive disposition:

1.   If I attempt to repress other religions, I shall meet stiff resistance which will issue in bloodshed and strife. That bloodshed and strife is too high a price to pay for eliminating false religions.

2.   I believe that my faith is correct, but sane and sensible people who subscribe to other faiths are no less convinced of the correctness of their beliefs. Hence there is scope for reasonable doubt and disagreement about what is the

---

[20] *Authority of Law*, p.18; *Morality of Freedom*, pp.37, 42.
[21] Raz, *Practical Reason and Norms*, pp.40, 46-7.

one true faith.   That gives me reason to refrain from enforcing what I nevertheless reckon to be the correct faith.

3.   We should give weight to people's own beliefs about how they should live. That weight is sufficient to give me reason not to coerce people into complying with the one true religion even though lives lived in accordance with that religion are better than those that are not.

Each of these arguments for toleration is entirely intelligible as an argument that functions through a first-order reason. In each case, if the argument for toleration wins out, that is because it outweighs my reason for repression. It neither excludes nor cancels the reasons I have for enforcing the one true religion; it simply overrides those reasons.

Consider now the remarks of Raz on a different sort of toleration. We might find someone's deliberate manner of speech or their slow and methodical way of considering every issue frustrating and annoying.   Nevertheless, these irritating features of a person may be inevitable accompaniments of characteristics of that we value. The reason people lack certain virtues or accomplishments may be, and often is, that they possess other incompatible virtues and accomplishments.   When we tolerate the limitations of others we may be aware that these are but the other side of their virtues and personal strengths. This may indeed be the reason that we tolerate them.[22] The rationale for toleration that Raz offers here is, again, one that conforms to the model of conflicting first-order reasons.   We find people's failings objectionable but we appreciate that those failings are simply the flip-side of their virtues and the value of those virtues provides adequate reason to tolerate the failings.   The virtues provide us with sufficiently strong first-order reason, rather than with an exclusionary second-order reason, for tolerating the failings.

Finally, consider an example given by Meckled-Garcia himself.[23] Some people engage in a freely chosen way of life that does not harm other humans but does involve animal cruelty. I have reason to repress views and practices that involve animal cruelty. But I also have reason to encourage people freely to choose their way of life and, in this instance, my repression of animal cruelty may set an example that militates against encouraging people freely to choose their way of life.   I consider this reason important enough not to act on my reason to prevent animal cruelty.   Meckled-Garcia identifies my reason to repress animal cruelty as a first-order reason and my reason to encourage people freely to choose their way of life as a second-order reason. But, again, the most obvious reading of this example is that it is one in which I have conflicting first-order reasons of unequal strength. I have a first-order reason to prevent animal cruelty and a competing and weightier first-order reason to allow someone to live the non-human-harming form of life that they have freely chosen. My concern for freedom simply outweighs my objection to animal cruelty.

It is certainly possible to characterise the respect that we should have for people's choice over their form of life as an exclusionary reason. If, for example,

---

[22] *Morality of Freedom*, p.402.
[23] "Toleration and Neutrality", pp.[296-7].

they have a *right* to live the form of life they have chosen for themselves, that constitutes an exclusionary reason for their not being prevented from living that form of life.[24]   But there is no obvious exclusionary reason in the example as Meckled-Garcia sets it out. Raz's formal definition of a second-order reason – "any reason to act for a reason or to refrain from acting for a reason"[25] – is potentially misleading. An overriding first-order reason could be described as a reason for refraining from acting for an overridden first-order reason. But that is clearly not what Raz intends his definition of a negative second-order reason to describe. A clearer brief description is "a reason to exclude reasons and not to act for them"[26]

TOLERANT PERSONS AND NEUTRAL CITIZENS

All of this is, of course, of no significance for Meckled-Garcia's attempt to prise apart the concepts of toleration and neutrality if he is right in claiming that neutralists, like Rawls, provide us only with first-order reasons for being neutral rather than with conflicting reasons whose resolution results in a case for toleration which, in turn, requires neutrality. So do Rawls's citizens need to practise toleration?

Rawls aims to provide us with reasons why people should enjoy fairly distributed liberties, opportunities and resources to pursue their conceptions of the good. He is not in the business of persuading us that we should use political power to prevent or impede people's pursuit of their conceptions of the good. Thus, if we are in search of reasons for repression, *A Theory of Justice* and *Political Liberalism* will not be good places to look. Nevertheless, Rawls's neutralist theory is clearly designed for a society in which people have different and conflicting beliefs and a society in which, in the absence of his political conception of justice, people could find reason to resort to state power to promote their own conceptions of the good and to repress the conceptions of others. Rawls is at pains to emphasize that the pluralist society for which he provides is one whose members are "profoundly divided by reasonable though incompatible religious, philosophical, and moral doctrines"[27] He describes the doctrinal beliefs of his citizens variously as 'conflicting', 'irreconcilable', 'incompatible', 'incommensurable', 'deeply divided', 'deeply opposed', and as offering 'no prospect of resolution'.[28] He traces the origins of liberalism in general, and of political liberalism in particular, to the Reformation of the sixteenth century and to the religious divisions that emerged from it.[29] Noting the 'clash' of conceptions of the good that developed after the Reformation, he observes that political liberalism "starts by taking to heart the absolute depth of that irreconcilable latent conflict".[30] Thus the world for which Rawls provides is one characterised by deep doctrinal conflict and one in which, without his political conception of justice,

---

[24] Cf. Peter Jones, *Rights* (Basingstoke: Macmillan, 1994), pp.54-5.
[25] *Practical Reason and Norms*, p.39.
[26] *Practical Reason and Norms*, p.62.
[27] *Political Liberalism*, p.xviii.
[28] *Political Liberalism*, pp.xviii, xxv-xxviii, 4, 10, 36, 133, 303.
[29] *Political Liberalism*, pp.xxii-xxvi.
[30] *Political Liberalism*, p.xxvi.

people could find ample reason to use political power to repress doctrines with which they disagreed and ways of life of which they disapproved.

It is precisely because his citizens subscribe to such different and conflicting comprehensive doctrines that Rawls tries to provide a theory of justice to which they can subscribe in spite of their doctrinal differences. That is, he seeks to find a theory of justice, including a reason for citizens to tolerate one another's conflicting doctrinal allegiances, that is independent of those doctrinal differences. Hence we have his idea of a specifically 'political' liberalism that uses a form of 'political' constructivism to generate a 'political' conception of justice. Hence too his concern to develop that conception as a 'freestanding view'. It is neither a comprehensive doctrine nor derived from a comprehensive doctrine; instead it is drawn from ideas implicit in the public political culture of a democratic society.[31] In the same spirit, the quality that Rawls claims for his political conception of justice is not 'truth' but 'reasonableness' so that, rather than competing with comprehensive doctrines, it can be seen to function on a different plane from them.[32]

Thus Rawls's political conception of justice is designed to leave in place, rather than to displace, the various (reasonable) comprehensive doctrines held by his citizens. So whatever reasons those comprehensive doctrines give their adherents for objecting to conflicting doctrines held by others will continue to be reasons for them in Rawls's just society. That is why Rawlsian citizens are called upon to engage in toleration. While they may have good reason (from within their own doctrines) for objecting to and repressing the doctrines and ways of life of others, Rawls gives them strong countervailing non-doctrinal reason not to use political power to act on these doctrinal reasons. He hopes, of course, that tension between comprehensive doctrines and his political conception of justice will disappear over time and be replaced by an overlapping consensus. I shall consider the implications of that idea for toleration in a moment but, in the first instance at least, there is ample scope for Rawlsian individuals to object to one another's doctrines and conceptions of the good and therefore ample opportunity for them to engage in toleration.

One thing that helps to obscure this simple feature of Rawls's society is his constantly addressing the members of his society as 'citizens'. Now to be a citizen is, for Rawls, to assume a 'political' role and, when an individual conscientiously assumes that role, he or she will act only on 'political' reasons. Thus, in their role as citizens, individuals will be guided by the political conception of justice and by public reason, rather than by the 'nonpublic reason' of their different comprehensive doctrines.[33] In making political decisions as citizens, they will take no account of whatever reasons for repression their comprehensive doctrines might contain; rather they will simply deliberate and decree - as justice requires - in a way that is neutral

---

[31] *Political Liberalism*, pp.12-14.

[32] *Political Liberalism*, pp.xviii-xxi, 94-5, 127.

[33] Rawls requires this only with qualification. The limits imposed by public reason apply to 'constitutional essentials' and 'questions of basic justice' rather than to less fundamental political questions, though Rawls thinks it highly desirable that even those less fundamental political questions should be settled by public reason insofar as that is possible (*Political Liberalism*, pp.214, 215, 230). Rawls also modifies the exclusionary character of public reason by "allowing citizens, in certain situations, to present what they regard as the basis of political values rooted in their comprehensive doctrine, provided they do this in ways that strengthen the ideal of public reason itself" (*Political Liberalism*, p.247).

between comprehensive doctrines. That is why Rawlsian citizens might seem to exhibit a commitment to neutrality that is bereft of toleration. But, of course, Rawls's individuals are not only citizens; they are also full persons possessed of comprehensive doctrines and it is as full persons that they exhibit toleration. Their toleration is manifest in their willingness, in spite of their doctrinal commitments, to limit their use of political power (as citizens, but in other political roles as well) in the ways that Rawls prescribes.

RAWLSIAN TOLERANCE AND SECOND-ORDER REASONS

This separation between the political and the nonpolitical, the public and the nonpublic, takes us on to the question of whether the reason Rawls gives for toleration is a first- or a second-order reason. To my knowledge, Rawls nowhere refers to Raz's distinction between these different types of reason or shows any indication of using it self-consciously to structure his theory. Nevertheless, he does present his conception of justice as one that should function in political decision-making in an exclusionary way. It matches Raz's idea of a 'protected' or 'peremptory' reason. It is a first-order reason in that it prescribes how we should settle fundamental political matters, but it is also a second-order reason in that it provides that, in dealing with those political matters, other sorts of reason - reasons drawn from our comprehensive doctrines - should be excluded from consideration. Similarly, in political matters, the associated idea of public reason operates in an exclusionary way. In their role as citizens, just individuals do not engage in political decision-making by weighing both public and nonpublic reasons and letting the balance fall where it may. Rather, they exclude nonpublic reasons from consideration and attend only to public reasons.[34] Thus, given that Rawls's argument for toleration forms part of his political conception of justice, there is a clear case for holding, *pace* Meckled-Garcia, that it provides us with a negative second-order reason for toleration. That is, on public or 'political' matters, it provides us with a reason for refraining from acting on reasons of another sort.

This interpretation of the logic of Rawls's position is not without complication. When he confronts the question of why we should settle issues of constitutional essentials and of basic justice by reference to political values alone, he answers that political values "normally have sufficient weight to override all other values that may come into conflict with them".[35] His use of the language of 'outweighing' and 'overriding' suggests that political values and values stemming from comprehensive doctrines relate to one another as competing first-order reasons rather than as reasons of a different order. Even so, that is consistent with my claim that, for the citizens of Rawls's society, the political conception of justice functions as an exclusionary reason. In dealing with constitutional essentials and matters of basic justice, including questions of toleration, citizens are to attend only to political values. But those citizens can also take a step back and ask why they should give those political values that exclusionary status. In other words, they can ask why the

---

[34] Subject again to the qualifications described in note 33.
[35] *Political Liberalism*, p.138; see also pp.146, 155-7, 218-9, 241.

political conception of justice should constitute an exclusionary reason and it is at that point that it is appropriate to answer that the "values of the political are very great values and hence not easily overridden".[36] We should distinguish between a reason's functioning as an exclusionary reason and the reason for its being an exclusionary reason.

I have previously argued that the distinction between first- and second-order reasons is not critical for toleration. The duality of reasons that is essential for toleration can be competing first-order reasons, and in most instances of toleration probably is. But suppose we accept that the reason that Rawls's citizens have for being tolerant is, indeed, a second-order reason. Should that lead us to invert the logic of Meckled-Garcia's analysis and hold that this reason cannot count as a reason for *toleration* precisely because it is an *exclusionary* reason? In excluding rather than outweighing whatever countervailing first-order reason we might have for intolerance, it might be thought to deprive us of the duality of competing reasons that is essential if we are to have a genuine instance of toleration. But that would be a thought too far. An exclusionary reason does not eradicate other reasons. It simply pre-empts them in determining what we should do. Thus, even if Rawls's principles of justice have an exclusionary character, they can still be reasons for toleration.[37]

Finally, there is the matter of overlapping consensus. The primary concern that has driven Rawls to reformulate his liberalism as political liberalism has been his concern for stability. Stability is achieved when the various reasonable comprehensive doctrines to which the members of a society subscribe overlap in supporting the political conception of justice. In some cases that may be achieved negatively. A comprehensive doctrine may be less than fully comprehensive in that it may be silent on matters that are the concern of the political conception of justice. In that case, the political conception can simply occupy the 'gap' or 'leeway' left by the comprehensive doctrine.[38] In other cases, stability may be achieved more positively. A comprehensive doctrine might come to be understood by its adherents as fully endorsing the political conception of justice so that they can find positive reason, within their comprehensive doctrine, for embracing that conception. By whichever of these routes overlapping consensus is achieved, it will remove conflict between the demands of an individual's comprehensive doctrine and the demands of the political conception of justice. Does that mean that, even if there is a place for toleration in Rawls's political liberalism, it is merely provisional: that, once the goal of overlapping consensus has been achieved, toleration will become redundant?

That does not follow. Where a citizen finds that his comprehensive doctrine endorses the political conception of justice, he has both public and nonpublic reason to be tolerant. The need for toleration does not disappear simply because it is required by a comprehensive doctrine. The duality of conflicting or competing reasons necessary for toleration can occur within a comprehensive doctrine as well as between a doctrine and an external principle. Consider, for example, Locke's

---

[36] *Political Liberalism*, p.139.
[37] Analogously, suppose that I promise to tolerate your objectionable conduct. That promise provides me with an exclusionary reason, but that is still a reason for my *tolerating* your objectionable conduct.
[38] *Political Liberalism*, pp.160, 246.

celebrated *Letter on Toleration*. Locke does not seek to neuter Christianity by pretending that Christians have no reason to object to heresy or infidelity. Rather, he produces a series of reasons, several of them specifically Christian reasons, why Christians should not persecute or coerce those whose religious beliefs and conduct they view, quite properly, as wrongful. So Locke's message is not that Christians should urge others to tolerate what they themselves find unexceptionable. Rather his message is that they, as Christians, have reason to tolerate what they, as Christians, have reason to condemn. Toleration therefore needs to be internal to Christianity itself. Thus the Christian who finds reason within his comprehensive doctrine for endorsing Rawls's political conception of justice does not lose the need to be tolerant; he simply discovers a congruence of reasons for being tolerant.

THE SIGNIFICANCE OF DEMOCRATIC TOLERATION

Set in the context of the long history of political toleration, both the circumstances of toleration that Rawls contemplates, and the main justification he gives for toleration, are unusual. Historically, political toleration has commonly taken the form of a state's officially subscribing to a doctrine, typically a religious faith or denomination, but nevertheless refraining from coercing or persecuting those who subscribe to other doctrines. Thus, there has been a clear distinction between the state that tolerates and the subjects who are tolerated. In Rawls's democratic society tolerators and tolerated are not dichotomised in that way. Toleration is multilateral rather than unilateral: all democratic citizens are committed to tolerating one another's different and conflicting but reasonable comprehensive doctrines and the ways of life based upon them. Thus, everyone simultaneously tolerates and is tolerated. Historically, Rawls's multilateral model of toleration may not have been the norm, but it is nonetheless entirely coherent as a model of toleration.

It is this democratic model of toleration that some of Rawls's critics seem unable to comprehend. John Gray, for example, writes

> Toleration as a political ideal is offensive to the new liberalism - the liberalism of Rawls, Dworkin, Ackerman and suchlike - because it is decidedly non-neutral in respect of the good. For the new liberals, justice - the shibboleth of revisionist liberalism - demands that government, in its institutions and policies, practise *neutrality*, not toleration, in regard to rival conceptions of the good life.[39]

Gray supposes that political toleration can be exhibited only by governments and only if those governments identify certain beliefs or practices as 'bad'. What he overlooks is the further possibility that the citizens of a democratic society, each of whom is "decidedly non-neutral in respect of the good", can engage in mutual toleration by refraining from using political power to impose or privilege their particular conceptions of the good. In this democratic model, the neutrality of a government manifests the tolerance of its citizens.

Why should democratic citizens behave in this mutually tolerant way? Rawls's main answer is: because that is what justice as fairness requires. To use political power to repress reasonable comprehensive doctrines, or otherwise to disadvantage

---

[39] John Gray, *Enlightenment's Wake* (London: Routledge, 1995), p.19.

people because of their doctrinal affiliations, is to behave unfairly. He arrives at that answer by taking ideas implicit in the public culture of a democratic society - particularly the ideas of society as a fair system of cooperation and of persons as free and equal - and applying them to the fact of reasonable pluralism. Now once again, this way of arguing for toleration has not figured prominently in the catalogue of reasons that have been used, in the past, to plead the case for toleration. It provides us nevertheless with an entirely intelligible and cogent case for toleration. For Rawls it is a peculiarly strong case; indeed, reasons of justice are peculiarly strong for most of us. But it would be perverse to hold that Rawls, in providing us with a peculiarly strong reason for being tolerant, somehow removes the need or occasion for toleration.

It is because Rawls locates toleration within fairness that he gives it such a far-reaching and thorough form. Gray protests that the neutralism of Rawls goes far beyond a policy of toleration since it rules out as wrong or unjust not only the coercive imposition of a favoured conception of the good, but also governmental encouragement of particular ways of life through education, subsidy, taxation, welfare provision, and the like.[40] But for Rawls, citizens who extend toleration fairly to one another will not use *any* of the levers of political power to privilege or disadvantage particular conceptions of the good. Political toleration can, of course, take less generous forms than this and Gray is right to point out the contrast between Rawls's policies and the more parsimonious forms of toleration exhibited by past 'tolerant' regimes. Even so, the generous and inclusive approach to toleration that we find in Rawls is still fully intelligible as a policy of toleration.

Finally, we might ask whether toleration has any special value or significance for a neutralist like Rawls. After all, Meckled-Garcia does not seek to criticise those who (as he sees it) substitute neutrality for toleration. On the contrary, he holds that a neutralist position is superior to one of toleration and argues that neutralists can dispense with the value of toleration without loss.[41] Toleration can, indeed, seem second best. Those who are tolerated would prefer to be accepted; they would prefer not to be objected to by their tolerators and so not to stand in need of their toleration. Those who tolerate would prefer that they did not have to: they tolerate only what they object to and they must surely prefer that what they object to did not exist. For both parties in the relationship therefore, toleration can seem unfortunate. It may be the best they can achieve in the given circumstances but, for each, it falls short of their most desired condition.

Rawls does not share this pessimistic view of toleration. The pluralism that he believes a democratic society should accommodate is not any sort of pluralism but reasonable pluralism - a plurality of reasonable comprehensive doctrines. Rawls is not wholly clear about what it is that makes a doctrine 'reasonable'. Sometimes it seems to be the doctrine's epistemic qualities[42], sometimes if and because it does not reject the essentials of a democratic regime[43], sometimes both of these[44], sometimes

---

[40] *Enlightenment's Wake*, pp.19-20. See also Meckled-Garcia, "Toleration and Neutrality", pp.[301-2, 304].
[41] "Toleration and Neutrality", pp.[309-13].
[42] *Political Liberalism*, p.59.
[43] Ibid, p.xvi.

its recognizing the burdens of judgement[45] and sometimes its actually supporting the political conception of justice.[46] I do not want to pursue that matter here. Clearly Rawls thinks that the fact that doctrines can be various yet reasonable contributes importantly to the case for toleration. Disagreement amongst reasonable persons arises because of the burdens of judgement. Reasonable persons will recognise those burdens and be willing to accept their consequences, including their consequences for the legitimate exercise of political power.[47] One such consequence is that there is a limit to what we can reasonably justify to others and that, in turn, makes it unreasonable to use political power to repress comprehensive doctrines that we do not share.[48] The burdens of judgement are, therefore, "of first significance for a democratic idea of toleration".[49]

Rather than excavate further the justificatory link between toleration and the reasonableness of pluralism, I want here to fasten on a related aspect of Rawls's thinking. Reasonable pluralism for Rawls arises from "the work of free practical reason within the framework of free institutions".[50] It is "the normal result of the exercise of human reason within the framework of the free institutions of a constitutional democratic regime".[51] As such, it is a normal and enduring feature of a democratic society. The multiplicity of doctrines and conceptions of the good that we find in modern democratic societies is not something that we should regret, nor something that we can reasonably hope will disappear over time, and certainly not something that we should try to eradicate or even discourage.

Now, if reasonable pluralism is an enduring feature of a democratic society, so must be toleration. Disagreement remains disagreement even when it is reasonable: people engaged in reasonable disagreement still have reason to regard one another's doctrines as wrong. It is crucial to Rawls's position that we can regard the doctrines of others as reasonable yet wrong, and our own doctrine as uniquely true if not uniquely reasonable. Thus, the reasonableness of pluralism does not diminish the need for toleration. On the contrary, as long as we are confronted with reasonable pluralism, we have both occasion and reason to respond to it tolerantly. Hence, if a diversity of reasonable comprehensive doctrines is not a contingent and temporary characteristic of a modern democratic society but "a permanent feature of the public culture of democracy"[52], toleration must also be an enduring feature of a democratic society. For Rawls, then, toleration is not second-best. It is neither a regrettable necessity in a regrettable world, nor a temporary expedient that we can look forward to abandoning. It is a central and permanent feature of a just liberal order.

---

[44] Rawls, *The Law of Peoples* (Cambridge, Mass.: Harvard University Press, 1999), p.87.
[45] Rawls, *Justice as Fairness: a Restatement* (Cambridge, Mass.: Belknap, 2001), p.191.
[46] Rawls, "The Idea of Public Reason Revisited", in his *Collected Papers*, Samuel Freeman, ed. (Cambridge, Mass.: Harvard University Press, 1999), pp.573-615, at pp.608-9.
[47] *Political Liberalism*, p.54.
[48] Ibid, pp.60-2.
[49] Ibid p.58.
[50] Ibid, *p.37.*
[51] Ibid, p.xvi; see also pp.xvii-ix, xxiv-v, 4, 36-7, 55-8.
[52] Ibid, p.36.

CHAPTER 7

NEUTRALITY, TOLERATION AND REASONABLE AGREEMENT

Colin Farrelly

INTRODUCTION

It is widely agreed, claims John Horton, "that the core of the concept of toleration is the refusal, where one has the power to do so, to prohibit or seriously interfere with conduct one finds objectionable".[1] Liberals champion toleration as one of the main political virtues of a just society. The tolerant society is one which protects a diverse array of fundamental freedoms ranging from freedom of conscience and religion to freedom of expression and freedom of association. Secure in the knowledge that the constitution guarantees these various freedoms, citizens can freely pursue the lifestyles they find most fulfilling, regardless of the fact that the majority of people may or may not find their choices objectionable. The tolerant society is thus one which respects citizens as autonomous persons.[2]

This connection between autonomy and toleration suggests that toleration is a virtue because it is *justice-promoting*. That is, by respecting the autonomy of its citizens the tolerant society comes closer to satisfying the requirements of fair social cooperation than the intolerant society. But this account of toleration quickly runs into problems. Consider the following example. Take two liberal societies (lets call them A and B) which both tolerant a range of diverse beliefs, practices and ways of life. The only difference between A and B in this respect is that society B does not tolerate practice X. The citizens of society B find X objectionable and have imposed a number of restrictions in an attempt to limit the influence of X. If toleration is

---

[1] J. Horton, "Toleration as a Virtue", D. Heyd, ed., *Toleration: An Elusive Virtue*, (Princeton: Princeton University Press, 1996), 28-43, at p. 28. Those who make this claim include, among others Horton cites, P. King *Toleration* (London: Allen and Unwin, 1976), p. 22; and D.D. Raphael, "The Intolerable", S. Mendus, ed., *Justifying Toleration: Conceptual and Historical Perspectives*, (Cambridge: Cambridge University Press, 1988), p. 139.

[2] For a discussion of the connection between autonomy and toleration see J. Raz, "Autonomy, Toleration and the Harm Principle", S. Mendus, ed., *Justifying Toleration: Conceptual and Historical Perspectives*, 155-175.

understood as "the refusal to prohibit or seriously interfere with conduct one finds objectionable" then it is obvious that society A is more tolerant than society B.

Does the fact that society A is more tolerant than society B mean that, in this respect, A is more just than B? What if the reason the citizens of society B object to X is that X interferes with the rights of others (e.g. security of the person)? In this case the basis for claiming that toleration is justice-promoting, that is, that it protects citizens' fundamental freedoms, is the same as the basis for saying that *intolerance* in this instance would be justice-promoting. Fundamental rights and freedoms often conflict. The extent to which toleration will be justice-promoting, and thus a political virtue, will depend on the extent to which it accommodates the other virtues of fair social co-operation- civility, reasonableness and the sense of fairness.[3] This is the focus of this paper. Contemporary liberals tend to neglect the importance of these other virtues when articulating what fair terms of agreement are. For example, many liberals emphasis the ideal of state neutrality.[4] But, as I argue in section I of this paper, this ideal does not get us very far. State neutrality does overlap to some degree with toleration but once we consider the contentious cases that liberal societies face it becomes clear that the ideal of neutrality does not necessarily secure fair terms of social co-operation. Unlike Meckled-Garcia,[5] I believe that neutralist liberals should not give up toleration in favour of neutrality. Toleration is often *a matter of degree*. A determination of what degree best achieves fair terms of co-operation will require legislators and judges to make a number of judgements concerning how best to reconcile the conflicting values which characterise a free and democratic society. The extent to which such judgements will be justice-promoting will be determined by how informed they are by the virtues of civility, reasonableness and the sense of fairness.

In section I I consider the ideal of neutrality and highlight the appeal and limits of this ideal. In section II I consider the issue of censoring hate speech, an issue which neutrality is ill-equipped to handle. I illustrate the various ways the virtues of fair social co-operation can inform the decisions of legislators and judges by focusing on the design of Canada's prohibition on hate propaganda. Such a measure sought to balance the concern for toleration with those of civility, reasonableness and the sense of fairness. Similar issues arouse in *R. v. Butler* (1992), in which the Supreme Court of Canada upheld Canada's regulation of pornography. I consider how the issue of harm was handled in this case in section III. This case further illustrates why neutralist liberals cannot dispense with the political virtue of toleration and that toleration is only justice-promoting when it is informed by the virtues of civility, reasonableness and the sense of fairness.

---

[3] In this paper I adopt the account of the virtues of fair social cooperation which John Rawls endorses in *Political Liberalism* (New York: Columbia University Press, 1993), p. 194.

[4] See, for example, J. Rawls *A Theory of Justice* (Cambridge, Mass.: Harvard University Press, 1971); R. Nozick, *Anarchy, State and Utopia* (New York: Basic Books, 1974); B. Ackerman, *Social Justice and the Liberal State* (New Haven: Yale University Press, 1980); R. Dworkin, *A Matter of Principle* (Cambridge, Mass.: Harvard University Press, 1985); C. Larmore, *Patterns of Moral Complexity* (Cambridge: Cambridge University Press, 1987); and W. Kymlicka, "Liberal Individualism and Liberal Neutrality", *Ethics*, 99 (4) (1989), 883-905.

[5] See his paper "Toleration and Neutrality: Incompatible Ideals?" in this volume.

STATE NEUTRALITY

In *Political Liberalism* John Rawls makes a distinction between three different types of neutrality. The first type of neutrality is procedural. That is, a decision is neutral if it is the result of a neutral procedure. Such a procedure would have to be impartial, consistent in its application of general principles to all reasonably related issues and provide equal opportunities for the contending parties to present their claims. Rawls makes it clear that his theory of justice as fairness is not procedurally neutral. He claims:

> Clearly its principles of justice are substantive and express far more than procedural values, and so do its political conceptions of society and person, which are represented in the original position. As a political conception it aims to be the focus of an overlapping consensus... This common ground is the political conception itself as the focus of an overlapping consensus. But common ground, so defined, is not procedurally neutral ground.[6]

A second type of neutrality is consequential neutrality or neutrality of effect. This version of neutrality requires neutrality in the consequences of government policy. If a policy benefits certain conceptions of the good life more than others then it violates neutrality of effect. Will Kymlicka argues that this is not the version of neutrality which Rawls endorses.[7] Neutrality of effect is incompatible with two basic tenets of Rawls's theory- respect for civil liberties and Rawls's explanation of the role of 'primary goods'. Moreover, Rawls himself rejects neutrality of effect, claiming that it is untenable. "It is surely impossible for the basic structure of a just constitutional regime not to have important effects and influences as to which comprehensive doctrines endure and gain adherents over time; and it is futile to try to counteract these effects and influences, or even to ascertain for political purposes how deep and pervasive they are".[8]

The third type of neutrality, and the one which both Kymlicka and Rawls want to endorse, is neutrality of aim or justificatory neutrality. This version of neutrality maintains that the justification for a law or policy should be neutral. It should not presuppose, for example, values particular to one conception of the good. Piety is a clear example of a value which would violate justificatory neutrality. The religious state is the archetype of the non-neutral state.

Justificatory neutrality is the type of neutrality which liberals like Rawls and Kymlicka defend. It is important to ask what the appeal is of this version of neutrality. Why argue for justificatory neutrality? Liberals endorse it for a reason. The neutral state is not something which liberals value as an *end-in-itself*. In *Beyond Neutrality* George Sher distinguishes three reasons why liberals defend state neutrality. These are:

1. because non-neutral government decisions violate the autonomy of citizens.

---

[6] Rawls, *Political Liberalism*, p. 192.
[7] See Kymlicka, "Liberal Individualism and Liberal Neutrality".
[8] Rawls, *Political Liberalism*, p. 193

2.   because non-neutral government decisions pose unacceptable risks of oppression, instability, or error.
3.   because non-neutral government decisions rest on value-premises that cannot be rationally defended.[9]

These reasons effectively illustrate the overlap between neutrality and toleration and thus help explain why liberals view neutrality and toleration as complementary. The neutral state will be a tolerant state because it does not use the coercive power of the state to pursue what Rawls calls a 'comprehensive doctrine'.[10] By remaining neutral among conceptions of the good life, the neutral state will ensure the inviolability of citizens' basic rights and freedoms.   I will now explain why neutrality alone falls well short of achieving this goal thus setting the stage for a fuller discussion of toleration.

The liberal ideal of neutrality is a useful ideal but it is important to recognise that it is one whose usefulness tends to be overemphasised by liberals who make it central to the liberal project.   Neutralists liberals like Rawls emphasis the 'neutrality constraint' because this constraint helps clarify what fair terms of cooperation are. By requiring the justification for a law or policy be neutral, the neutrality constraint ensures that only those laws or policies that rest on value-premises reasonable citizens of a pluralist society could accept are legitimate.   The neutrality constraint thus rules out many intolerant measures.   For example, it rules out laws against religious heresy.   The religious state is non-neutral because its laws and policies are based on values (e.g. piety) particular to one conception of the good.   A non-neutral value like piety should not trump the political values of liberty and equality.   The religious state thus fails to take seriously the requirements of public reason.[11]

Before turning to the shortcomings of the neutrality constraint let me show the potential difficulties it faces when dealing with a repressive policy liberals might feel it can easily dismiss- a prohibition on homosexuality.   Such a prohibition might be defended in a way that makes it obvious that such a law is non-neutral.   For example, the defence that such behaviour is a sin.   But the most influential arguments in favour of such a prohibition are not usually framed in such a way that its violation of the neutrality constraint is so obvious.   In *The Enforcement of Morals* Lord Devlin criticised the Wolfenden Report (1957) which recommended that homosexual acts between consenting adults in private be decriminalised.   Devlin's argument for such a prohibition was premised on a conception of legal moralism. He argued:

> If men and women try to create a society in which there is no fundamental agreement about good and evil they will fail; if, having based it on common agreement, the

---

[9] G. Sher, *Beyond Neutrality: Perfectionism and Politics* (Cambridge: Cambridge University Press, 1997), p. 15.

[10] "A doctrine is comprehensive when it includes conceptions of what is of value in human life, and ideals of personal character, as well as ideals of friendship and of familial and associational relationships, and much else that is to inform our conduct, and in the limit to our life as a whole.   A conception is fully comprehensive if it covers all recognized values and virtues within one rather precisely articulated system". (*Political Liberalism*, p. 13)

[11] For a discussion of public reason see *Political Liberalism* Lecture VI and J. Rawls, "The Idea of Public Reason Revisited", *The University of Chicago Law Review*, 3(64) (1997), 765-807.

agreement goes, the society will disintegrate. For society is not something that is kept together physically; it is held by the invisible bonds of common thought. If the bonds were too far relaxed the members would drift apart. A common morality is part of the bondage. The bondage is part of the price of society; and mankind, which needs society, must pay its price.[12]

Neutralist liberals might dismiss Devlin's argument on grounds that a prohibition on homosexuality is non-neutral. That is, that the aim of such a measure is to promote a particular conception of the good life (i.e. heterosexuality). But such a characterisation of Devlin's argument would be misleading. Devlin did not justify his argument on the grounds that heterosexuality is the good life or that homosexuality is merely offensive. His argument was that the decriminalisation of such behaviour would be harmful to society. His argument could thus be framed in terms more congenial with the neutrality constraint. Neutralist liberals themselves recognise that the state should not be neutral between all conceptions of the good, but only between permissible conceptions of the good.[13] Devlin would argue that the behaviour targeted by such legislation is 'impermissible' because it threatens the social cohesion necessary to maintain stability. By prohibiting homosexual behaviour the state is taking the steps necessary to establish and secure the minimal standards of behaviour necessary for society to be stable.

Framed in these terms, Devlin's argument is perhaps more formidable to the neutralist liberal than one might have initially expected. But one does not have to establish that a prohibition on homosexuality violates the neutrality constraint in order to establish a persuasive case against such a provision. Emphasising this point is important for it highlights the other demands of public reason. Namely, that not only must the objectives of legislation be neutral, but the means chosen must be reasonable and demonstrably justified. Prohibitions on homosexuality fail these requirements. In order to substantiate that the means chosen in this instance are reasonable and demonstrably justified Devlin would have to support a number of claims he fails to substantiate. Firstly, he would have to provide evidence to show that decriminalising homosexuality would cause the harm he claims it would cause. Devlin's failure to do this is more than sufficient grounds for rejecting the legitimacy of a prohibition on homosexuality. Secondly, Devlin would also have to show that less restrictive measures (e.g. education) are insufficient for establishing and securing the minimal standards of behaviour necessary for society to be stable. And thirdly, even if Devlin could substantiate his claim that such behaviour harms society, such a policy would only be reasonable if the benefits of the prohibition clearly outweighed its costs. Given the gross violation of individual liberty such a prohibition entails, the harm at issue would have to be very substantial. Devlin's failure to establish these points reveals the different ways his proposal fails to satisfy the demands of public reason. The requirements of public reason go well beyond the requirements of the neutrality constraint. I will now show how such a constraint is ill-equipped to deal with the repressive measures of the neutral state itself.

The neutral state could pursue a number of aims we feel are necessary for ensuring that the interests of all citizens are cared for. It could enforce a number of

---

[12] P. Devlin, *The Enforcement of Morals* (Oxford: Oxford University Press, 1965), p. 10.

[13] See, for example, *Political Liberalism*, p. 193.

restrictions on our freedom through various traffic laws (e.g. speed limits, seat belt laws, etc.) building regulations and taxes. These laws and policies are legitimate, the neutralist liberal will argue, because they are premised on values no one could reasonably reject (e.g. public safety). But does the fact that they are neutral *necessarily* mean that these policies are publicly justified? There is nothing in the ideal of neutrality itself that ensures that measures be *reasonable* as well as premised on neutral values. The state could justify a number of repressive measures that are consistent with neutrality of aim. For example, the government could justify a prohibition on motorised vehicles on grounds of public safety. In this case we have a neutral aim but an unreasonable policy.

Two features of such a law are worth emphasising to reveal how, despite its being neutral, it is unreasonable. Firstly, while we recognise that the aim of public safety will require limitations on our freedom we also expect legislators to take a responsible approach to pursuing such an aim. Comparable levels of public safety can be secured by varying degrees of restrictive policies and we expect law-makers to opt for those measures that impair our freedom as little as possible. Opting for the most extreme form of restriction in the name of public safety is unjustified if a less restricted policy, say one that permitted motorised vehicles but imposed a number of various traffic laws, would secure a comparable level of public safety. Furthermore, even if a prohibition on motorised vehicles secured a substantially higher degree of public safety such a proposal would still qualify as unreasonable and unfair. Public reason demands that there be a proportionality between the effects of the measure and the objective in question (i.e. public safety). In the case of prohibiting motorised vehicles there is no such proportionality. The gains secured in public safety do not outweigh the burdens imposed on freedom and efficiency. People prefer to live with the higher degree of risk which comes with permitting motorised vehicles because it also brings with it benefits which outweigh these risks (e.g. greater mobility).

The coercive power of the state is not necessarily legitimate when it is consistent with the requirements of the neutrality constraint. In addition to pursuing neutral aims, the requirements of public reason, at least when applied to important issues such as a limitation on a fundamental freedom, requires that measures be rationally connected to their objectives, that they impair the freedom as little as possible and that there be a proportionality between the effects of the measure and the objective which the measure is designed to achieve.[14] I now turn to the issue of toleration to show that, unlike the ideal of neutrality, this political virtue can help resolve these issues. Toleration is often a matter of degree. The degree to which we should tolerate beliefs, practices and ways of life that are potentially harmful will depend on the social and political values at stake in the particular case at hand. I will focus on the issues of hate speech and pornography, issues which the ideal of neutrality is ill-equipped to handle. But the political virtue of toleration, when informed by the other virtues of fair social cooperation, can help liberal societies find a reasonable

---

[14] These are the requirements adopted in Canadian *Charter* Jurisprudence with respect to section 1 of the Canadian *Charter of Rights and Freedoms*. This section of the *Charter* guarantees the rights and freedoms set out in it subject only to such reasonable limits prescribed by law as can be demonstrably justified in a free and democratic society. See, for example, *R. v. Oakes* in 26 D.L.R. (4th) 200 (1986).

balance between the conflicting values which characterise a free and democratic society.

TOLERATION AND HATE SPEECH

The neutrality constraint is useful in ruling out the repressive measures of the perfectionist state but it is not very helpful once we consider the difficult cases which liberal societies typically face. Take, for example, the issue of hate speech. Should liberal societies tolerate the incitement of racial hatred? Section 70 of the British Race Relations Act (1976) makes it a criminal offence to incite racial hatred. Section 319 of Canada's Criminal Code is a similar provision which prohibits "the wilful promotion of hatred, other than in private conversation, towards any section of the public distinguished by colour, race, religion or ethnic origin". The justification of such provisions are framed in neutral terms. The Race Relations Act included a number of other provisions (e.g. prohibitions against discrimination) and it also established a Commission for Racial Equality to help enforce the legislation and to promote equality of opportunity and good relations between people of different racial groups generally. The aim of racial equality is not premised on one particular conception of the good and thus fulfils the requirements of the neutrality constraint. Similarly, the objective of Section 319 of the Canadian Criminal Code was also neutral. In its decision to uphold Section 319 in *R. v. Keegstra* (1990) the Supreme Court of Canada argued that the provision sought to restrict material deemed not merely offensive, but harmful. Hate propaganda, Chief Justice Dickson argued, caused two sorts of injury.

> First, there is harm done to members of the target group. It is indisputable that the emotional damage caused by words may be of grave psychological and social consequence....A second harmful effect of hate propaganda which is of pressing and substantial concern is its influence upon society at large... It is... not inconceivable that the active dissemination of hate propaganda can attract individuals to its cause, and in the process create serious discord between various cultural groups in society.[15]

The aims of racial equality and prevention of harm are neutral aims and thus neutralist liberals could endorse prohibitions on certain expressions in a manner consistent with the neutrality constraint. But neutrality alone will not get us very far in resolving the complicated issues which are bound to arise as law-makers contemplate how best to pursue this neutral aim. Prohibitions against the incitement of racial hatred could vary widely in terms of how restrictive they are on freedom of expression. The following represent some of the different expressions which could be targeted to protect minority groups:

1. restrictions on publishing hate propaganda.
2. restrictions on distributing hate propaganda.
3. restrictions on using words in any public place or at any public meeting that promote racial hatred.

---

[15] *R. v. Keesgstra*, J. Bickenbach eds., *Canadian Cases in the Philosophy of Law* (Peterborough: Broadview Press, 1993), pp. 70-71.

4.   restrictions on using words in private conversation that promote racial hatred.

There is nothing in the ideal of neutrality itself that will help us determine the extent to which we should prohibit the incitement of racial hatred. The neutrality constraint is designed to ensure that non-political values do not trump political values, but it does not help us in cases where two political values conflict. The more stringent the restrictions on freedom of expression the more the aim of racial equality comes into conflict with respect for individual autonomy. The political virtue of toleration plays an important role in resolving these kinds of conflicts. Toleration is often a matter of degree. A determination of the degree to which we should tolerate expressions of racial hatred requires legislators and judges to make judgements informed by the other virtues of fair social cooperation, such as civility, reasonableness and the sense of fairness.

To illustrate how these various virtues can inform the decisions of both legislators and judges I will focus on some of the issues raised in *Keegstra* (1990). Four features of s. 319 are worth emphasising as they played an important role in convincing the Supreme Court that the measure was a reasonable limit on a constitutional right. Firstly, the provision sought to minimise its impairment of freedom of expression by excluding private conversation from its scope. While the aim of protecting minorities might be further secured by a more stringent measure such an infringement upon the privacy of the individual would not be fair or reasonable. Respect for the autonomy of the individual should, in the case of statements made in private conversation, trump the goal of protecting minorities. But the stakes at risk change once we turn to expressions that are made publicly and the provision targeted expressions in this category. This aspect of the provision is reasonable as these expressions are more likely to harm minorities than those made in private conversation which are very limited in terms of the influence they will have. Furthermore, a restriction on public expression is less of an infringement on individual freedom than a provision that also applied to private conversations. Wayne Sumner describes the balancing act s. 319 attempts to accomplish as follows:

> The optimal trade-off, or balance, is that at which any further gains in one of the values would be outweighed by greater losses in the other. Freedom of expression would be better protected were there no legal constraints whatever on the circulation of hate propaganda, while the security of minority groups would be more effectively safeguarded by legislation a good deal more restrictive than s. 319(2). Somewhere between the two extremes we seek a balance point at which the greater protection for minorities afforded by stronger legislation would be outweighed by the chilling effect on political speech, while the greater protection for expression afforded by weaker legislation would be outweighed by the increase in racial hatred.[16]

Three other features of the measure which reflect this balancing exercise are worth noting as they illustrate the importance of the political virtues of civility, reasonableness and the sense of fairness. In addition to excluding expression which is made in private conversation, the provision stipulates that the promoting of hatred

---

[16] W. Sumner, "Hate Propaganda and Charter Rights", W. Waluchow, ed. *Free Expression: Essays in Law and Philosophy* (Oxford: Oxford University Press, 1994), p. 160.

must be *wilful*. Chief Justice Dickson argued that this feature of the provision imposed a stringent *mens rea* requirement, "necessitating either an intent to promote hatred or knowledge of the substantial certainty of such".[17] This is a reasonable feature of such a provision for a number of reasons. As Chief Justice Dickson pointed out, lawmakers should concern themselves not just with whom they want to catch, but also with whom they do not want to catch. There are, for example, instances were members of a minority group publish hate propaganda against their own group in order to create controversy or to agitate for reform.[18] Insertion of the word 'wilfully' in s. 319(2) ensures that the provision is invoked in cases consistent with the aims of the provision.

Thirdly, the provision invoked the word 'hatred' and, despite the difficulties of stipulating exactly what hatred is, it is possible to distinguish between expressions that promote hate and those one finds merely offensive. The latter are not legitimate grounds for restricting a fundamental freedom like freedom of expression. The meaning of the word 'hatred', argued Chief Justice Dickson, must be defined according to the context in which it is found. The purpose of s. 319(2) is to prevent the pain suffered by target group members and to reduce racial, ethnic and religious tension in Canada. Taken in this context, "the word 'hatred' is restricted to the most severe and deeply-felt form of opprobrium".[19] The reasonableness of a provision against the promotion of racial hatred depends on the degree to which it targets those expressions most likely to inflict harm.

Finally, the provision includes a number of defences. These are (a) truth; (b) good faith opinion on a religious matter; (c) public interest; (d) good faith opinion to point out, so as to remove, matters producing feelings of hatred toward an identifiable group. These defences represent cases where tolerating racial hatred could be publicly justified. The first defence, that the statements communicated are true, recognises the importance of John Stuart Mill's argument against censorship.[20] Censorship not only mistakenly presupposes the censor's infallibility, argued Mill, it also undermines the conditions necessary for us to gain a better understanding of the truth. The inclusion of this defence is another example of how law-makers can attempt to find a reasonable balance between competing social interests. In this instance it was judged that the social interests in protecting the truth was of greater value than the interests in protecting minorities. The other three defences- good faith opinion on a religious matter, public interest, and good faith attempt to point out, so as to remove, matters producing feelings of hatred toward an identifiable group- were intended to aid in making the scope of the wilful promotion of hatred more explicit.

These defences are further instances of how the virtues of reasonableness and the sense of fairness, for example, should inform the political virtue of toleration. Laws that seek to limit expressions deemed harmful should be designed so that they are not overbroad or unduly vague. Chief Justice Dickson interpreted the inclusion of the defences in s. 319(3) as an indication of Parliament's commitment to the idea

---

[17] *Keegstra*, p. 77.
[18] See, for example, *R. V. Buzzanga and Durocher* (1979)
[19] *Keegstra*, p. 77.
[20] J.S. Mill, *On Liberty* (Harmondsworth, UK: Penguin, 1982).

that an individual's freedom of expression should not be curtailed in borderline cases.

The design of s. 319 of the Canadian Criminal Code exemplifies the myriad of issues liberal societies face as they attempt to determine to what extent they should tolerate expressions which threaten to undermine important social values like racial equality. Tolerating even the potentially harmful expressions of racists can be justice-promoting in certain circumstances. By tolerating such expressions in private conversation, for example, we recognise that the price of intolerance in this instance is too costly. A provision which prohibited such expressions would intrude upon the privacy of the individual and this would be more unfair than tolerating such expressions. Furthermore, by targeting expressions which are deemed 'hateful' as oppose to ones we merely dislike, s. 319 takes the necessary steps to ensure that the provision will only be applied in those cases where expressions do instil detestation, enmity, ill-will and malevolence in another. The defences included in s. 319(3) are further examples of how the case for toleration can be strengthened when other important values are at stake (e.g. truth). The degree to which the political virtue of toleration will be justice-promoting depends on the degree to which it coheres with the virtues of civility, reasonableness and the sense of fairness.

PORNOGRAPHY AND THE ISSUE OF HARM

The political virtue of toleration is justice-promoting when the beliefs, practices and ways of life we accord constitutional protection do not violate the rights of others. But as the example of racial hatred makes clear, the issue is not always as clear-cut as saying that we either tolerate or do not tolerate certain beliefs, practices and ways of life. Toleration is often a matter of degree, and thus the degree to which it will be justice-promoting will depend on the degree to which legislators and judges exercise this virtue in a way that is informed by and supports the other virtues of fair social cooperation. An important issue which I only briefly addressed in section II, but will now discuss in more detail, is that of harm. Toleration would be much easier to execute as a political virtue if all beliefs, practices and ways of life fell into one of two categories- those that harmed others and those that did not. In such a scenario reasonable agreement could perhaps be secured by simply according those that fall into the latter category greater freedom. But what constitutes these categories is itself a source of much debate among legal scholars and many actions which do not fall into the category of 'harmful to others' still fall within the legitimate purvey of the criminal law. As Joel Feinberg's masterful four volume *The Moral Limits of the Criminal Law* effectively illustrates, there are a diverse array of possible coercion-legitimising principles including the harm principle, the offence principle, legal paternalism and legal moralism.[21]

---

[21] See J. Feinberg, *The Moral Limits of the Criminal Law: Vol.1 : Harm to others* (Oxford : Oxford University Press, 1984); *Vol.2 : Offense to Others* (Oxford : Oxford University Press, 1985); *Vol.3 : Harm to Self* (Oxford : Oxford University Press, 1989); and *Vol.4 : Harmless Wrongdoing* (Oxford : Oxford University Press, 1988). For a summary of the various coercion-legitimising principles see the definitions provided in *Harm to Self*, pp. xvi-xviii.

I do not intend to provide a lengthy analysis of what constitutes 'harm' but instead wish to limit my discussion to two issues related to harm in the hopes of further illustrating how the virtue of toleration is intertwined with the other virtues of fair social cooperation. The first issue is to recognise that harms occur along a broad spectrum in varying degrees of seriousness. Harms can range, for example, from physical and mental injury to harming someone's reputation. The second issue is that in many cases there is only a risk, not a certainty, that the harm in question will be realised. In some cases the certainty of inflicting a harm is guaranteed. For example, when someone is physically assaulted. In other cases there is only a risk of inflicting a harm on others. The risk could vary from the probable to the implausible. What degree of risk is sufficiently high enough to warrant state intervention to prevent harm and what degree is low enough to warrant tolerance? This question cannot be answered in the abstract, detached from any definite context. Consideration must be given, for example, to the value of the freedom at stake, the risk of harm as well as the importance of the harm involved. Consider, for example, laws against drinking and driving. The potential harm of such actions is very substantial (e.g. injury or even death to the driver and others). The impairment of individual freedom is very minimal. These considerations lead us to conclude that laws should set stringent limits on the level of blood alcohol content drivers can have in an attempt to minimise the risk of harm.

The fact that harms vary in both degree and probability raises a number of complications for the political virtue of toleration. The degree to which we should tolerate potentially harmful beliefs, practices and ways of life will depend on the degree of harms at issue as well as the likelihood that such harms will be realised. The virtues of civility, reasonableness and the sense of fairness are indispensable for determining the degree to which we should tolerate potentially harmful beliefs, practices and ways of life. I will now illustrate how these virtues can help resolve some of the contentious issues which arise in the case of restricting pornography.

One might think that the neutrality constraint will prove useful when assessing the legitimacy of restrictions on sexual representations. The justification typically given for obscenity legislation is that such measures are offensive and immoral. The neutrality constraint could thus go a long way in undermining these kinds of legislation. But some countries justify such restrictions on grounds consistent with the neutrality constraint. Canada is a good example of this. In his study of the right to freedom of expression in Canada Richard Moon describes the shift in the justification of restrictions on pornography as follows:

> The public justification for the censorship of sexually explicit representations no longer emphasizes the offensive or immoral character of such material. Censorship is now justified on the grounds that sexually explicit representations sometimes have harmful consequences. With this change in justification has come a shift in the focus of restriction from sexually explicit material in general to sexually explicit material that depicts violent and degrading activity and a change in the language used to describe the restricted material from obscenity to pornography.[22]

---

[22] R. Moon, *The Constitutional Protection of Freedom of Expression* (Toronto: University of Toronto, 2001), p. 105.

In the much debated case of *R. v. Butler* (1992), the Supreme Court of Canada upheld s. 163 of the Criminal Code which adopted this 'harm based' approach to restricting pornography. I will not go through the details of this decision nor all of the merits and demerits of this legislation. But I do wish to briefly discuss the two issues of the degree and probability of harm to illustrate how the virtues of civility, reasonableness and the sense of fairness can inform the virtue of toleration. What harm, if any, does tolerating sexually explicit representations cause? The harm at issue in *Butler* was that of predisposing persons to antisocial behaviour. For example, the physical or mental mistreatment of women by men. Related to this issue is that of the risk that exposure to such materials will cause this harm. Can the claim that tolerating such materials will cause these harms be demonstrably justified? The empirical evidence on this issue, as the Supreme Court acknowledged, is divided and inconclusive. In such a scenario, what is the fair and reasonable course of action?

When the values of liberty and equality conflict, as they do in the case of censoring certain forms of sexually explicit representations, civility requires us to listen to the concerns raised on both sides of the debate. Civil libertarians oppose restrictions on pornography because they believe that restrictions on these types of expressions will lead us on the path to a repressive state. Those who argue in favour of censorship claim that such legislation is necessary if we are to take equality seriously. Catharine MacKinnon, for example, praises the Canadian Courts for recognising the reality of inequality in the issues before it:

> ...this is not big bad state power jumping on poor powerless individual citizen, but a law passed to stand behind a comparatively powerless group in its social fight for equality against socially powerful and exploitative groups. This positioning of forces- which makes the hate propaganda prohibition and the obscenity law of Canada (properly interpreted) into equality laws, although neither was called such by Parliament- made the invocation of a tradition designed to keep government off the backs of people totally inappropriate.[23]

Civility, once coupled with the other virtues of fair social coopeartion- tolerance, reasonableness and the sense of fairness- guides us to measures which are a sensible compromise between the dangers of the repressive state and the state that ignores the realities of inequality. Other things being equal, the stronger and more probable the harm, and the less weighty the aspect of freedom at stake, the lesser the likelihood of tolerance. This was the guideline that informed both the design of s. 163 and the decision to uphold the law in *Butler*.

Section 163 does not target all explicit sexual representations, but only those with violence and those which subject people to treatment that is degrading or dehumanising. These are the representations that are not only those most likely to cause harm, but those that will cause harms substantial enough to warrant state intervention. By limiting itself to these particular representations the Supreme Court concluded that, despite the lack of conclusive empirical evidence, Parliament had a reasonable basis for presuming that exposure to these images bears a causal relationship to changes in attitudes and beliefs. Furthermore, the legislation contained an 'artistic defence' so that materials which have scientific, artistic or

---

[23] C. MacKinnon, *Only Words* (Harvard: Harvard University Press, 1993), p. 103.

literary merit are not captured by the provision. The function of this defence clause was to ensure that greater protection be accorded to expressions which are not primarily economically motivated. This further demonstrates the reasonableness of this particular piece of legislation. Section 163 and the decision reached in *Butler* are good examples of how legislators and judges can be guided by the virtues of fair social cooperation and come to decisions which, at least the most part, exemplify the ideal of public reason.

CONCLUSION

Like hate speech, pornography poses a challenging dilemma for liberal societies. It forces us to search for a reasonable balance between the values of freedom and equality. The ideal of neutrality does not help us with these difficult cases because the issues at stake are not 'conceptions of the good' but fundamental social and political values. For this reason, neutralist liberals must not treat toleration and neutrality as two complementary solutions. By emphasising the limits of the neutrality constraint I hope I have made an effective case in favour of remaining faithful to the importance of toleration as a political virtue. In this paper I have also emphasised the limits of toleration as a virtue. Toleration will remain an 'elusive virtue'[24] because the degree to which it is a virtue depends on our ability to reconcile it with the other virtues of fair social cooperation- the virtues of civility, reasonableness and the sense of fairness.

---

[24] D. Heyd, *Toleration: An Elusive Virtue.*

CHAPTER 8

JOHN STUART MILL AS A
THEORIST OF TOLERATION

Graham Finlay

John Stuart Mill has not featured as prominently as one might expect in discussions of diversity and toleration, even as the author of *On Liberty*.[1] There may be various reasons for this neglect. One reason may be the more general belief that utilitarianism is inherently unable to cope with these problems, presumably because any account of them in terms of utility seems to deny that they are problems at all, to deny that differences between the conceptions of the good held by competing groups resist translation into a common utilitarian calculus. This perceived inability on the part of utilitarianism is bolstered by the classical objection that utilitarianism does not offer sufficient guarantees that individuals or minorities will not be sacrificed to the majority's well being whenever that sacrifice leads to greater general good. That utilitarians are insensitive to the *interests* of minorities is also coupled with the charge that utilitarian policy-makers are insensitive to their subjects' *beliefs*; that the historic relations between utilitarianism and colonialism help explain a pernicious 'Government House Utilitarianism' (one might say 'India House Utilitarianism'), where a utilitarian elite sharply distinguish between the demands of the utilitarian theory of the rulers and the committed practices of the ruled.[2] Another reason for the specific exclusion of *On Liberty* from recent discussions of toleration may stem from the increasing emphasis on groups, rather than individuals, as the objects of toleration. Mill's individualism, as classically expressed in *On Liberty*, may seem inadequate to deal with the problems of 'multiculturalism' and the situation of individuals in groups that provide them with their 'conceptions of the good'.

---

[1] This statement is less true of the literature of toleration in the United Kingdom than it is of the same literature in the United States. See, especially, the anthologies produced by the Morrell Centre at the University of York: e.g. S. Mendus, ed., *Justifying Toleration*, (Cambridge: Cambridge University Press, 1988), J. Horton and S. Mendus, eds., *Aspects of Toleration*, (London: Methuen, 1985) and J. Horton and P. Nicholson, eds., *Toleration: Theory and Practice*, (Aldershot: Avebury, 1992).

[2] See B. Williams, 'A critique of utilitarianism', *Utilitarianism: For and Against*, (Cambridge: Cambridge University Press, 1973), 75-150 at pp. 135-140, *Ethics and the Limits of Philosophy*, (Cambridge, MA: Harvard University Press, 1985), pp. 108-110 and 'The point of view of the universe: Sidgwick and the ambitions of ethics', *Making Sense of Humanity*, (Cambridge: Cambridge University Press, 1995), 153-171 at p. 166.

Criticisms of both types inform what commentary there is on Mill's thinking about diversity. Mill's famous remarks on nations and colonies in *Considerations on Representative Government* , his notorious claims about 'barbarians' in *On Liberty* and his position within the East India Company have led both friendly and unfriendly commentators to characterize Mill as an uncomplicated assimilationist, insensitive to the claims of true cultural diversity and the benefits of a multicultural state.[3] Against these interpretations, I argue that John Stuart Mill's later work, properly understood, presents a coherent and viable response to cultural diversity and the demands of political action, one which avoids the pitfalls of an unreal primacy of the individual and an uncritical conception of the social. According to this interpretation, awareness of and commitment to specifically cultural diversity is fundamental to Mill's social scientific method and utilitarian policy-making. The particular form that Mill's utilitarian commitment to diversity takes marks him as a theorist of toleration, but not of state neutrality, and as an instrumentalist about diversity, not a theorist of fundamental respect. I will try to illustrate this difference by contrasting Mill's theory with that of the pre-eminent deontological theorist of state neutrality and equal respect, John Rawls.

Mill's views on nations and civilization, expressed in *Considerations on Representative Government*, have formed the basis of the interpretation of him as an assimilationist and imperialist. Nations are identified by 'common sympathies', 'community of language', 'community of religion' and 'strongest of all', 'identity of political antecedents; the possession of a national history, and consequent community of recollections; collective pride and humiliation, pleasure and regret, connected with the same incidents in the past.'[4] Parallel to this discussion of nations and self-government is an account of civilization's centrality to representative government and the problems posed by a more advanced nation's government of a more backward one.[5] These two considerations are combined in the passages that are most frequently cited as proof of Mill's insensitivity to diversity. In the *Representative Government*, Mill talks about the 'indubitable benefit' that 'an inferior and more backward portion of the human race'—like the pre-British Highlanders and Welsh and pre-French Basques and Bretons—gains from absorption into another:

> Nobody can suppose that is not more beneficial to a Breton, or a Basque of French Navarre, to be brought into the current of the ideas and feelings of a highly civilized and cultivated people--to be a member of the French nationality, admitted on equal terms to all the privileges of French citizenship, sharing the advantages of French protection, and the dignity and *prestige* of French power--than to sulk on his own rocks, the half-savage

---

[3] See, especially, W. Kymlicka, *Multicultural Citizenship*, (Oxford: Oxford University Press, 1995), pp. 52-53. Perhaps the most significant and seriously considered rejection of Mill's usefulness for problems of social conflict is John Rawls' rejection of Mill's 'comprehensive liberalism' in favour of a 'political liberalism' in his *Political Liberalism*, (New York: Columbia University Press, 1993), of which more below.

[4] John Stuart Mill, *Considerations on Representative Government*, in *Collected Works* , (Toronto: University of Toronto Press, 1963-1991), XIX, p. 546. All future references to the *Collected Works* will give the work's title in parentheses followed by CW and the volume and page number.

[5] *Ibid*, pp. 376-379, 394-398, 415-420. See also the notorious claim of *On Liberty*, CW XVIII, p. 224: "Despotism is a legitimate mode of government in dealing with barbarians, provided the end be their improvement, and the means justified by actually effecting that end."

relic of past times, revolving in his own little mental orbit, without participation or interest in the general movement of the world.[6]

Perhaps the location of Mill's discussion of nations and minorities in the *Representative Government* accounts, in part, for the individualist interpretation of *On Liberty*. *On Liberty* has been most frequently interpreted as a plea for the liberty of individuals, not of cultural, religious or political minorities. Minority rights are thought to be solely protected by the mechanisms of proportional representation.[7]

To ignore *On Liberty*'s relevance to problems of cultural diversity, however, is to ignore those aspects of Mill's thought that mark him as an important theorist of toleration. Classically, arguments for toleration have been addressed to the state, because the state has been viewed as the greatest threat to the free expression of one's beliefs or practices. The signal turn of *On Liberty* is to argue that the rise of mass society and majoritarian politics makes a more extensive and sinister form of intolerance possible: the enforcement of majority opinion and beliefs both directly through social pressure and indirectly through their influence on the political interventions of the state. Mill argues that the widening of the franchise, the spread of literacy and the availability of newspapers and the increased contact and interdependence between groups make for a more uniform, extensive and powerful majority culture. Mill describes this transformation as a loss in the 'variety of situations':

> The circumstances which surround different classes and individuals, and shape their characters, are daily becoming more assimilated. Formerly, different ranks, different neighborhoods, different trades and professions, lived in what might be called different worlds; at present, to a great degree in the same. Comparatively speaking, they now read the same things, listen to the same things, see the same things, go to the same places, have their hopes and fears directed to the same objects, have the same rights and liberties, and the same means of asserting them. Great as are the differences in position which remain, they are nothing to those which have ceased. And the assimilation is still proceeding. All the political changes of the age promote it, since they all tend to raise the low and to lower the high. Every extension of education promotes it, because education brings people under common influences, and give them access to the general stock of facts and sentiments. Improvements in the means of communication promote it, by bringing the inhabitants of distant places into personal contact, and keeping up a rapid flow of changes of residence between one place and another. The increase of commerce and manufactures promotes it, by diffusing more widely the advantages of easy circumstances, and opening all objects of ambition, even the highest, to general competition, whereby the desire of rising becomes no longer the character of a particular class, but of all classes. A more powerful agency than even all these, in bringing about a general similarity among mankind, is the complete establishment, in this and other free countries, of the ascendancy of public opinion in the State.[8]

This long passage should put us on our guard against identifying Mill as an enthusiast for assimilation. But it does identify Mill as a theorist of 'culture': the

---

[6] *Representative Government*, CW XIX, p. 549.
[7] See, for example, F. R. Berger, *Happiness, Justice and Freedom*, (Berkeley: University of California Press, 1984), p. 227.
[8] *On Liberty*, CW XVIII, pp. 274-275.

variety of considerations that Mill appeals to in this passage and their hold over individuals betray an awareness of a specifically 'cultural' influence on 'character'.[9]

Of course, Mill does not describe this 'social control' as the influence of 'culture' but 'custom'. Once we note that Mill's notion of custom plays the role we assign to culture, we can then begin to reevaluate Mill's views about assimilation and its relation to cultural and religious diversity. This is because, for Mill, custom is also centrally related to knowledge, both as a condition on the knowledge an individual can have and as the object of social scientific knowledge. This is an important connection, because the problems that religious and cultural diversity presents can be seen as problems of knowledge and conflicts over the truth. It is because we think others are mistaken about what is true or good that we seek to change or suppress the beliefs or practices of the sincere members or adherents of other cultures or other faiths. These problems also raise difficulties for Mill's specifically utilitarian defense of liberty, since promoting the good requires some knowledge both of what is good and what will promote it. One might well ask: how can a utilitarian be committed to the promotion of diversity?

To see this connection between custom and knowledge, we need to consider Mill's wholesale reworking of the notion of 'custom' he found in the empiricist tradition. There custom appears interchangeably with 'habit' and, in particular, habitual association. Habit is itself nothing but the repeated experience of a particular association between two things, so that soon the mind makes the association between those things by itself whenever one is present to it.[10] A custom, then, is the habitual associations of a group of individuals, and serves to explain any beliefs that are either irrational or not universally shared and so delimits the boundaries of different cultural groups. Before Mill, it always remains a mere description of the behaviour of groups, never an active power forming the individual characters of individuals who are raised in the customs of a particular cultural or social group. Even in Hume, where custom and habit are important to his political thought, it is merely the ground of practical certainty for action and belief, including political beliefs.[11]

The use of this individualist notion of custom is especially marked in the psychological theory with which Mill was most familiar, his father's *Analysis of the Phenomena of the Human Mind*. James Mill ascribes all belief to habit and custom; all beliefs are the product of repeated association.[12] In his notes to the *Analysis*,

---

[9] Raymond Williams notes this historical contribution in *Culture and Society*, (New York: Harper and Row, 1958), pp. 58-59. Mill, of course, means by 'culture' something closer to our notion of 'cultivation', for example, 'self-culture'.

[10] See, e.g., J. Locke, *An Essay Concerning Human Understanding*, Peter Nidditch ed., (Oxford: Clarendon Press, 1979), Book II, Chapter XXXIII "Of the Association of Ideas", pp. 394-401.

[11] See D. Hume, *A Treatise of Human Nature*, L.A. Selby-Bigge ed., (Oxford: Clarendon Press, 1888), Book II, Part III, Section V, "Of the effects of Custom", pp. 422-424. For political matters, see *Ibid*, Book III, Part II, Section 10, "Of the Objects of Allegiance", pp. 555-557 and Hume, *Essays Moral, Political, and Literary*, (Indianapolis: Liberty Fund, 1987), "Of the Original Contract", p. 474-475. For the form of this idea with which Mill probably was most familiar, see William Paley, *The Principles of Moral and Political Philosophy*, Book I, Chapter V, cited by J.B. Schneewind in *Sidgwick's Ethics and Victorian Moral Philosophy*, (Oxford: Clarendon Press, 1977), p. 124. I am indebted to Schneewind for this reference.

[12] J. Mill, *Analysis of the Phenomena of the Human Mind*, (London: Longmans, Green, Reader and Dyer,

John Stuart Mill argues that this passive, individualist account of belief does not sufficiently distinguish between truth and error or describe their causes, and does not provide any explanation of progress in the sciences. Mill notes that 'Indissoluble belief' characterizes the beliefs both of the scientist and the fool and argues that a purely passive and 'mechanical' relation to experience leaves the inquirer prey to whatever associations he or she may happen to have.[13] What is needed is an active attention to the evidence with the goal of keeping those observations as free as possible from the influence of uncritical habit, prejudice or interest. This is particularly the case when considering moral and political matters.[14] Against both the crude empiricism of his father and the uncritical intuitionism of his conservative opponents, he emphasized that many propositions or beliefs that are considered to be indubitable—because their negation is 'inconceivable'—can in fact be doubted, because their negation has been believed by people living in different societies or periods. To guard against this lazy, passive tendency to accept the beliefs your own immediate class or society offers you, Mill advocates a wide-ranging interest in the beliefs of other cultures and times.[15] Similarly, G.W. Smith has noted that Mill's determinism requires 'social diversity' for there to be any social improvement, since only if we are aware of alternative ways of going on are we able to modify our own characters, which would otherwise succumb to the regularities of custom and habit.[16]

Unlike these crudely individualist theories, Mill's notion of custom is much more like our notion of 'culture'. It is a broad social fact about groups and unites all the major conditions on individuals' situation in society. As a cultural process, it combines the operations of language, our 'mother tongue', the influence of tradition and collective wisdom and the economic, legal, social and political institutions that we find ourselves born into.[17] Because custom is the most significant of the circumstances that form people's beliefs and characters, it forms the limit of a people's imagination. As such a limit, Mill notes how it is held to be immune to criticism:

> the people of any given age and country no more suspect any difficulty in it, than if it were a subject on which mankind had always been agreed. The rules which obtain among themselves appear to them self-evident and self-justifying. This all but universal illusion is one of the examples of the magical influence of custom, which is not only, as

1869), Volume I, pp. 380-381, p. 368.

[13] *Ibid*, John Stuart Mill's editorial comments, Volume I, p. 407.

[14] J. Mill, *Analysis*, John Stuart Mill's editorial comments, Volume I, pp. 117-120. For moral and political matters, see *A System of Logic*, CW VIII, p. 777.

[15] See e.g. *Logic*, CW VII, p. 564-565. Paul Feyerabend has, of course, drawn attention to Mill's insistence on the importance of knowledge of the entire history of science for scientific investigation in 'Introduction: proliferation and realism as methodological principles' in his *Realism, Rationalism and Scientific Method: Philosophical Papers*, Vol. 1, (Cambridge: Cambridge University Press, 1981.), p. 140-143 and *Against Method*, (London: Verso, 1978), p. 47-48.

[16] G.W. Smith, "Social Liberty and Free Agency", in *J.S. Mill on Liberty in Focus*, J. Gray and G.W. Smith eds. (London: Routledge, 1991), 239-259 at pp. 254-255. See also, G.W. Smith, "J.S. Mill on Edger and Réville: An Episode in the Development of Mill's Conception of Freedom", *Journal of the History of Ideas* 41, 1980, reprinted in J. C. Wood, ed. *John Stuart Mill: Critical Perspectives*, (London: Routledge, 1988) 550-566.

[17] For language, see *Logic*, CW VII, p. 663; for tradition, see *Ibid*, p. 238, cited above, and "Coleridge", CW X, 117-164 at pp. 119-120; for economic institutions, see *Principles of Political Economy*, CW II, pp. 240-244, for legal and political institutions, see *Logic*, CW VIII, pp. 911-912.

> the proverb says, a second nature, but is continually mistaken for the first. The effect of custom, in preventing any misgiving respecting the rules of conduct which mankind impose on one another, is all the more complete because the subject is one on which it is not generally considered necessary that reasons should be given, either by one person to others, or by each to himself.[18]

The limits that custom imposes on imagination and criticism constitute its threat to liberty and individuality. Individuality is living out a life plan one has chosen, customary or not. Liberty is being allowed to live the way one chooses, free from the unnecessary or intrusive impositions of state and society. The critique of custom is the most important way we secure liberty, and the first step in this critique is to point out the actual diversity we find in the world and history, to note that the appearance of unanimity custom imposes on our minds is a false one.

It is central to Mill's account of custom that it motivates human beings to impose 'rules of conduct' on each other. Mill is ambivalent about this factor in social life: on one hand, he notes that some rules must necessarily be imposed, on the other, he remains profoundly concerned that this imposition will be informed by class interest and power. Mill's suspicion that human beings are frequently motivated by 'love of domination', pervades his political and polemical writings. In *On Liberty* he describes the 'natural intolerance' of mankind:

> The disposition of mankind, whether as rulers or as fellow-citizens, to impose their own opinions and inclinations as a rule of conduct on others, is so energetically supported by some of the best and by some of the worst feelings incident to human nature, that it is hardly ever kept under restraint by anything but want of power.[19]

Uncriticized custom is too often the expression of a particular class interest, whether the group is an economic class or a religious, cultural or ethnic group.

The most brutal and obvious cases of such class oppression are the cases in which no effective legal and institutional safeguards are in place to protect the subjected group. This is the case with slaves, women and many colonial subjects.[20] With regards to the last case, Mill defends, in 'The Negro Question', the black inhabitants of the West Indies against Carlyle's charge that they are naturally inferior in terms of industry, respect for law and wisdom. Outraged by the violently repressive measures used against black West Indians and supported by Carlyle, Mill attacks the idea of natural inferiority as such, and denies any 'original' differences between human beings, especially ones supposed to be based on race. Mill's belief in the 'infinite malleability of man', combined with his concern with the way superior classes exercise power, leads him to explain the differences between the colonizing masters and the colonized subjects in terms of the historical oppression of the latter by the former. The current social and material state of the black and white inhabitants is irreducibly involved with the power exercised by masters over subjects. Mill argues that just as the difference in height between trees is no argument for the superior vigour of the taller's original seed, because accidental

---

[18] *On Liberty*, CW XVIII, p. 220. That the 'tyranny of opinion' is on the increase and possesses its own historical dynamic, see *Ibid*, p. 269, 227.
[19] *Ibid*, p. 227.
[20] For women and slaves, see, e.g., *On the Subjection of Women*, CW XXI, pp. 267-270.

variations in soil, exposure, insects etc. all contribute to its growth, so superior power is no argument for the superiority of the more powerful:

> If the trees grew near together, may not the one which, by whatever accident, grew up first, have retarded the other's developement by its shade? Human beings are subject to an infinitely greater variety of accidents and external influences than trees, and have infinitely more operation in impairing the growth of one another, since those who begin by being the strongest, have almost always hitherto used their strength to keep the others weak.[21]

In *On Liberty*, Mill uses the same image of a tree's growth and the costs to its neighbours in his description of the spread of Christian domination over Europe.[22] The use of the same image in the two contexts shows that the domination of society by one class of people operates on both a political and religious or cultural level; in both cases, control by a dominant group deforms and stunts the growth of subordinate groups. It also shows that we should be hesitant to find an uncritical Romantic organicism in *On Liberty*'s contrasts between the natural and the mechanical.

Mill's concern with power as it figures in culture represents another improvement over the theories of Bentham and James Mill. James Mill identified 'sinister interests' exclusively with the aristocracy and their influence in the state and explicitly invoked the working classes' submission to the opinions of the middle class as the guarantee for the stability of a reformed state. In contrast, John Stuart Mill was concerned by the danger to freedom and rationality posed by any dominant class, and was suspicious of the tendency to take one's cues from the classes above oneself.[23] Because of the comprehensiveness of the influence of culture and class power, John Stuart Mill is not only concerned, in *On Liberty*, with individuals, but with conflicts between religious, political and cultural attitudes and with the persecution of religious views—Muslims' abhorrence of pork, Hindu notions of purity—or alternative social forms like the (then) polygamous Mormons of Utah.[24] Many of the ways of life, the 'experiments in living', that Mill advocates can only be conducted by or in groups, and the groups to which Mill appeals usually have a religious or cultural identity. So we find him advocating not only a diversity of opinions, but a diversity of ethics, where an ethic requires a group of practitioners:

> I believe that other ethics than any which can be evolved from exclusively Christian sources, must exist side by side with Christian ethics to produce the moral regeneration of mankind; and that the Christian system is no exception to the rule, that in an imperfect state of the human mind, the interests of truth require a diversity of opinions.[25]

Mill's vision of a free society, in *On Liberty*, essentially contains a lively diversity of religious, cultural and political groups. The references to 'an imperfect state of the human mind' and the 'interests of truth' in the passage cited above give

---

[21]'The Negro Question', CW XXI, 85-96 at p. 93.

[22] *On Liberty*, CW XVIII, p. 241.

[23]"They ask themselves, what is suitable to my position? what is usually done by persons of my station and pecuniary circumstances? or (worse still) what is usually done by persons of a station and circumstances superior to mine?", *Ibid*, p. 264.

[24]*Ibid*, pp. 284-285, 290.

[25] *Ibid*, pp. 256-257.

Mill's theory of toleration a particular cast. The diversity of practices that Mill advocates are fundamentally justified by the demands of knowledge. As my earlier discussion of habit and observation showed, it is only by interesting ourselves in other ways of going on that we are able to free ourselves, to the extent that we can, from our prejudices and pre-conceptions. Similarly, it is only because of the contingent, *de facto* tendencies of any dominant group to exercise class power that it is necessary to maintain this diversity of attitudes through political institutions. Deep as Mill's commitments to individual autonomy, equal treatment and respect for others are, they are not fundamental. What is fundamental is that people who are seeking knowledge, especially about what is morally and politically good, must not be hemmed in by their local situation and its partial experience. Mill has an instrumental view of toleration, since it is encouraged as the means to some other goal. Furthermore, in the end, Mill's theory is also non-neutral. The goal of inquiry is the production of knowledge, including knowledge of the political sphere, and this knowledge is to guide our deliberations. Since, to be effective, this knowledge will have to be relatively concrete, it may well clash with other people's beliefs about what should be done, on the basis of their conceptions of the good. The trick, for Mill, is to allow this knowledge to guide political policy without it becoming oppressive.

Mill's prescriptions for how knowledge of the good is to be turned into practice are found in the institutional structures advocated by both *Considerations on Representative Government* and *On Liberty*. In those writings, Mill is concerned about any class coming to dominate the state, even the 'instructed few' whose political participation he encourages in the *Representative Government* and whose liberty he seeks to protect in *On Liberty*.[26] His solution to the problems presented by class power is to build in institutional safeguards that prevent the domination of political and cultural institutions by any one class. So education--the institution which is central to the formation of individuals' characters and the most divisive site of cultural conflict--is too important to be subject to the direct control of the state: its teachings will be too likely to reflect the views of public opinion, the state and the governing class.[27] Just as diverse practices are required for the preservation of liberty and the production of knowledge, so the government should permit and, if necessary, support competing educational experiments.[28]

We can now reconsider the remarks from the *Representative Government* that have been cited as proof of Mill's assimilationist tendencies. If we look at the wider context in which these remarks appear, we find that Mill insists that none of these commonalities of language, sentiment or history are either necessary or sufficient conditions of a viable nationality, and cites the examples of Switzerland, Belgium

---

[26] For the former see, *Representative Government*, CW XIX, p. 506, and p. 476. For the latter see, e.g., *On Liberty*, CW XVIII p. 269.

[27] "All that has been said of the importance of individuality of character, and diversity in opinions and modes of conduct, involves, as of the same unspeakable importance, diversity of education.", *Ibid*, pp. 302-303.

[28] This recommendation has obvious parallels with Mill's suggestion that competing socialist cooperatives may be the solution to the problems of class power, where 'class' is construed in a narrow economic sense. See "Chapters on Socialism", CW V, 703-756 at pp. 739-748.

and a unified Italy.[29] We find that the goal of improvement is not served by assimilation, but by blending the best qualities of the participating cultural groups:

> Whatever really tends to the admixture of nationalities, and the blending of their attributes and peculiarities in a common union, is a benefit to the human race. Not by extinguishing types, of which, in these cases, sufficient examples are sure to remain, but by softening their extreme forms, and filling up the intervals between them. The united people, like a crossed breed of animals (but in a still greater degree, because the influences in operation are moral as well as physical), inherits the special aptitudes and excellences of all its progenitors, protected by the admixture from being exaggerated into the neighbouring vices.[30]

This is an image of diversity, but not a neutral one. The making of a nation, when done best, does not involve leaving the participant groups as they are but combining them in some harmonious whole, in which they all can learn from each other. This is not done by 'extinguishing types', but by the formation of a new, more harmonious public culture, necessitated by the need to live together under the same institutions and laws.

This complex process, with its twin demands for mutual compromise and respect, requires that the 'liberal self' interest itself in other ways of going on. Just as a familiarity with the attitudes of other cultures and periods is essential to the pursuit of knowledge and self-improvement in *A System of Logic*, so it is essential to the education of 'competent judges' in *Utilitarianism*. Knowledge of other ways of life is essential to the mental cultivation of the individual and, accordingly, to individual happiness.[31] On the political level, an anthropological understanding of others is an essential part of the knowledge Mill's utilitarian planners need to possess, if they are to improve society by judging existing institutions and promoting just institutions. Instead of ignoring the practical commitments of the ruled, Mill's theory of diversity is best understood as a response to the depth of those practical commitments, to their diversity and to the conflicts that deep commitments to diverse practices produce. Policy makers' navigation of the conflicts which emerge from a diverse society is crucially concerned with the threat society poses to these diverse commitments, rather than the threat they pose to society. Accordingly, in the *Representative Government*, Mill places a tremendous emphasis on the government and its bureaucracy's need to justify their actions to all the members of society. More important, because of the difficulties of assuming another's viewpoint, each person's voice itself must be heard, insofar as this is possible.[32]

Similar concerns for the point of view of other groups animate the aspect of Mill's career that is thought to be most telling against the idea that he was sensitive to the needs of other cultures. In his role as servant and defender of the East India

---

[29] *Representative Government*, CW XIX, pp. 546-547.

[30] *Ibid*, pp. 549-550.

[31] Mill declares: a "moral or human interest" in nature, art, poetry, history and "the ways of mankind past and present, and their prospects in the future" to be chief among the sources of happiness. *Utilitarianism*, CW X, pp. 215-216

[32] "it is a personal injustice to withhold from anyone, unless for the prevention of greater evils, the ordinary privilege of having his voice reckoned in the disposal of affairs in which he has the same interest as other people....There ought to be no pariahs in a full-grown and civilized nation; no persons disqualified, except through their own default." *Representative Government*, CW XIX, pp.469-470.

Company, Mill produced a large body of work on the problems of governing a very different culture. His writings in defense of the Company and his references to India in his writings and letters all emphasize the importance of knowledge and consideration of Indian tradition and culture.[33] Throughout his career, Mill resisted attempts to coerce the Hindus and Muslims of the sub-continent into accepting English ways of education and religion. Lynn Zastoupil has described how Mill's resistance was initially justified by an appeal to Coleridge and the Orientalists of the East India Company; later, in *On Liberty*, he resists the forced anglicisation of religious minorities on the ground of liberty alone.[34]

Mill's defense of the East India Company, under threat from absorption into the British government, was phrased in both anthropological and institutional terms and presented the company as the best protection for the native inhabitants. East India Company officials, Mill argued, were more likely to promote just treatment of the Indian peoples and respect their customs than a government more sensitive to the opinions of the English public than the Indian one. The complexities of Indian culture and its otherness require a professionalized bureaucracy:

> India is a peculiar country; the state of society and civilization, the character and habits of the people, and the private and public rights established among them, are totally different from those which are known and recognized in this country; in fact the study of India must be as much a profession in itself as law or medecine.[35]

Mill claims that the problem is not simply a lack of information, but results from real cultural difference:

> It is always under great difficulties, and very imperfectly, that a country can be governed by foreigners;...Foreigners do not feel with the people. They cannot judge, by the light in which a thing appears to their own minds, or the manner in which it affects their feelings, how it will affect the feelings or appear to the minds of the subject population. What a native of the country, of average practical ability, knows as it were by instinct, they have to learn slowly, and after all imperfectly, by study and experience.[36]

Finally, the situation is irreducibly caught up in the power relations of governance. The task of learning about Indian cultures is complicated by the power relations between a ruling colonial government and its subjects. The suspicion of the ruled makes getting a true account of the culture difficult: the rulers must trust their native informants, but they are most likely to be sought out by those seeking some gain, so that they tend to rely on the servilely submissive. For similar reasons, the

---

[33] Lynn Zastoupil, the only scholar to make an exhaustive investigation of the India House collection of Mill's dispatches, has drawn on those dispatches to show that Mill's career with the company is marked by an increased insistence on sensitivity to native customs and native opinion, in contrast with his father's hostility and indifference to those aspects of Indian life. See Lynn Zastoupil, *J.S. Mill and India.* (Stanford: Stanford University Press, 1994).

[34] Zastoupil, *J.S. Mill*, pp. 42-46. For Mill's later views, see *On Liberty*, CW XVIII, pp. 240-241, note, in which the connection between toleration and liberty is emphasized: "I desire to call attention to the fact, that a man who has been deemed fit to fill a high office in the government of this country, under a liberal Ministry, maintains the doctrine that all who do not believe in the divinity of Christ are beyond the pale of toleration. Who, after this imbecile display, can indulge the illusion that religious persecution has passed away, never to return?"

[35] 'The East India Company's Charter', CW XXX, 31-74 at p. 49.

[36] *Representative Government*, CW XIX, p. 568-569.

hard-won anthropological expertise of the Company is the best guarantee ordinary Indians have against oppression, since only powerful individuals and classes will have the opportunity to influence English public opinion.[37]

The greatest danger to the rulers of a colony is 'the feelings inspired by absolute power'.[38] This tendency to 'despise' Indians cannot, in fact, be kept from less experienced company officials and is the dominant attitude of the 'rapacious' English colonists and the missionaries who would 'force English ideas down the throats of the natives'.[39] As a check on this tendency of the English classes to oppress the Indian, Mill again appeals to the Company officials' superior knowledge: the anthropological expertise of the Company's government means that its decisions are informed by the public opinion of Indians. If the East India Company was replaced, as planned, by a Cabinet Minister of the English government, the government's decisions would be informed by English public opinion, through England's parties and press, and the decisions would reflect both public's ignorance and their ignorant sympathy with those English colonists and missionaries.[40]

Whether in India or in England, the solution to conflicts between different cultures and groups, where there are differences in power, is the institutional constraints Mill describes in *On Liberty*. The proper response to conflict is to set up institutions that promote critical reflection on policies through the preservation of diverse views. In the case of India, this takes the form of the complex process of policy review embodied in the structure of the East India Company.[41] In England, also characterized by diverse views and class conflict, it takes the form of the institutions advocated in the *Representative Government*. After a long discussion of the need for an expert Commission of Legislation to adjust means to ends, Mill balances it with his emphasis on the opposing need to preserve discussion and debate through the participation of the widest variety of citizens possible, so that workers and religious minorities may argue their own case. Mill sums up:

> The representative system ought to be so constituted as to maintain this state of things: it ought not to allow any of the various sectional interests to be so powerful as to be capable of prevailing against truth and justice and the other sectional interests combined. There ought always to be such a balance preserved among personal interests as may render any one of them dependent for its successes on carrying with it at least a large proportion of those who act on higher motives and more comprehensive and distant views.[42]

---

[37] "For in the subject community also there are oppressors and oppressed; powerful individuals or classes, and slaves prostrate before them; and it is the former, not the latter, who have the means of access to the English public.", *Representative Government*, CW XIX, p. 572.

[38] *Ibid*, CW XIX, p. 571.

[39] *Representative Government*, CW XIX, pp. 570-571. 'Minute on the Black Act', CW XXX, 11-16 at pp. 14-15.

[40] *Representative Government*, CW XIX, p. 570.

[41] In England, the experts of the Examiner's Office, of which Mill eventually became the head, guided the decisions of the Court of Directors, who in turn proposed policies to the Board of Control, which had a veto over policies it considered unwise. Policies produced through this complex process of revision eventually were eventually sent, as despatches, to the government in India, both as comments on the Indian government's previous actions and as guides to its future action.

[42] *Representative Government*, CW XIX, p. 447.

Representative government is essentially concerned both with resolving conflicts and the production of truth. Resolving conflicts on the basis of 'comprehensive and distant views' is the way to overcome class domination and thus promote just government.

I have argued that Mill's account of the nature of government needs to be seen as a response to the problems of diversity and the dangers of governmental and class intolerance. Clearly, profound worries remain about Mill's attitudes towards India and his role in governing the subject peoples there as part of a corporation that had no institutional responsibility to its subjects. Further worries are raised both by his 'Orientalist' sources and his confident ranking of groups and cultures in terms of differences in civilization. Despite these faults in Mill's practice, which might be allayed by an improved anthropology, Mill's claims about the centrality of anthropological and sociological knowledge to government, about the maintenance of diversity through institutional structures and about the need to continuously guard against class domination retain their relevance to contemporary debates about diversity. Nevertheless, for contemporary liberals, Mill's account of how to arbitrate cultural and religious conflict may shock, because it seems to eschew 'liberal neutrality' to an unacceptable extent. Although non-neutral conservative, socialist, humanist and communitarian thinkers are not hard to find,[43] most of the efforts of professedly liberal thinkers after Rawls' carefully neutral *A Theory of Justice* and *Political Liberalism* have been devoted to devising *more* neutral versions of liberal theory. In what follows, I suggest some reasons why we might prefer Mill's account to Rawls', recognizing, however, that space makes it impossible to do justice to so large a subject or so sophisticated a theory.

If my account of Mill's view is correct, he provides a strong case for both toleration of minority communities and for a liberal state's refusal to tolerate intolerant groups within it, insofar as they are intolerant. Crucial to maintaining both these positions at once is the development of a particular culture and the public opinion that goes with it: a relatively more harmonious culture of diversity and mutual respect I have described above. In this culture, knowledge of diversity is a value; it is a culture which is 'open' to other opinions and ways of life. The necessary correlative of this culture is a political arrangement in which the central public institutions are not under the control of any particular class or group. That said, political decisions still have to be made, including decisions about cultural and educational matters and, in particular, about the resolution of cultural conflicts. That such conflicts will arise needs no argument. What needs to be argued for is a particular understanding of their resolution, which helps justify Mill's particular notion of a liberal political culture and its relationship to the political institutions of a liberal and democratic society.

---

[43] The best example of which, especially the last three appellations, is C. Taylor, "The Politics of Recognition", in A. Gutmann, ed., *Multiculturalism*, (Princeton: Princeton University Press, 1994) 25-74. Gutmann herself is an exception to the above claims about 'liberal neutrality'. See, e.g., A. Gutmann, "Why Go to School?" in A. Sen and B. Williams, eds. *Utilitarianism and Beyond.* (Cambridge: Cambridge University Press, 1982), 261-278, as is J. Raz, *The Morality of Freedom*, (Oxford: Clarendon Press, 1986) and 'Multiculturalism: A Liberal Perspective', *Dissent*, Winter, (1994), 67-79.

A powerful and influential deontological understanding of this relationship already exists, of course, in the form of John Rawls' recent work. There he argues for a 'political liberalism', which restricts its goals to spelling out the commitments of our shared 'democratic public political culture' rather than proposing a 'comprehensive doctrine' which is intended to cover every aspect of life for every member of society. The stability of this political liberalism, in the face of diversity, is maintained through an 'overlapping consensus': a set of principles, values and judgments that all citizens who make up a 'reasonable pluralism' would endorse from the standpoint of their comprehensive religious, philosophical or moral positions.[44] Indeed, the citizens of this pluralism *will* endorse such an overlapping consensus, since they will have acquired the appropriate 'sense of justice' in the course of growing up under just institutions.[45] They will, then, agree on the importance of certain 'very great political values' and on a conception of all citizens as free, equal and rational[46] and will as a result be committed to "equal political and civil liberty; fair equality of opportunity, the values of economic reciprocity;' and 'the social bases of mutual respect between citizens".[47]   This description of the political culture of the society Rawls envisions makes it clear that Rawls is concerned with 'ideal theory' and is describing an 'ideal overlapping consensus'.[48]

I will list very briefly the differences between my interpretation of Mill's response to diversity in terms of the priority of knowledge and Rawls' emphasis on the priority of consensus and suggest ways in which Mill's may be a more satisfactory view. First, Mill's theory, like Rawls', relies on the presence of democratic and representative institutions and equal access to them.[49] Unlike Rawls' 'ideal theory', however, Mill's account does not require the development of a reasonable pluralism as a ground for the convergence on democratic institutions. Rather, it provides policy makers with an articulated justification of their pursuit both of the development of democratic institutions and of the preservation of diversity, a justification stated in terms of their understanding of the concrete trends of modern society, the imperfect institutions therein and the persistent possibility that that society will contain unreasonable or imperfectly reasonable groups. Policy makers' knowledge-based justification of democratic institutions allows them to legitimately impose on these recalcitrant groups whatever minimal restraints are necessary for a functioning diverse society.

Second, Mill's account recognizes the homogenizing and controlling effects of power which are found in any set of institutions, even liberal ones. Where Rawls' 'overlapping consensus' expresses his hope for a society where these power effects are absent, Mill's concern with the danger power poses to diversity makes him erect permanent safeguards against the worst of these effects. On the other hand, Mill's liberalism does not aspire to a neutrality which—in the face of the real, unreasonable pluralism that characterizes modern societies—is unlikely to be realized in any

---

[44] Rawls, *Political Liberalism*, p. 141.

[45] *Ibid*, pp. 141-143.

[46] *Ibid*, p. 169 and p. 143, respectively.

[47] *Ibid*, p. 139.

[48] *Ibid*, p. xxi.

[49] In, of course, Mill's sense of 'equal access', which famously does not mean, at least not necessarily, equal participation in terms of voting.

actual set of democratic institutions. Liberals like Will Kymlicka and Amy Gutman have noted excellent examples of existing Canadian and American religious or national groups who do not support the notion of autonomy found in Rawls' 'overlapping consensus': for example, Tennessee fundamentalists or Wisconsin Amish who want to limit their children's access to information about other ways of living, so that they will not be tempted to question the religious views of their parents.[50] If even a policy that encourages the greatest possible diversity compatible with democracy involves assimilation of some aspects of or interventions in the lives of intolerant and illiberal groups, it may be counted among the virtues of Mill's liberalism that it honestly recognizes the limits of liberal neutrality.[51] Mill did, in fact, license paternalist interventions into the lives of anti-educational groups. Because of the centrality of knowledge to Mill's theory, and in particular knowledge of other ways of life, Mill claims that requiring parents to educate their children, even if they are opposed to such education or have no desire for it, does not violate the principles of liberty and laissez-faire.[52]   Third, Rawls' basing reasonable pluralism on citizens' growing up under just institutions and, as a result, developing the appropriate 'sense of justice' depends on the same insight into the way institutions mould individuals that characterizes Mill's fundamental methodological concerns in the *Logic* and the *Liberty*. Mill's theory, however, adds an extra concern about the dangers inherent in that socialization, a worry that Rawls seems unwilling to entertain.

Fourth, Mill's account provides a strong justification for interventions into the practices of intolerant groups. Institutional power and the pernicious effects of custom are at work in the smaller 'worlds' as in the wider—groups who want to make their custom a law unto individuals, preventing them from leaving the group or from criticizing any aspect of the group's activities, may be made to respect the rights of their members in the interests of diversity of views and critical reflection within the group. Finally, where Rawls' political liberalism is a concept abstracted from one aspect of social life, like 'perfect competition' in economics,[53] Mill's account of custom is central to what he deems the most concrete social science possible. Mill generates what amounts to a formal principle out of the conditions of positivist and materialist social science. Since diversity is essential to the progress of that social science, any group which does not oppress its members--in a relatively narrow interpretation of 'oppression'--has a *prima facie* claim to the freedom to explore and maintain its own modes of action, regardless of what those modes of action are or how they are viewed by non-adherents.

Theorists of certain sympathies may object that I am merely substituting Millian domination for Rawlsian hegemony. Establishing this requires that the particular mechanisms Mill recommends to remedy the dangers posed by any dominant class-- in the *Representative Government*, the *Liberty*, *Chapters on Socialism* and

---

[50] The example of Tennessee fundamentalists is from A. Gutman, "Undemocratic Education", in Nancy L.. Rosenblum, ed.,*Liberalism and the Moral Life*, (Cambridge, MA: Harvard University Press, 1989), 71-88 at pp. 81-82. The Amish are discussed in W. Kymlicka, *Multicultural*, p. 161.
[51] John Gray notes this in *Enlightenment's Wake*, (London: Routledge, 1995), p. 142.
[52] See *On Liberty*, CW XVIII, pp. 301-302, *Principles*, CW III, p. 947.
[53] Rawls, *Political Liberalism*, p. 154, note 20.

elsewhere--are unable to overcome the more general dangers posed by an institutionalization of expert opinion and by state institutions generally. This debate can only be arbitrated, and only in part, by an examination of the fate of minorities in countries which have adopted these reforms—e.g. proportional representation—but such an examination also requires an estimation of those countries' commitment to diversity as the lens through which social life must be viewed. Only if states adopt Mill's methodological recommendations will his account receive a fair test. It is, perhaps, enough if we recognize that Mill's claim that the 'professional' study of the diverse groups that make up society is essential to coming up with any solutions to the resulting problems has already been accepted wherever policies on diversity exist. Whether the issue is Afro-centric school curricula in the United States or refugee policy in Ireland, decisions are being made about what and who are in and who and what are out and these decisions require understandings of who and what these policies are for and about. That understanding these internal minorities' points of view is essential to a particular society's self-understanding and vice versa is a strong argument in favour of Mill's account of the problem, and warrants consideration of his solution.

PART III

TOLERATION AND DEMOCRACY

CHAPTER 9

IS DEMOCRATIC TOLERATION
A RUBBER DUCK?

Glen Newey

INTRODUCTION

A tacit Whiggism reigns in political philosophy which holds that history is a long birth-pang of liberal values, that among these values are democracy and toleration, and that they now march in happy consort together. My less sanguine argument is that democracy and toleration are in endemic conflict with each other. This casts doubt on whether toleration can be a coherent political value.[1]

The pressure on toleration, I will argue, follows from some empirical, but nonetheless very well-corroborated, observations about the political culture of democracy, together with some more analytical reflections on the structure of toleration. In the first part of the discussion I aim simply to set the scene within which the politics of toleration are transacted—or, more precisely, the circumstances in which the question of toleration becomes politically urgent. My treatment will be fairly schematic. It does, however, seem to me to provide a recognisable representation of many contemporary interest-group and single-issue conflicts.

THE CONDITIONS OF TOLERATION

I shall assume without argument that questions of toleration conform to a certain three-part structure.[2] This provides three kinds of reason which may be engaged when a decision has to be made (whether in personal life or in the public sphere) as to whether something is to be tolerated. I shall refer generically to this thing as a

---

[1] To this extent the situation may be more dire than that envisioned by those who think that toleration cannot be instituted politically as a moral value (e.g. because of moral disagreement) but that it can be given a purely political grounding, in roughly the sense of 'political' adopted by Rawls in *Political Liberalism* (New York: Columbia University Press 1993). For more on this conception of toleration, see Elisabetta Galeotti's contribution in this volume.

[2] For further discussion of this structure, see my *Virtue, Reason, and Toleration: the place of toleration in ethical and political philosophy* (Edinburgh: Edinburgh University Press 1999), ch. 1.

'practice', which of course may include the expression of an opinion, or the writing of a book. The decision whether to tolerate the practice is structured by the following kinds of reason:

(a)   a reason for disapproving of the practice
(b)   a reason for failing to intervene in order to prevent or censure the practice despite (a) (though it should be noted that 'non-intervention' is a term of convenience, since toleration will on most views sometimes require active intervention)
(c)   a reason for not failing to prevent or censure certain practices, which reason may or may not be identical with (a).

Some analyses of toleration, though not all, restrict the categories of reason involved, at least in (b) and (c), to moral reasons. Contrary to some accounts, toleration does not require pluralism of reasons or of values, since there is nothing in the three-part structure which requires that the reasons mentioned in (a) to (c) must be of different kinds, or based on different values. The distinction between the reasons may be between different applications of the value of autonomy, for example, or of liberty.

It follows from this that the tolerator is necessarily situated in a force-field of opposing reasons: for tolerating the practice, in spite of the reasons covered by (a) and (c). I take it (as some accounts of agency do not, such as W.D.Ross's)[3] that the fact that a reason to tolerate is acted on does not, by itself, annul the force of the other kinds of reason. It simply has greater force. It is an important fact about the phenomenology of toleration that this is so, and that the main taste left in the tolerator's mouth may be not be the milk of concord, but blood and ashes.

This suggests that if toleration is a virtue at all, it should be understood as an *executive* virtue.[4] In other words, unlike some (though not all) other virtues, toleration requires that thought about the agent's own agency be incorporated directly into deliberation, and that the deliberation reflect certain structural features of that agency, including other ethical dispositions of the agent. In contrast with, say, courage, the tolerant agent necessarily has thoughts about his or her own dispositions (a similar example of a classical virtue would be that of *temperance*). The courageous agent may simply act in the face of danger without any dispositional thoughts at all, whereas the tolerator has to feel the competing pull of reasons for intervention and reasons for restraint. My tolerance of vegetarianism, for instance – for example, if I do not merely refrain from force-feeding vegetarians with meat, but also forgo the pleasures of veal or beef myself when I invite them to my home for dinner – requires that I have reflected on my own dispositions, and have decided to respond to them in a certain way (for example, by checking my own carnivorous

---

[3] See Ross, *The Right and the Good* (Oxford: Oxford University Press 1930). See also J.Dancy, *Moral Reasons* (Oxford: Blackwell 1993), ch. 1.
[4] For further discussion of the structure of toleration as a virtue, see Barry Barnes' contribution to this volume.

impulses out of respect for my guests). I would have responded in a different way if, for example, I simply decided to cook what *I* liked.

The thought which characterises the virtue of toleration concerns the agent's own powers. Even if toleration does conform to the broad three-part structure, the analysis is over-simplified. One simplification lies in the *type* of reason which is eligible to answer (b), i.e. the reason to tolerate. Not just any reason will do. It is not sufficient for my tolerating a practice, for example, if my reason for not intervening is that someone has bribed me to do so, or that someone else will beat me into insensibility if I do intervene. It seems that what has to be involved must be in some respect a matter of principle (the source of the view mentioned earlier that only *moral* reasons can answer (b)). Also obviously, intervening must be something it lies within the tolerator's *power* to do – or at least must be believed to be so. I do not tolerate someone else's views if I would dearly love to gag them but lack the means to do so, as with internet regulation.

As this example itself suggests, however, expanding this last remark into a plausible constraint on when toleration is practised proves elusive. The problem lies in specifying the *kind* of power which the agent needs to wield in order for the (b)-type reasons to be relevant. Here we are looking at the different forms of incapacity to which agents can fall prey. Most of the formulations which come to mind are unhelpful when delineating the difference between eligible and ineligible forms of incapacity: that, for example, the incapacity must not lie in purely external circumstances, rather than in the agent. One reason why this way of putting matters is less than helpful is that personal incapacities themselves may be inadequate to ground a (b)-type reason. Cowardice or squeamishness provide obvious examples.

On the other hand, certain ethical commitments may themselves be the grounds for an agent's inability to bring about a certain outcome.[5] In other words, powerlessness may result from the agent's normative commitments, which could themselves be seen as expressions of the agent's deliberative (e.g. moral) powers. This is a form of incapacity which need not refute an agent's claim to tolerate a practice. Even if the good of toleration is supererogatory,[6] this does not entail that an agent has the capacity not to (seek to) produce it. To suppose otherwise is to confuse moral obligation with practical necessity.

It is hard to avoid the conclusion that in deciding whether an action is tolerant, we are really determining the eligibility of reasons to figure in a certain account of a person's conduct. And that determination depends, as often when reasons are assessed, on the relations between action, character, and deliberation. To suppose otherwise is liable to engender paradox: that someone might become more tolerant, for instance, simply by expanding the range of practices of which he or she

---

[5] It is over-simplistic to think that this is not really an incapacity, in contrast with the obstacles which are imposed by external objects or physical impossibility – though there are significant differences between them as forms of incapacity. See B.Williams, "Moral Incapacity", repr. in Williams, *Making Sense of Humanity* (Cambridge: Cambridge University Press 1995), 46-55.

[6] As I argue in my "Against Thin-Property Reductivism: Toleration As Supererogatory", *Journal of Value Inquiry* 31 (1997), 231-249.

disapproves, with other behaviour held constant – what elsewhere I have called the *censorious tolerator problem.*[7]

Acts of toleration have to satisfy plausible conditions for attributing responsibility to agents. This tends to be obscured by too mechanical an application of the 'acts and omissions' doctrine, which is often interpreted to mean that since the non-intervention characteristic of toleration is an 'omission', responsibility for it must either be diluted in comparison with an 'act', or annulled entirely. What is needed, if the reason supporting non-intervention is to count as a reason for *toleration*, is that the powers of the agent as an agent are engaged. And it is the engagement of these powers which makes the attribution of responsibility intelligible.

THE POLITICAL CIRCUMSTANCES OF TOLERATION

Any political theory which aims to engage realistically with the practical problems of toleration needs to envisage the circumstances in which it becomes politically urgent. I consider these next. The treatment will of necessity again be schematic. My main concern here is to identify a certain shape for issues of political toleration, relating it to the three-part structure already set out. I will mention one or two real examples in passing, but make no further attempt to show how well the following sketch fits the political circumstances of toleration in general.

Suppose that there is some practice, and that it is carried on or supported by one group, while being opposed by another. Of course, the latter may choose to suffer in silence, or adopt low-level methods of expressing its disapproval, to which the first group takes no exception. This happens a lot of the time. In this case, it seems, there is no political question to address: the two groups have arrived at a peaceful, if not wholly satisfactory, *modus vivendi.* But now suppose that matters go further than this, and the members of the second group begin to call for action against the first, unless the latter desists from the practice. These may initially be demands for political action, but may turn to incitement or direct violent action. I take it that by the time this point has been reached, questions of toleration have become politically relevant.

We can note first that in these circumstances – assuming that it develops into conflict – each side proposes to do something of which the other disapproves.[8] Of course, the authorities can let matters lie like this, as long as public order is not under threat, though there is no obvious reason why this course of action is more tolerant than any other. But in any case, this is not really the point. The issue has already become a political one by this stage, and those in power have to respond to first-order expressions of disapproval. In the circumstances of toleration, democratic

---

[7] For the original formulation of this problem, see J.Horton, "Three (Apparent) Paradoxes of Toleration", *Synthesis Philosophica* 9 (1994), 7-20, at p. 16f. For further discussion, see also Horton, "Toleration As A Virtue", in D.Heyd (ed.) *Toleration: An Elusive Virtue* (Princeton, N.J.: Princeton University Press 1996), p. 34f, and my *Virtue, Reason and Toleration*, pp. 107-111.
[8] Here I adapt remarks which first appeared in *Virtue, Reason and Toleration*, p. 161.

politicians have to respond to those who argue, not that the practice should be permitted *despite* their own disapproval, but that the practice should be suppressed *because* they disapprove of it.

Second, there is little inclination on either side to tolerate the other's behaviour in spite of this disapproval: if there were, the members of the first group might have been prepared to discontinue or modify the practice to meet the concerns of the second, while members of the latter might have thought that the practice should be permitted despite their own feelings of disapproval. Very often in conflicts of this nature there is a reactive dynamic, whereby one party's disapproval of another's activities prompts reciprocal disapproval by the second party of this very disapproval. This is not very conducive to a peaceful resolution of the conflict, but it is liable to arise in situations where one party sees toleration as the path of submission and as a result asserts what it takes to be its entitlements – a move which unsurprisingly arouses a counter-assertion by the other party of *its* entitlements. To this extent the situation favours confrontation.

Third, it is an important, if obvious, empirical fact about political conflicts in democratic polities that they simplify the structure of single-person deliberative conflicts in certain respects.[9] We can bring out this point by considering the *claims* made by the groups involved on the politicians who are accountable to them. In conflicts like the one described, it is not tolerant dispositions which are engaged. Neither party calls for a certain outcome (toleration) *despite* its disapproval of the other group; rather, each group characteristically expresses itself by demanding that what it disapproves of should be suppressed.

In so far as the confrontation is liable to come down to logically incompatible demands – that the practice be prohibited, and that it be permitted – each course of action is prone to excite charges of intolerance. In either case, the course of action favoured will be one which the other side has branded as intolerant. The political authorities are caught in the middle of the dispute, and lie open to the charge of tolerating what is really intolerable whichever side they favour. The problem of 'tolerating the intolerant' is often treated as an anomalous or marginal case in theories of toleration, such as that of *A Theory of Justice*.[10] But the political circumstances of toleration suggest, by contrat, that the question of whether to 'tolerate the intolerant' is not a marginal one, but arises at the very point when toleration becomes a political issue.

The structure of conflict here is symmetrical. The courses of action determined upon by the two groups are incompatible. Moreover, each group strongly objects to the other's (actual or projected) action, and is apt to brand the other side as intolerant, while calling for toleration for its own favoured course of action. We can

---

[9] This is, incidentally, a reason for doubting the reducibility of public to private deliberation, or *vice versa*, as argued recently in S.Hampshire, *Justice Is Conflict* (Princeton, N.J.: Princeton University Press 2000), p. 11ff.

[10] See J.Rawls, *A Theory of Justice*, rev. edn. (Oxford: Oxford University Press 1999), §35: "Toleration of the Intolerant", pp. 190-194. It is a marginal case for Rawls both because the intolerant are thought to lack dispositions characteristic of most citizens in the well-ordered society, and because they are thought to justify derogations from the equal liberty principle (p. 193).

note here in passing the need for part (c) of the three-part structure, since in distinguishing its own actions from those of the opposing side, each group has to be able to contrast disapproval (which can be overridden) from judgements that certain practices are intolerable. And each side, *ex hypothesi*, lacks the means to enforce its views.

The symmetrical structure limits the practical options available to those in power. I mean this not only in the sense that there are certain actions which may not be open to them (or, what comes to the same, may not be possible without unacceptable cost); it limits the descriptions, and hence justifications, available to the political decision-makers. The three-part structure holds that there are legitimate occasions for withholding toleration, and few, apart perhaps from some anarchists, are likely to deny that this is so. If there are such occasions, then the only question is when it is legitimate to act intolerantly – when, in other words, to act against practices which really are intolerable. The fashionable political rhetoric of 'zero tolerance' provides a debased expression of this way of thinking, designed to subvert the public culture of toleration by appropriating its vocabulary of commendation.[11]

Toleration is an executive virtue, and can be displayed by persons with very different first-order values. This is also true of some non-executive virtues, such as courage: a person does not act the less courageously if it is in a cause which I deplore. But the three-part structure and executive character of toleration also leaves scope for conflicting judgements about whether another person is acting tolerantly, even relative to that person's first-order values. For an observer could accept that the person had these values, while denying that they had been *applied* correctly to a particular case. This includes the important possibility that the person may have been too tolerant, rather than too harsh, towards a practice.

Thus the scope for conflict arises even if we confine our attention to the values held by a single person. This scope naturally increases when we consider the fact of 'reasonable pluralism' – the fact that modern societies are culturally diverse, and partly as a result, contain an indefinite number of ethical outlooks or 'forms of life', none of which may be demonstrably more or less reasonable than the others. As I argue elsewhere,[12] 'reasonable pluralism' is not a very happy label for this phenomenon, but it remains plausible to say that reason may be unable to adjudicate between the different outlooks when they conflict. The structure of toleration still makes it *possible* to see inhabitants of other forms of life as acting tolerantly, but 'reasonable pluralism' is prone to make clashes of the kind exemplified by the symmetrical structure all the more implacable when they arise.

---

[11] In this regard the talk of 'zero tolerance' provides a case in point of the rhetorical transformations described by Quentin Skinner in his writings. See e.g. "The Principles and Practice of Opposition: The Case of Bolingbroke versus Walpole", in N.McKendrick (ed.), *Historical Perspectives* (London 1974), 93-128.

[12] "Rawls, Reasonable Pluralism and Public Justification", forthcoming. The main line of argument is that, to the extent that pluralism of outlooks is reasonable, it undermines itself, since then *ex hypothesi* the reasonableness of outlooks conflicting with one's own follows. For an initial statement of this position, see my "Floating on the LILO: John Rawls and the content of justice", a review of J.Rawls, *Collected Papers, Times Literary Supplement*, 10 September 1999.

The executive structure of toleration, combined with the facts reported by the 'reasonable pluralism' doctrine, makes questions of political toleration peculiarly intractable. There is no obvious reason why in this environment an 'overlapping consensus' can be constructed out of the contending 'comprehensive doctrines'.[13] The executive structure allows each side to depict itself as operating within an intelligible conception of toleration, with different substantive values as raw materials. For this reason, the concept of toleration is in some ways peculiarly *un*suited to resolve the political conflict. But, in any case, irrespective of the question of objective justification, there is still a political issue to address once the conflict between the groups is out in the open. In fact, in a sense, there is *only* a political issue to address if this is so. I shall return to this at the end.

At this point it may be said that the symmetry identified in the political circumstances of toleration has been exaggerated.[14] Surely, it may be said, there may be alleged circumstances of toleration in which there is asymmetry. For example, if someone objects to my reading a book, the person may be charged with acting intolerantly. But it sounds very implausible to say that if I persist with my reading, I balance up the symmetrical structure by also acting intolerantly: I'm just sitting there, reading. So surely in cases like this one, at least, the symmetrical structure fails to apply.

One reply would simply be to deny that these are in fact circumstances of toleration. But this would be bland and stipulative. A better response is to try to understand why the objection seems plausible. What action could be less objectionable, particularly to an academic observer, than somebody's reading a book? But the point at which reflective individuals retreat to the fastness of first-order normative judgments is precisely the point where toleration becomes practically urgent. It should be remembered that the analysis does not pretend to be a normative one. We can all fill in values in the three part schema – for example, Millian liberal values which hold that the sole basis for legitimate interference itself lies in interference. But emphatic pointing a particular value will not address the political problems which arise when that value is confronted with something quite alien. That values can be alien to each other in this way is, after all, the point from which toleration historically took its rise.

So we have to attend to the practical circumstances in which questions of toleration become politically urgent. Part of what is owed – epistemically – in the practical circumstances of toleration, on which hypothetical examples are liable to default, is an account of *why* the anti-reader is behaving in this way. Certainly it's hardly difficult to imagine situations where the 'mere' act of reading might be objectionable ('What's the matter with you? I'm just sitting quietly in this synagogue, reading *Mein Kampf*'). It's easy enough to elaborate a situation in which we can make no sense of the objector, and then confidently pronounce that there is

---

[13] As has already been often observed in commentary on Rawls's *Political Liberalism*. See e.g. U.Wolf, "Übergreifender Konsens und öffentliche Vernunft", in W.Hinsch (ed.), *Zur Idee des politischen Liberalismus* (Frankfurt a.M.: Suhrkamp 1997), esp. pp. 63-66.

[14] I owe the following objection to John Horton, who cited the book-reading example given (written communication).

nothing here to object to. By contrast, in filling out the real details of practical conflict, one may come to an appreciation of why the objector is acting like this even if the values concerned are quite alien ones. Once we move beyond our own tribal norms, in all their glutinous thickness, all we have is the fact of confrontation, and a description of why, given the value-orientations of the protagonists, it has arisen.

This does not entail relativism: nothing that has been said is inconsistent with the view that some specific value or set of values are the right or true ones. All that has been said is that there is a hypothetical vantage-point from which we can regard the protagonists' dispositions as symmetrical. Perhaps, having filled out all the circumstantial information, we still feel that the person who wants to interfere with my reading is unjustified. But this does not necessarily mean that my response is therefore not intolerant. We have to distinguish between the case where someone is not being intolerant and where their intolerance is justified: maybe this is just a case of justified intolerance, as is fully consistent with the three-part schema identified earlier. I am certainly likely to disapprove of this person's attempts to interfere with my reading, and think of my attitude as justified. Not to be intolerant towards one's own intolerant dispositions is just part of what it *is* to to have the value-orientation constitutive of a theory of toleration.

If it is a fantasy to think that there is a human perspective on agency which is devoid of normative commitments, then for each person there will be cases warranting 'zero tolerance'. But to acknowledge this does not by itself transcend politics: rather it sounds out one of its conditions. This is what makes politics, in a certain sense, transcendental: like any ideology, particular systems of value aim at an *umfassende Weltauffassung*, while the alienness of values makes the scope for clashes between perspectives inexhaustible. To point beyond the pale is not to point beyond politics, but to its central arena.

DEMOCRACY AND TOLERATION

When the ideal of toleration was formulated by thinkers such as Locke, Bayle, Walwyn, Milton and Spinoza during the early modern period, the predominant form of government in Europe was personal and prerogative rule – compare Louis XIV's 'l'état, c'est moi'. The sovereign stood as individual person to the collectivity of the citizenry or subjects, a point made explicit in *Leviathan*'s account of authorisation. In these circumstances, toleration could be exercised on a basis strictly analogous too – in fact, as a special case of – the interpersonal situations already considered. A century later, Kant could still write in 'What is Enlightenment?', that "[a] prince who does not regard it as beneath him ... in religious matters, not to prescribe anything to his people, but to allow them complete freedom, a prince who thus even declines to accept the presumptuous title of *tolerant*, is himself enlightened".[15]

---

[15] Kant, "An Answer to the Question: 'What is Enlightenment?'", in H.Reiss (ed.), *Kant: Political Writings* rev. edn. (Cambridge: Cambridge University Press 1991), p. 58.

But Kant's remarks here look forwards as well as back. His underlying point (one also emphasised later by Tom Paine in *The Rights of Man*)[16] is that to tolerate is to exercise power, in circumstances where power should be absent. The following argument will suggest that the exercise of power in democratic polities is liable to make toleration impossible precisely because the personal-prerogative use of power, which provided Kant and Paine with their tacit working model of political action, can no longer be justified within democracies.

I take it that popular sovereignty is at the core of democratic theory, and this is standardly taken to require that the populace exercises standing control over the political process. This control embodies the core democratic values of political equality and autonomy: each citizen has an equal say in political decision-making, and their participation in it is the only way in which the citizens can genuinely be subject to a law which they have given to themselves. Provided that a suitable procedure exists for putting the popular will into effect, the test of democratic legitimacy, as applied to a given measure, is whether it owes its existence to the popular will as effectuated by this procedure.[17]

The question now is how well this account of democratic legitimacy can accommodate toleration. Earlier, in explaining the reasons which figure in the three-part structure, I said that it was important that the *type* of reason for non-intervention be of the right kind. There I offered only brief remarks as to how reasons of the relevant type might be identified, but suggested that one restriction on eligibility was to be found in the local circumstances of agency. The question now is how far this restriction carries over from the personal to the public realm.

We have already seen that in the circumstances of toleration, advocates of a practice are pitted against their opponents in a way which becomes politically contentious precisely when toleration is no longer a possibility. Certainly, one response to this would be to argue that there is a certain range of practices which are tolerant, that others are not, and to redescribe these disputes accordingly. But this would risk misrepresentation, for more than one reason.

The first point to note is that an important difference marks the political circumstances of toleration in comparison with interpersonal cases. Whereas in the standard inter-personal situation the tolerator stands to the tolerated as first party to second, the authorities, in the political circumstances of toleration, are typically related to the conflicting groups as a third party. This is particularly clear in neutralist theory, where the state or political authority is thought of as a normative vacuum. Since toleration requires that the tolerator have reasons for disapproving of the practice, and must nonetheless have reasons for regarding non-intervention as

---

[16] Cf Paine, *Rights of Man*, ed. H. Collins (Harmondsworth: Penguin 1969), p. 107: "Toleration is not the *opposite* of Intolerance, but is the *counterfeit* of it. Both are despotisms. The one assumes to itself the right of withholding Liberty of Conscience, and the other of granting it. The one is the pope armed with fire and faggot, and the other is the pope selling or granting indulgences." As with Kant's remarks, this presupposes the discretionary and personal exercise of political power.

[17] I omit, among others, public-goods and other telic justifications of democracy.

good, the normative vacuum is filled, and neutrality disappears.[18] Nonetheless, some liberal neutralists, like Charles Larmore,[19] apparently believe that toleration is not merely consistent with, but *entailed* by neutrality.

Therefore, the reasons in question are likely to be of a different kind from the interpersonal case, when the political authority acts as a third party with respect to two vying groups in civil society. A fundamental difference is that the introduction of a third party brings with it the exercise of *power* over others. If those in political power (or those exercising the executive right of nature) act to stop the second party acting against the first, coercion has entered the picture. *Prima facie* this demands justification, since it is one thing to restrain myself from intervening against a practice I disapprove of, and another to restrain somebody else from doing so. For one thing, the value of autonomy, which justifies democracy, is engaged when I use my power to prevent another from acting as he or she would otherwise act. So the grounds for enforcing non-intervention on others may well have to be stronger than those for restraining myself.

But the introduction of coercion is not the only new development in the three-party case. This comes out if we compare the authorities' reasons for action with those of the original protagonists – those carrying on the practice, and those disapproving of it. Clearly the reasons on which the authorities act, if they act tolerantly, cannot merely duplicate those of the protagonists, since the political problem is created by their failure to tolerate one another: it makes little sense to say of either party that it tolerates itself. But, whatever they decide to do, the authorities act on reasons which map but poorly onto the three-part structure.

Suppose that they decide to enforce *acceptance* of the practice. Then it will be a matter of coercing the objectors so that they do not intervene against it. The reasons which support this policy concern the consequential benefits of using force in this case, and the actions of the objectors to the practice will not be tolerated. If, on the other hand, they enforce prohibition of the practice, they again use coercion. Again the animating reasons will concern the consequential benefits of force, and those carrying on the practice are not tolerated. So, whatever the authorities' reasons justify, they justify withholding toleration. This problem is inherent in the symmetrical structure, since each side has at its disposal the resources for accusing the other of intolerance. This is true *a fortiori* when political power is mobilised to enforce either acceptance or prohibition of the disputed practice.

Of course it could be argued that there is no good reason for liberals – let alone others – to accept neutrality. What is then in view is a 'perfectionist',[20] confessional, or 'romantic-expressivist'[21] state instead. Such a state freely makes normative judgements in formulating public policy and deliberating executive actions, some of which fit into the three-part structure. So the state may, for instance, decide to

---

[18] For more on the tension between neutrality and toleration, see the article by Saladin Meckled-Garcia in this volume. See also my "Metaphysics Postponed: liberalism, pluralism and neutrality", *Political Studies* 45 (1997), 296-311.

[19] See Larmore, *Patterns of Moral Complexity* (Cambridge: Cambridge University Press 1987), e.g. p. 51.

[20] Joseph Raz's term. See his *The Morality of Freedom* (Oxford: Clarendon Press 1986).

[21] Larmore's term in *Patterns of Moral Complexity*.

tolerate cannabis use by failing to enforce laws against possession of the drug, or by decriminalising possession (but not the act of supplying it); the state may do this despite its upholding the belief that it is better not to use cannabis. It may nonetheless strictly prohibit the dissemination and consumption of 'hard' drugs. In doing so, it acts in a way which is fully consonant with the structure of toleration.

There is nothing incoherent in this picture, assuming that the three-part structure itself is coherent. The state can indeed *adopt* certain kinds of reason for non-intervention on its own account, and this qualifies my main line of argument. In fact, a good deal of social policy seems to involve a structure of this sort: for example, aspects of the state's regulation of pornography, speeding and some other road traffic offences, prostitution, homosexuality, cigarette smoking, reliance on state pensions, certain kinds of state-funded prophylaxis, gambling, and the availability of certain drugs. In such cases the state may be thought of as a first party in relation to the second (such as gamblers, homosexuals, etc.) and this seems to offer a fair analogy with the interpersonal case.

However, it is important to notice that the fact that certain practices occupy a legislative *demi-monde* between outright prohibition and straightforward acceptance does not show that the practices themselves are in fact being tolerated. As in the interpersonal case, we have to examine the antecedents of action. It is also necessary to be clear about the *aspect* under which politicians act when legislating or imposing policy. I will take these points in turn.

Where the state (or its policy-making arm) disapproves of a practice, but decides in spite of this not to intervene to prevent it, some of its reasons for doing so will not constitute this decision as an act of toleration. In many cases, given the clash between different lobby- or interest-groups over a particular practice, the concerns which guide policy may be more pragmatic in character. The most obvious type of situation is one in which those in power hold views *qua* private citizens about the practice, but are guided in their political actions by other considerations. This has certainly been true in the United Kingdom of past members of Conservative governments, for example, with regard to certain aspects of penal and social policy, such as the availability of abortion on the National Health Service or the (effective) abolition of capital punishment. Where the conflict is fierce, for example, policy-makers may be less concerned about their appraisal of the practice's merits than the wider consequences of the courses of action open to them. Very familiarly, what then emerges is a compromise in which both lobbies get some, but not all, of what they want; this is often true *regardless* of whether those who make the decision have conscientious views of their own about the practice.

The reasons for formulating such a compromise, or indeed for coming down on one side or the other, are less significant than the way in which the decision is reached, and its relation to the ethical dispositions of the legislators. These reasons include political considerations, more or less broadly construed, such as electoral advantage, party strategy, or the need to appease influential lobbies (such as newspaper editors). But they also include a *bona fide* concern with public goods. Prominent among these is public order, but those in power may also be concerned to protect the constitution, to nurture diplomatic or foreign trading links, to promote social engineering, and so on.

The point is not that it is *impossible* that acts of toleration might be based on reasons of this kind. Reasons to tolerate need both to be of a certain sort, and to play the right role in deliberation. It is rather that the relation between the (in this case, corporate) agent and the policy is quite different here from the interpersonal case. As argued earlier, toleration is an executive virtue, and the tolerator's deliberation reflects certain features of his or her agency, including other ethical dispositions (such as dispostions to value) of the agent. Thus the deliberation which issues in an act of toleration involves critical reflection on the deliberator's own characteristics as an agent.

But in the case of political toleration, deliberation is about the actions of others, together with the valuations which accompany these actions. The very fact that the valuations mount politically pressing claims is what calls for a political decision in the first place, and the conflicts to which they give rise have to be negotiated politically, unless politics itself cedes to civil unrest. Essentially the conflicting valuations say on the one hand that the disputed practice should be permitted, and on the other that it should not. But these valuations in no sense duplicate the reasons covered above under (a) and (b) for disapproving of the practice while nonetheless not intervening to stop it. The conflict is between two opposed but equally single-minded bodies of opinion. They cannot be used to model the tension between the reasons which, when both motivate a single deliberator, may lead to toleration.

The reasons for tolerating are, after all, not those on which the defenders of the disputed practice characteristically mount their political claims, though they may find it rhetorically convenient to use this vocabulary. It is itself a significant fact about the political culture of toleration that there are also strong forces opposing use of the language of toleration, which result from the lobbying pressures already mentioned. The main reason for this is the fact that to be *tolerated*, as I have assumed, requires disapproval, whereas the characteristic demand made by pressure groups is for equality, if not more. Their claims are, for example, that this practice is demanded by the one true religion. And each side has available to it, given the circumstances of political toleration, the opportunity to brand the action demanded by the other as being intolerable. So the reasons which animate the protagonists in the conflict cannot simply be taken over, so to speak, by the political decision-makers. The reasons behind any particular attempt at a political resolution will necessarily differ from those which made the question politically pressing to start with.

We saw before that in cases of interpersonal toleration, an agent's lack of power to determine outcomes could annul his or her claim to tolerate a practice. This was contrasted with the powerlessness which might result from the agent's normative commitments, which could themselves be seen as expressions of the agent's deliberative powers. It might be, for example, that a certain action was something which a particular agent could not do, in the sense that the action was not deliberable for this agent, or if deliberable, the agent could not bring him- or herself to do it.

Toleration may result when the agent experiences an inability of this kind to intervene against a practice.

But if we compare the circumstances of political toleration, it is unclear what analogue there is in these circumstances for the deliberative powers. One problem is that there is no obvious counterpart for the ethical dispositions on which reflection has to work. A related problem is that the deliberative incapacities also lack any precise analogue in the political case. But if we cannot even define these incapacities, the interplay, characteristic of the tolerator's agency, between character, action and deliberation, seems inapplicable in the political case.[22]

Some versions of democratic theory (which are sometimes *ex post facto* justifications of political practice) allow that legislators or policy-makers are able to act on private and conscientious reasons in certain situations – the 'free vote' possibility. This means that political actors are endowed with a dual aspect in their professional lives. Since there is nothing to stop these actors acting within the three-part structure under the 'free vote' aspect, there is nothing to stop them tolerating a practice under this aspect. United Kingdom legislators' opposition to reintroducing capital punishment, against overwhelming popular support for its reintroduction, currently illustrates this.

The dual aspect of the legislator in representative democracies is telling: it provides a case where those directing law or policy may genuinely stand as one party to a second, as in the interpersonal case. But it is significant that this form of representative democracy marks the survival of personal prerogative into the age of democratic politics: representatives take decisions as private individuals, e.g. on conscientious grounds, rather than being delegated by their electors. But in a pure direct or delegatory form of democracy, these interstices for private conscience no longer exist within the political process. Here, the possibility of toleration requires local derogations from democracy in political systems which are, on the whole, democratic.

TOLERATION, POLITICS, AND POLITICAL PHILOSOPHY

Modern philosophical liberalism seeks a basis for agreement on fundamental political institutions and procedures in general normative considerations. The interpretation of these considerations varies, of course, from one theory to the next. The mention of a 'basis for agreement' is not intended to imply that contractarianism is the sole or paradigmatic version of modern liberalism, but contractarianism does make explicitly a move typical of liberal theory in general: it attempts to argue that the terms of the agreement are such that persons *should* accept them, whether or not they in fact *would* do so.

John Rawls states at the start of *Political Liberalism* that "[t]he aim of justice as fairness, then, is practical: it presents itself as a conception of justice that may be

---

[22] For some suggestive remarks on the relation between agency and virtue, see see R.Audi, "Acting From Virtue", *Mind* 104 (1995), 439-472, and Williams, "Moral Incapacity". For further discussion see also my *Virtue, Reason and Toleration*, ch. 3.

shared by citizens as a basis of a reasoned, informed, and willing political agreement".[23] This has been criticised on the grounds that it substitutes actual for ideal agreement, and thus ignores the normative dimension of political justification.[24] But even in Rawls's account of agreement in *Political Liberalism*, the agreement does not reduce to the terms which, as a matter of brute fact, the parties to it will accept: Rawls makes it clear that he is not aiming at a mere *modus vivendi*. A normative conception of reasonableness frames the contract.[25]

Most of the difficulties are rolled up in this quotation, from "The Idea of Public Reason Revisited":

> Citizens are reasonable when, viewing one another as free and equal in a system of social cooperation over generations, they are prepared to offer one another fair terms of cooperation according to what they consider the most reasonable conception of political justice; and when they agree to act on those terms, even at the cost of their own interests in particular situations, provided that other citizens also accept those terms.

The latter part of this quotation seems to countenance a fairly drastic relativisation of the notion of reasonableness, since it depends on what the advocates of particular 'comprehensive' conceptions of the good *regard* as reasonable: but it is clear that Rawls is not endorsing out-and-out relativisation here, as the reference to the need by *all* citizens to regard one another 'as free and equal' indicates. Rawls perhaps believes that the 'overlapping consensus' doctrine ultimately effaces this difference, since the doctrine holds that different comprehensive conceptions can each ratify the principles of political agreement from its own perspective. But either there is no good reason to think that each comprehensive conception will ratify *any* set of principles, or the reasonableness of those who hold such conceptions will be held to depend on their propensity to ratify the principles which Rawls favours. A condition of securing agreement on these principles is a normatively augmented conception of reasonableness.[26]

I now want to suggest that toleration exposes a blind spot in this approach to political philosophy. We have already seen a version of the normative approach in discussing the political problems of toleration: the view that there is some right answer to the question of whether or not a practice should be tolerated, and a political authority acts tolerantly if and only if its action in respect of a practice conforms to this answer. The 'normative agreement' approach adds that the practice

---

[23] J.Rawls, *Political Liberalism* (New York: Columbia University Press 1993), p. 9.

[24] See e.g. G.Gaus, *Justificatory Liberalism: An Essay on Epistemology and Political Theory* (Oxford: Oxford University Press 1996), p. 4f and section II *passim*.

[25] Rawls, "The Idea of Public Reason Revisited", *University of Chicago Law Review* 64 (1997), 765-807; repr. in Rawls, *Collected Papers* ed. S.Freeman (Cambridge, MA.: Harvard University Press 1999), p. 578.

[26] Similar remarks apply, e.g., to Brian Barry's neo-Scanlonian contractualism, which attempts to produce agreement on terms "which nobody can reasonably reject". See Barry, *Justice As Impartiality* (Oxford: Oxford University Press 1995). Barry explicitly acknowledges that this relies on a normative conception of what is reasonable (p. 8).

of toleration is justified only if it is justified by an agreement to which those involved (would, or should) have given their consent.[27]

As the parentheses indicate, however, there are problems in formulating this notion of justification while retaining the intuitive appeal of an agreement-based approach. The basic problem, as the circumstances of toleration themselves show, is that unless actual agreement is forthcoming, the attempted justification will shift to talking about the agreements by which the parties, were they rational or moral, would or should have bound themselves – and then the 'agreement' itself begins to look otiose, since what then matters is that the parties were required to agree anyway. But once the political circumstances of toleration have been reached, the obligations the protagonists are under is part of what is in dispute.[28]

If so, the approach risks ignoring or misconstruing the facts which made toleration politically urgent to start with. For the political circumstances of toleration arise precisely when action is either unstructured by obligations, or the obligations themselves are disputed. There is in fact a further possibility, that one party fails to act on an obligation which they have already accepted. Then, something along the lines of the 'normative agreement' approach may be appropriate. But this situation is rather rare, and the reason why is fairly obvious. Either the party climbs down – accepts that this is the case – and the political impasse is cleared; or it does not because it denies that *this* action is required by the obligation. The history to date of the 'Good Friday Agreement' provides a case in point.[29] To adapt the old saying of Epicurus about death: when toleration is there, politics is absent, and when politics is there, toleration is absent.

We can now see the underlying truth in the remarks of Kant and Paine quoted earlier. The practice of toleration essentially requires the use of power, since the political circumstances only arise when one party or the other, or both, have failed to act tolerantly, and so have to be compelled to adopt a different form of action. This is true even in the 'free vote' case discussed earlier, where legislators seen under one aspect are in a position analogous to that of interpersonal toleration. For even here the position is at best *analogous*, since using my powers over my own agency in the cause of non-intervention is very different from using political power to control the actions of others. Power is mobilised to enforce public policy against those who oppose it. This need not itself involve intolerance, or refusal to tolerate, but it may do.

---

[27] As I argue in *Virtue, Reason and Toleration*, esp. ch. 5, philosophical argument about toleration's structure cannot provide a definitive account of what should be tolerated. For related reasons, it is also very difficult to furnish an unambiguous content for toleration from within liberalism.

[28] Note that this need not doom attempt to provide an agreement-based justification for *morality* itself. There are, in any case, different conceptions of what such a justification should aim to do. One is simply that it should replicate the *content* of morality. Another is that tell us what the *bindingness* of morality consists in, i.e. to provide an answer to the question, "Why be moral?". Yet another is to provide a perspicuous procedural model for alleged formal properties of morality (e.g. its applying categorically) which would otherwise be obscure.

[29] For further argument on this point, see my "Discourse Rights and the Drumcree Marches: a Reply to O'Neill", forthcoming in the *British Journal of Political and International Relations*.

democracy and toleration can arrive at an easy accommodation, optimism is misplaced. Nor should we regard more toleration as being *necessarily* better than less – at least if toleration is identified with non-intervention, or permissiveness. If on the other hand, toleration as a practice or as a virtue is invested directly with normative content as an intrinsic good, then more is indeed better than less; but the first-order values on which toleration works, as well as judgements about how they apply in particular circumstances, are the subject of dispute. Moreover, the three-part structure implies that particular acts of toleration are only intelligible within a system of values which regards some practices as intolerable.

So, while it is a good thing that there are tolerant people, it is also a good thing that the strong valuations on which the goodness of toleration depends limit the practical scope of toleration. The worth, as well as the scope, of toleration depends on the constitutive attachments whose practical public import it is the business of politics to articulate.

CHAPTER 10

THE ENFORCEMENT OF TOLERATION

Frederic R. Kellogg

The nature of our discussions of toleration has changed. How about the essential problem? John Locke's 1689 *Letter Concerning Toleration* famously advanced the proposition that "the care of souls cannot belong to the civil magistrate, because his power consists only in outward force; but true and saving religion consists in the inward persuasion of the mind, without which nothing can be acceptable to God. And such is the nature of the understanding that it cannot be compelled to the belief of anything by outward force."[1] In this last remark, Locke was addressing state enforcement of an affirmative belief, of an approved religion. Now that the western democratic state has abandoned that enterprise, the danger appears to lie elsewhere. With some extraordinary exceptions, concern in the West has largely focused on private, rather than governmental, intolerance. If the care of souls cannot belong to the civil magistrate, what can the state do to advance civility among conflicting visions? What are we to conclude about the powers of the magistrate to enforce or encourage toleration itself?

The moral and political environment has drastically changed since Locke wrote, and even more only recently. His words take on new meaning, as do the words of the essayists in this book, who wrote in large part before the events of September 11, 2001. Many of their questions are rendered more compelling, their observations more acute. As the introduction to this volume notes, the shrinking world has made it impossible for any person or group to escape from those with whom they differ. What now constitutes tolerance? What does it demand? What can be done to create and sustain not just a standoff between conflicting beliefs, an institutional *modus vivendi*, but a widespread regime or culture of tolerance? And precisely what form would it take?

A prime issue addressed by these essays is the distinction between the moral and political dimensions of toleration. What is the relation between the moral attitude and the institutional arrangements designed to promote it? My purpose in this paper is to reflect on the relationship of toleration to law—or, more generally, to the system or process of social ordering that is embodied in law and rules.

---

[1] John Locke, *A Letter Concerning Toleration*, in *Works* (London: Tegg et al., 1823), VI, p. 11

Several authors divide between an exploration of toleration understood as a moral attitude and as a practical political ideal. I suggest that we should approach this question by examining the relationship of the two. By law I do not mean simply the clear role for law enforcement in addressing the worst forms of conflict among fanatical groups or acts of individual violence. The issue is broader, and encompasses many of the questions dealt with in this volume: disagreement over the meaning of tolerance, and the pursuit of coherence; seeking both a culture of tolerance and the rationale for its justification; reconciling the independent virtue of tolerance with the need for stark choices among competing first-order conceptions of the good. Tolerance cannot survive at the expense of principled action. It cannot be enforced simply on instrumental, traditional, sceptical, or pragmatic grounds, and be maintained at the expense of vigorous pursuit of truth, or legitimate difference. We must concern ourselves not just with the fanatic fringe but with effects upon competing mainstream interests.

Locke wrote that

> [i]t may indeed be alleged that the magistrate may make use of arguments, and thereby draw the heterodox into the way of truth, and procure their salvation. I grant it; but this is common to him with other men. In teaching, instructing, and redressing the erroneous by reason, he may certainly do what becomes any good man to do. Magistracy does not oblige him to put off either humanity or Christianity. But it is one thing to persuade, another to command; . . . I affirm, that the magistrate's power extends not to the establishing of any articles of faith, or forms of worship, by the force of his laws. For laws are of no force at all without penalties, and penalties in this case are absolutely impertinent; because they are not proper to convince the mind.[2]

The issue of importance here is the distinction between *persuasion* and *command*, its role in the analysis of law and the maintenance of order, and how it must be kept in mind in the pursuit of tolerance. Legal proscription and law enforcement is a rough tool, but it serves to set limits and preserve the institutional arrangements that permit discourse and change amidst conflict. Intolerance is a phenomenon that has emerged in different forms and in distinct circumstances; it is evident within society and without, against individuals and against groups, local, national, and worldwide. As Michael Walzer has shown,[3] there have been several distinct forms or regimes of toleration, as well as a great diversity of forms of intolerance.

Intolerance may be religious, racial, cultural, geographical, economic, class, linguistic, tribal, political, educational, sexual, any combination of these, or others more difficult to specify, such as who arrived sooner. The framework for analysis of toleration is substantially expanded. No longer is the issue limited to the protection of freedom of religion, it is extended to the protection of privacy, community, culture, thought, language, family, expression in general and in all its possible manifestations. Just as intolerance reaches into every branch of life, issues of toleration reach into all the branches of law, whether local, customary, national, or constitutional. The debate reaches into the law of family, legislation, education,

---

[2] Locke, *Letter Concerning Toleration*, p. 11-12
[3] M. Walzer, *On Toleration* (New Haven and London: Yale University Press, 1997)

privacy, abortion, affirmative action, voting rights, and especially constitutional law and the burgeoning law of human rights.

Against this background the moral and political dimensions of toleration cannot readily be distinguished. Both are in continuing development, and the two constantly inform each other. We should not be surprised to find that there may be no fixed and uniform answer to the questions regarding toleration's definition or implementation. There is no uniform nor clear answer to the question, What is toleration, nor the question, What is the 'regime of toleration' that works best for society. *Which* society? If the answer is *our* society, itself undergoing constant transformation, we cannot be altogether sure of the relevant conditions in the not-too-distant future, not to mention what will ultimately prevail over the long run.

Nevertheless, I would like to consider the bearing of an issue addressing the nature of law in general. This is again the distinction between *persuasion* and *command*, and its role in the analysis of law and the maintenance of order. Law functions through command and sanction; if that were the end of the matter, we might conclude that its role in toleration is limited to the exercise of 'outward force.' But the common law has from its distinctive appearance in the thirteenth century been part of a civil conversation, engaging the parties to disputes with juries in their communities as well as with royal officialdom. The distinction between persuasion and command reflects the question whether law is essentially endogenous, or embedded in society and acting within it, or exogenous, autonomous, apart from society and acting upon it. Both concepts are found within our jurisprudential tradition. Simply stated, the first emphasizes the intimate relation of law with social custom and preexisting values, and the second has emphasized the aspect of law as sovereign command. The answer given regarding the nature of law affects the manner in which intolerance is addressed as a matter of policy—even where answers to the more specific questions are only dimly perceptible. Indeed, it matters all the more *because* those more specific answers are so uncertain.

First, what are the dimensions of uncertainty to which I allude? There are two principal ones: one is the difficulty of perceiving how legislated social policy will influence broad patterns of conduct affecting toleration, or in colloquial terms, what will be the unseen and unintended consequences of legislation directed at an abstract goal. The second lies in the paradoxes of coexistence between individualism and group identity. There is a sense in which toleration is meaningless without individualism, and meanwhile individualism is shaped and strengthened by strong group affinities. How then can coercive sanctions be employed to strengthen both toleration *and* the prosperity of group identities that may otherwise threaten it? Our goal cannot be an idealized but unreal harmonious and peaceful coexistence; toleration and group identity must prosper together.

Walzer provides an account of the difficulty in the task of understanding the contradictions involved. Experience with toleration demonstrates a diversity of approaches suggested by history: multinational empires, such as ancient Persia, Egypt and Rome, in which an overall order was imposed and various groups had no choice but coexistence; international society, in which sovereign states of varying degrees of internal tolerance are all tolerated by a 'society of states'; consociations, like Belgium, Switzerland, and Lebanon, in which an arrangement among several communities is negotiated among the parties; nation-states, where greater tolerance of individuals may accompany lesser tolerance of groups; and immigrant societies like the United States, in which group identities are themselves transformed as they become 'hyphenated,' such as African-American and Italian-American. All have produced distinct approaches to, and different degrees and kinds of, toleration. With this background we may see how toleration of *groups* is a distinct question from toleration of *individuals*. Regimes that protect insular groups from state intolerance may leave the individual less protected from intolerance from within the group—and *vice versa*.[4]

In his final chapters Walzer addresses the impossibility of the goal of social harmony. Recent writers, like the Bulgarian-French writer Julia Kristeva, have portrayed multiculturalism as pointing toward an idealized model of 'postmodern' toleration. This is a vision of social life in which differences have become so dispersed that they are encountered everywhere. Boundaries among ethnically or culturally distinct groups are softened to the point of near disappearance. "Individuals escape from their parochial entanglements and mix freely with members of the majority, but they don't necessarily assimilate to a common identity. The hold of groups on their members is looser than it has ever been before, but it is by no means broken entirely. The result is a constant commingling of ambiguously identified individuals, intermarriage among them, and hence a highly intensive multiculturalism that is instantiated not only in the society as a whole but also in a growing number of families, even in a growing number of individuals."[5] Walzer asks, "Isn't the postmodern project, considered without its necessary historical background, likely to produce increasingly shallow individuals and a radically diminished cultural life?"[6]

The United States, for example, has recently witnessed a steady weakening of associational life. This has bred new anxieties and resentments and produced new forms of intolerance and bigotry, as in the more extreme forms of 'political correctness' and exaggerated claims of ethnic and racial mythology. America is a pluralism of groups as well as individuals, its regime of toleration focused on personal choices and lifestyles. Yet even the most robust individualism cannot survive a continuing associational weakness. The freedom to mix and mingle in different cultures, as an advantage of an immigrant society like the United States, does not make for strong or cohesive associations, nor, ultimately, for strong individuals.[7]

> Individuals are stronger, more confident, more savvy, when they are participants in a common life, when they are responsible to and for other people. . . . For it is only in the context of associational activity that individuals learn to deliberate, argue, make decisions and take responsibility.
> [N]o regime of toleration can be built solely on such 'strong' individuals, for they are the products of group life and won't, by themselves, reproduce the connections that

---

[4] Walzer, *On Toleration*, pp. 14-36.
[5] ibid., p. 87
[6] ibid., p. 91
[7] ibid., pp. 101-2

made their own strength possible. So we need to sustain and enhance associational ties, even if these ties connect some of us to others and not every one to everyone else.[8]

In short, toleration is not to be mistaken either for social harmony nor for a *formula for* harmony. It cannot be gained at the expense of a robust environment of associations and groups, many of which are themselves disinclined to practice toleration internally—nor , given the authority, would they be naturally inclined to practice it in relation to the society at large.

There are several ways in which this observation might affect our approach to law. First, as Walzer suggests, it is a matter for consideration in the crafting of national policy.[9] Walzer's concern with the strengthening of association prompts him to focus on the distribution of benefits, in taxation and otherwise; government programs should support citizens acting directly in local communities. Walzer is neither specific nor comprehensive on what such programs should be. I suspect that this is due to his sense of the difficulty of influencing the private realm though state action, and of the problem of unintended consequences.

But beyond this lies the question of the general degree of reliance on law and legal sanctions for the maintenance of basic standards of toleration. In thinking about the role of law we naturally focus first on its ability to control conduct through state distributions and sanctions. When law is conceived programmatically, as the tool for implementing social policy, it is seen as operating autonomously, *upon* society; but it acts indirectly in regard to its intended effects. Programs designed to promote associational vitality may or may not result in engendering specific kinds of tolerance among or within them. Laws directly affecting conduct through penal sanctions, such as those against hate speech, are directed specifically to guard the outer limits of acceptable conduct. They address the more notorious cases, in which drastic legal intervention is the only recourse. Such legal interventions are often the final resort due to failure to perceive the utility of other resources available to address the generic problem at an earlier stage.

But the law also works as part of the civic conversation, in ways wherein its greater effect lies in persuasion. Constitutional jurisprudence under the Bill of Rights in the United States, and human rights law in Europe, is given a prominent place in the maintenance of toleration in the West. According to constitutional scholar David A. J. Richards, toleration is the central constitutional ideal. It is "at the very moral heart of the dignity of constitutional law, and is thus the central or paradigm case of the rights that constitutionalism protects."[10]

But this is not the case purely as a result of the sanctions that are administered in constitutional litigation. What is the ultimate source of the 'dignity of constitutional law'? Does it come from the words of the document, or from the traditions and practices that produced them? Does the dignity of the words automatically translate into the power to enforce them? Finally, is toleration dependent upon the reasoning that accompanies judicial enforcement? Is toleration defined by the rulings of the

---

[8] ibid., p. 105
[9] ibid., p. 106
[10] Richards, David A.J., *Toleration and the Constitution* (New York and Oxford: Oxford University Press, 1986)

courts on fundamental rights, or does it derive from a more democratic source and process?

It is here that that the distinction between moral and political dimensions of toleration are of heightened importance. It is at the constitutional level that legislation is weighed alongside constitutional values, such that something akin to 'public reason' must be engaged. But even constitutional courts are not in a position to wrestle over the meaning of toleration, and the pursuit of coherence. They cannot explore the problems of seeking both a culture of toleration and the rationale for its justification, or reconciling the independent virtue of toleration with the need for stark choices among competing first-order conceptions of the good. They and we must accept their natural limits. The courts are not well positioned to accept full responsibility for the articulation of tolerant standards. The responsibility must be shared with the public at large, and thus the element of persuasion is a mutual one.

The problem of toleration has occupied a central role in the works of John Rawls.[11] In *Political Liberalism* Rawls makes the claim that "public reason in a constitutional democracy with judicial review is the reason of its supreme court."[12] Rawls' approach exemplifies what Walzer calls a 'proceduralist' turn in philosophy: "the philosopher imagines an original position, an ideal speech situation, or a conversation in a spaceship. Each of these is constituted by a set of constraints, rules of engagement, as it were, for the participating parties. The parties represent the rest of us. They reason, bargain, or talk within the constraints, which are designed to impose the formal criteria of any morality: absolute impartiality or some functional equivalent thereof. Assuming that the imposition is successful, the conclusions the parties reach can plausibly be regarded as morally authoritative. We are thus provided with governing principles for all our actual reasoning, bargaining, and talking—indeed, for all our political, social, and economic activity—in real world conditions."[13]

Rawls gives the unfortunate and perhaps quite unintended impression that something like an ideal speech situation may occur in an appellate court. The political process responsible for nomination and confirmation, the nature of legal education and practice, indeed the history of the United States Supreme Court, do much to offset that notion that the relatively high level of toleration in the United States hinges upon the work of its appellate courts. Proceduralist analysis suffers two disadvantages. One, it is disembodied, unattached to real (not hyothetical) cases and circumstances, and thus difficult to evaluate; and another, it is concomitantly inadequate to explain and meliorate the actual conditions of toleration. Rawls implicitly has in mind that high court judges may somehow profit from knowing such fundamental principles, such that a tolerant reflective equilibrium may thereby flourish. The danger in this attitude lies in its insufficient caution, its tendency to rely too much on a system of dispute resolution to maintain an important social characteristic.

So we may conclude that constitutional and human rights practice raises again the issue Locke identified, in a very different context: Can adjudication and

---

[11] See generally J. Rawls, *A Theory of Justice* (Cambridge, MA: Harvard University Press, 1971)

[12] Rawls, *Political Liberalism* (New York: Columbia University Press, 1993) p. 231

[13] Walzer, *On Toleration*, p.1

enforcement of legal principles guaranteeing toleration (such as those found in the United States Bill of Rights) maintain—or might they even undermine—the very culture of toleration they are designed to preserve? As Judge Learned Hand said in "The Contribution of an Independent Judiciary to Civilization," A society so driven that the spirit of moderation is gone, no court can save;...a society where that spirit flourishes, no court need save; ... in a society which evades its responsibility by thrusting upon courts the nurture of that spirit, that spirit in the end will perish."[14] Here again is the concern that, paraphrasing Locke, the care of tolerance itself cannot belong to the civil magistrate because his power consists only in outward force.

The most extreme statement of this viewpoint is found in an opinion of the American Supreme Court Justice Felix Frankfurter, dissenting in a case involving the enforcement of a state law requiring participation in the flag salute in public school during the 1940s, at the height of the Second World War:

> Of course patriotism can not be enforced by the flag salute. But neither can the liberal spirit be enforced by judicial invalidation of illiberal legislation. Our constant pre-occupation with the constitutionality of legislation rather than with its wisdom tends to preoccupation of the American mind with a false value. The tendency of focussing attention on constitutionality is to make constitutionality synonymous with wisdom, to regard a law as all right if it is constitutional. Such an attitude is a great enemy of liberalism. Particularly in legislation affecting freedom of thought and freedom of speech much which should offend a free-spirited society is constitutional. Reliance for the most precious interests of civilization, therefore, must be found outside of their vindication in courts of law. Only a persistent positive translation of the faith of a free society into the convictions and habits and actions of a community is the ultimate reliance against unabated temptations to fetter the human spirit.[15]

Both comments are equally concerned not only with redressing intolerance but optimizing conditions for tolerance, two different aspects of the same problem, deriving from pluralism, from the inclusion in civil society of people with radically different principled visions. In Frankfurter's case, the subject of the dispute was a student from a religious sect whose belief committed him to refusing to salute the American flag. The law in question required his expulsion from school. We feel a natural revulsion to that outcome and a relief that there exists a system of court-enforced constitutionalism available to overturn such a law and order the school to reinstate the student. Frankfurter's dissent has served less as a guide than as a caution, a warning that there exists a point beyond which automatic resort to the courts cannot preserve individual rights.

Between the attitudes of Rawls and Frankfurter appears to lie a substantial gulf of incompatibility. But they arise from a common concern, which involves the element that Rawls calls 'public reason.' Their divergence is a matter of difference over precisely what public reason is, and how best to engage in, encourage, and maintain it. Rawls path to his court-privileging attitude is complicated, and it bears extended attention that I am not able to give it here. But he does appear to speak for many, if not most, observers in placing notable reliance on court-enforced constitu-tionalism as the bulwark of public reasoning in matters of toleration.

---

[14] L. Hand, *The Spirit of Liberty: Papers and Addresses of Learned Hand* (I. Dilliard ed 1959), p. 144
[15] *West Va. State Bd. of Educ. v. Barnette*, 319 U.S. 624, 650 (1943).

Whence derives this sharp difference between Frankfurter and Rawls? Both Felix Frankfurter and Learned Hand were influenced by James Bradley Thayer, who taught constitutional law for many years at Harvard Law School at the turn of the last century. In the final paragraph of James Bradley Thayer's 1893 essay, "The Origins and Scope of the American Doctrine of Constitutional Law," is found the following passage:

> [T]he safe and permanent road towards reform is that of impressing upon our people a far stronger sense than they have of the great range of possible harm and evil that our system leaves open, and must leave open, to the legisla-tures, and of the clear limits of judicial power; so that responsibility may be brought sharply home where it belongs.[16]

If the courts are not the principal vehicle for averting massive constitutional harm, Thayer is suggesting that the public should retain, in some degree and manner, an ongoing constitutional responsibility akin to that exercised in its adoption. In his view the judges should defer lest the public cede the ultimate responsibility to interpret—though perhaps not in the academic sense—and *implement* its own constitution. These comments suggest that there is an important difference between promoting tolerance and redressing intolerance, and that the judiciary may not be well suited as the primary custodian of this virtue. For John Rawls, the 'public reason' essential to toleration is found in the highest judicial deliberations. Thayer, Hand, and Frankfurter place the responsibility squarely with the public.

Public engagement is the only way to develop both the moral and political dimensions of tolerant constitutionalism. The public cannot be commanded, and it also cannot simply be persuaded; it must be engaged in a conversation of *mutual* persuasion. Failure to to so runs the risk of separating the judicial from the public understanding of constitutionalism. Mark Tushnet, in *Taking the Constitution Away from the Courts*,[17] asks us to distinguish between two constitutions: the constitution *inside* the courts and the one *outside*. He argues at length that the standards that are applied by and within the courts in interpreting and enforcing the constitution are not necessarily those that we should accept for all public officials in their deliberations, or for the public at large in carrying out their civic duties.

Tushnet takes as an example the First Amendment requirement that Congress shall make no law respecting an establishment of religion. This has led to a line of decisions that are interpreted as having erected a metaphorical 'wall of separation' between religion and government. But, he asks, should the wall of separation be applied to elected representatives in their deliberations in parliament or Congress? Should such a wall be applied by people in their discussions among themselves on matters of public policy?

Tushnet points out that there are groups within society that will not refrain from presenting certain of their arguments in religious terms. And, there may be valid reasons relating to democratic deliberation that warrants their arguments to be presented in such terms, for example in registering the genuineness and intensity of

---

[16] J.B. Thayer, "The Origin and Scope of the American Doctrine of Constitutional Law," 7 Harvard L. Rev. 129 (1893), p. 156

[17] M. Tushnet, *Taking the Constitution Away from the Courts* (Princeton: Princeton University Press, 1999)

those opinions. Jeremy Waldron has observed that "there ought to be continuity between whatever discourse is appropriate among the people and whatever discourse is appropriate among those whom they represent."[18]   Yet a strict application of a wall of separation on all public officials would require an essential discontinuity. Tushnet asks why some requirements should be imposed on delegates and different ones on those whom they represent:

> The depth of disagreement about religion might caution legislators—and judges even more strongly—to do what they can to explain their actions without invoking religious premises. But in the end if they find it appropriate to use such premises in public arguments, the Constitution outside the courts ought not to limit them.[19]

From this and other examples, Tushnet concludes at length that judicial involvement in constitutional jurisprudence works at cross purposes from the necessary engagement of the public at large in shaping optimal constitutional values, including those of religous toleration. His ultimate recourse is the abandonment of judicial review of legislation.[20]

The concern common to Tushnet and Frankfurter, and shared by Hand and Thayer, is that of fully engaging the public in the shaping of legal standards that implement constitutional values. The moral dimensions of toleration, to which exacting analysis has been given by many of the authors in this volume, need not be irrevocably detached from the political dimensions, which have also been carefully addressed by others. I have suggested that both are in continual development. Something akin to what Rawls fruitfully calls 'public reason'—a broad-based public reason—must be hewn from however messy and unwilling a reality. For the moral dimensions to be comprehensive and effective, their shaping must engage the public, in a process that is part of the institutional arrangements whereby toleration is maintained and promoted.

---

[18] J. Waldron, "Religious Contributions in Public Deliberation," 30 *San Diego L. Rev.* 817 (1993) p. 830

[19] Tushnet, *Taking the Constitution Away from the Courts*, p. 94.

[20] Id. at pp. 154-176. A perhaps better approach, which I have discussed elsewhere, is the process known as 'judicial restraint', wherein the formation of general rules awaits a gradual community consensus. See Kellogg, "Learned Hand and the Great Train Ride," 56 *American Scholar* 471 (1987)

CHAPTER 11

THE FRAUGHT RELATION BETWEEN TOLERATION AND DEMOCRACY

Maurizio Passerin d'Entrèves

In recent years, a number of prominent thinkers (Rawls, Nagel, Waldron) have argued that democratic arrangements tend to favour the flourishing of toleration among groups with radically different comprehensive worldviews. My paper examines one of the most insightful attempts to demonstrate such a positive connection between democracy and toleration. In two recent essays, 'Three Faces of Toleration in a Democracy' (1996) and 'Toleration without Liberal Foundations' (1997), Sheldon Leader has presented a powerful case for grounding the practice of toleration on the values of democracy. I argue that Leader's attempt to ground the practice of toleration on a common understanding of democracy faces a number of fundamental obstacles. Such obstacles could only be overcome if both liberals and their opponents were to reach an agreement on the value of democracy and thereby converge in their support for toleration. I argue that, far from providing a common ground that liberals and their opponents can share, the so-called 'shareable understanding' of democracy appeals primarily to liberals. The difficulty resides in the fact that not every group in a liberal constitutional regime can be convinced of the priority of democratic principles over their other fundamental value-commitments.

DEMOCRACY AND TOLERATION

Sheldon Leader has presented what, in my view, is one of the most compelling arguments linking the practice of toleration to the acceptance of certain fundamental democratic values. By grounding the practice of toleration on what he believes is a set of shared democratic values, Leader advances an original argument, quite distinct from the usual defences of toleration. His originality resides in the fact that rather than defending toleration on the standard liberal arguments about the value of individual autonomy or the neutrality of the state with respect to competing and often incommensurable conceptions of the good life, he defends it on the basis of the value and importance of democracy. The value of democracy, in his view, should enable liberals and their opponents to converge in their support of toleration, understood either as a basic right, or as an equal right, or as a special right. Toleration would thus be based not on liberal foundations, but on a 'shareable understanding' of democracy. By shareable understanding he means a conception of democracy on which liberals and their opponents would agree independently of the other commitments that set them apart. If both liberals and non-liberals were to agree on certain democratic principles, they might find themselves in agreement on what an adequate principle of toleration requires, along the three dimensions he identifies.[1]

This strategy is quite similar to Rawls's method of avoidance, namely, the hope that by avoiding the appeal to comprehensive moral, religious, or philosophical doctrines in our justification of principles of justice, we might find a basis of agreement based on a more restricted, but stable, overlapping consensus. The premium that we—citizens of a modern democratic constitutional regime—put on certain political virtues—such as fairness and impartiality—should enable us to overcome our differences when deciding matters pertaining to constitutional essentials. The difference resides in the fact that while Rawls assumes that we have to agree only on a restricted number of political virtues to arrive at an overlapping consensus on basic principles of justice, Leader believes that we have to agree on a very substantial value—democracy—in order to reach an agreement on basic principles of toleration. This is a bold and courageous hypothesis, which finds me in sympathetic agreement, but which may give more hostages to fortune when applied to contexts characterized by non-liberal forms of life and by long-running disputes about the meaning, scope, and implications of the principles of democracy.

In my assessment of Leader's arguments, I shall focus initially on the paper he delivered at the UNESCO Conference on Tolerance and Law, April 1995, and will go on to examine two recent essays, 'Three Faces of Toleration in a Democracy' (1996) and 'Toleration without Liberal Foundations' (1997). The first of these essays reformulates the arguments of the UNESCO paper, while the second extends and considerably modifies the arguments presented in the first essay. My examination will thus proceed in two stages, tracking the development of Leader's views. I shall start by looking at the initial formulation of his arguments in the UNESCO paper, and will then examine their reformulation and extension in the two published essays of 1996 and 1997.[2]

---

[1] As Leader puts it in "Toleration without Liberal Foundations", *Ratio Juris*, vol. 10, no. 2 (1997), p. 142: "A wide range of groups, some strongly illiberal, demand their rightful place by virtue of a society's claim to being a democracy. Cultural groups, churches, families, through to trade unions, corporations, and single or loosely associated individuals - all argue that democracy confers on them a right to build up and live through these institutions. In doing so, they all share a general support for toleration, since that is what allows them each to survive in the face of outsiders' objections to what they do. But they differ strongly over the fine grained interpretations to give to that right as they impinge on one another ... It is at this point that it becomes interesting to see what their common support for democracy commits them to ... Either they hold onto their initial, preferred notion of toleration and frankly admit that after due reflection they don't care that much about democracy after all; or they hold to the latter, and then accept the need to alter their initial understanding of what toleration commits them to."

[2] Sheldon Leader, "Toleration without Liberal Foundations", paper presented at the UNESCO Conference on Tolerance and Law, April 1995, Pontignano, Italy; "Three Faces of Toleration in a Democracy", *Journal of Political Philosophy*, vol. 4, no. 1 (1996), pp. 45-67; "Toleration without Liberal Foundations", *Ratio Juris*, vol. 10, no. 2 (1997), pp. 139-64.

THREE TYPES OF TOLERATION

Leader opens his UNESCO paper by noting that a theory of toleration can fail to be adequate to the problems confronting modern pluralist societies in at least two ways, namely, by being biased or by being too narrow. The failure of bias can emerge, he says, 'when a community agrees that toleration is a virtue of its institutions, but a particular interpretation of that virtue held by some is forced onto others who may agree on endorsing it, but construe it in quite a different way.'[3] The second possible failure in a theory of toleration is that of having too narrow a range. Most theories, he claims, 'provide what can be loosely called a 'live-and-let-live' conception of toleration. They will sketch out radically different domains appropriate for toleration, but once those are fixed then within them all parties are enjoined to mutually refrain from interfering with one another.'[4] After having examined a series of cases showing the bias and narrowness of certain current conceptions of toleration, Leader puts forward a threefold taxonomy of rights to toleration that is meant to overcome such inadequacies. He calls these three distinct rights to toleration, respectively, (1) a claim to toleration as a basic right; (2) as an equal right; and (3) as a special right.

The first, he says, 'is a demand that one not interfere with an activity on the ground that it is not unduly interfering with or inconveniencing another; the second is a demand for fair access to some common space or scarce resource, and in the process of gaining it to be entitled to interfere with or inconvenience another if that proves necessary; and, finally, the call for toleration as a special right is a demand for exemption from standards normally governing the exercise of power in a community. Our theory—he says—must offer a ground for, and set plausible limits to, each of these types of right; and it must do so in a way that avoids the kind of bias pointed to at the outset, drawing on principles that liberals and non-liberals are able to share without feeling that the only way to reach agreement is for one side totally to capitulate to the other.'[5]

TOLERATION AS A BASIC RIGHT

Let us now look at the arguments that Leader develops in support of each distinct right to toleration. Consider the first species of toleration, namely, toleration as a basic right against interference. Leader defends a standard liberal position: he argues that the individual enjoys a *prima facie* right to be free from majority rule, while the majority does not enjoy a *prima facie* right to rule over the individual. He argues this on two grounds. First, in a democracy, liberty from majority rule is not a product of delegation: it concerns those matters which have not formed part of any delegation of authority and must therefore be left to individual discretion. Second, the state must be neutral with respect to competing conceptions of the good life, because there is no basis for expecting universal agreement on any single or overarching

---

[3] "Toleration without Liberal Foundations", p. 1; 'Three Faces of Toleration in a Democracy', p. 45.
[4] "Toleration without Liberal Foundations", p. 2; 'Three Faces of Toleration in a Democracy', p. 46.
[5] "Toleration without Liberal Foundations", p. 5; 'Three Faces of Toleration in a Democracy', pp. 48-9.

conception, and thus no basis for the state to enforce it on an unwilling minority. The examples chosen to illustrate the basic right against interference have to do with sexual and religious preference: here the right of the individual to be free from state interference has *prima facie* priority, unless valid independent arguments for overriding it can be given in the particular case. By contrast, recognition of a new and independent state, such as Croatia, or the decision about the acceptable level of violence in a society, can be left legitimately in the hands of the state or its controlling majority.

Notice, however, that these last two examples are relatively non-controversial, while those pertaining to sexual and religious preference are not, since they have to do with conflicting and at times incommensurable conceptions of the good. The standard liberal answer to conflicts of this type is to restrict them, if possible, to the private domain, so that they may be treated as matters of private choice. Sexual preferences and religious convictions would thus be considered, in the standard liberal view, as matters of private conscience or personal morality. Many non-liberal groups, however, would resist such a solution: they see matters pertaining to sexual preference and religious belief as not simply private, but as having a public dimension, as affecting the moral character or the moral tone of a society. Hence, they feel entitled to ask for the restriction of the public display of unorthodox sexual preferences or the public expression of what they perceive as offensive moral beliefs, since in their view they would erode the moral fabric of society. They would do so, to be sure, on the basis of non-detachable reasons, i.e. reasons that cannot be separated from the particular outcome they are seeking to achieve. But I doubt that this would count as a fundamental objection, as Leader believes. His central claim is that in a democracy central control (e.g. control by a central authority such as parliament or the judiciary) is legitimate 'only when justified for detachable reasons: where the reasons for central control can be separated from the particular outcomes that a party advancing such a solution would like to see emerge from it. Only in this way can the materials exist on which to base a principle by which all should reasonably be called on to assent to delegate a decision to the centre, despite the fact that they disagree over how the centre should use the power so delegated to it.'[6]

In advancing this argument Leader presents what may be called the democratic—as distinct from the liberal—answer to deep-seated conflicts about the good. I remain sceptical, however, that such an answer would satisfy the claims of many groups, whether liberal or non-liberal. In a democratic society, I would argue, there are often non-detachable reasons for allocating an issue to central control: in the case, say, of policies to prevent racial and sexual discrimination, the reasons for central control cannot be separated from the particular outcome that groups supporting state intervention in these matters would like to see emerging, namely, the ending of racial and sexual discrimination. In such cases it is impossible to separate the reasons in favour of central control from the particular outcome being sought by those groups advocating racial and sexual equality.[7]

---

[6] "Toleration without Liberal Foundations", p. 8; 'Three Faces of Toleration in a Democracy', p. 51.

[7] In the 1997 essay, "Toleration without Liberal Foundations", (footnote 16, pp. 152-53), Leader attempts to provide an answer to this criticism of mine. His answer picks out an example which is the exact opposite of the one I provided, namely, one where an individual discriminates against another by refusing

We may thus conclude that neither the liberal answer—the state must be neutral with respect to competing conceptions of the good life—nor the democratic answer—central control is legitimate only when justified for detachable reasons—would seem to be sufficient to convince non-liberal groups to refrain from attempting to impose their conception of the good on matters of religion or sexual morality. Far from providing a common ground that liberals and their opponents can share, Leader's 'shareable understanding' of democracy seems to appeal primarily to liberals. The implication to be drawn, to paraphrase Brian Barry, is that the only people who can be relied on to defend toleration as a basic right are—as you might expect—liberals.[8]

TOLERATION AS AN EQUAL RIGHT

Consider now the second species of toleration, namely, toleration as an equal right of access to some common space or scarce resource, and in the process of gaining it, to be entitled, if necessary, to interfere with or inconvenience another. Here, to demand toleration means not simply to have the freedom to live and act as one thinks is right and acceptable in public, but to have a right to share in the determination of the common standard of what is publicly acceptable. The example given is that of two homosexuals who were convicted of insulting behaviour for engaging in a public display of affection of the sort found acceptable among heterosexual couples. The decision against them failed to respect their equal right to toleration, since the definition of 'insulting behaviour' had been adjusted to reflect the moral preference of the heterosexual majority.

The second example is more controversial, insofar as it involved the attempt to reshape the perception of the sacred by a gay artist whose poem described homosexual acts on the body of Christ. Here the opinion of the majority cannot simply be overridden by claims of authenticity or sincerity on the part of the artist. In matters of religious doctrine, as Leader himself notes, the community of believers may well fix its central beliefs undemocratically.[9] The attempt by a believer to widen the conception of the sacred may find support among the religious community if it is seen to enrich or expand their notion of the sacred. But since every religion

---

to employ him on grounds of his religiuos beliefs. In such a case there is clearly no basis for granting the individual who discriminates a basic right to toleration, since his actions damage the civil interests of the person being discriminated against, while there is every reason to favour central control so as to prevent such an act of discrimination. Leader's answer attempts to show that in such a case we are not dealing with the basic right to toleration, but either with an equal or with a special right to toleration. But he does not answer the objection that in cases, say, of racial, sexual or religious discrimination, there are non-detachable reasons for allocating an issue to central control. Rather, his example seems to confirm it.

[8] Cf. Brian Barry, "How Not to Defend Liberal Institutions", in R. B. Douglass, G. M. Mara and H. S. Richardson (eds.), *Liberalism and the Good* (New York: Routledge, 1990), pp. 44-58, at p. 44: "I want to ask what arguments are available to persuade people who are not liberals ... that they ought nevertheless to subscribe to liberal institutions. I will examine four such arguments ... and conclude that they are either limited in scope or dependent on dubious factual premises. The implication to be drawn is the rather depressing one that the only people who can be relied on to defend liberal institutions are liberals."

[9] "The rights to religious freedom of, say, Jews and Catholics must include a right that their theology be fixed in a way they see fit, and this is not, of course, done democratically", Leader, "Toleration without Liberal Foundations", p. 17; "Three Faces of Toleration in a Democracy", p. 64.

embodies a dogmatic content that defines the identity of the believers, it is up to the relevant religious community to decide whether the attempt by one of its members to widen their conception of the sacred is an expansion or a distortion of their central religious beliefs. To claim that a religious community should act democratically by allowing the understanding and sensibilities of a minority always to inform the content of their central religious beliefs is to view the whole question of religious belief from a purely secular standpoint. We can't expect religious communities to act democratically with respect to the codification of their central religious beliefs. What we should expect, instead, is that in a liberal constitutional regime no religious group should have the power to appeal to the state to legally enforce its currently accepted dogmas upon the rest of society or upon its own dissenting minorities.[10] And this is precisely the conclusion that Leader reaches in his 1997 essay in response to this line of criticism. In that essay he claims that: 'There is an inevitable gap, and tension, between the internal and external ways of understanding and justifying the power of a community within a larger democratic polity. Internally, a particular Christian community may consider that its truths are delivered in ways that have nothing to do with democracy ... Democracy, they would say, is a secular principle that is irrelevant to matters of faith. While this may certainly be true across a wide range of issues, it ceases to be a sufficient guide when the proper use of the criminal law is in question ... The external view may well count someone as having a Christian belief that the internal view would disqualify.' The external view, he notes, 'would not be a substitute for the very different internal view among various Christian churches; it would rather function as a substitute only for the limited purpose of defining the reach of the crime of blasphemy, where an internal definition of a Christian belief must cede to an external one.'[11]

TOLERATION AS A SPECIAL RIGHT

Consider, finally, the last species of toleration, namely, as a special right to be exempt from standards that would normally regulate the exercise of power within a group. According to Leader, this special right to exemption applies only to the central set of beliefs and practices that constitute, rather than regulate the evolution of, the identity of a group. Thus a group may fix its constitutive beliefs undemocratically, but it is up to the wider democratic community to decide how it is to implement those beliefs inside its own structure. It does so by demanding that the leaders of the group acknowledge and represent the interests of all those who subscribe to its central tenets. The democratic community expects all members to have a right to shape the practices that regulate the evolution of the identity of the group. However, as Leader notes, the distinction between constitutive and regulative practices in not water-tight: by allowing every member to shape the practices regulating the evolution of the group's identity, its central constitutive practices may

---

[10] This implies that laws against blasphemy, as currently extant in the UK, carry no democratic legitimacy, since they grant to Christian religious groups the right to appeal to the state to legally enforce their views of the sacred upon the rest of society as well as upon their own dissenting minorities.

[11] "Toleration without Liberal Foundations", p. 156.

well be affected in the long term. But this change, he argues, is not imposed from the outside: democratic principles have only encouraged a wider range of individuals to be accounted as members in good standing of the group, leaving everything else to the internal procedures of the group.

Moreover, as Leader notes in his 1996 and 1997 essays, many of the regulative practices which can negatively affect the interests of the members of a group have a purely instrumental character: they do not form part of the group's identity, but are, at best, means to helping the group to maintain its identity. They either function, he says, 'as badges of membership, such as some dress codes or circumcision, or as instruments of control for maintenance of adequate membership, such as restrictions on access to certain types of secular education, or marriage partners. If these instrumental practices damage civil interests, they cannot find their countervailing justification by invoking them as part of what makes the group the particular group that it is. Instead, they will usually be one among a set of instruments used by the group to carry on.' It follows that 'if one of their instruments is removed or weakened out of respect for background rights it is doubtful that they could not improve or add to the remaining set in order to carry on.' The special right to toleration is thus properly grounded 'on those practices which truly cannot be pulled away without pulling away the constitutive elements of the group. It has a far weaker purchase when the group tries to impose the means it prefers to use to retain its identity: the onus instead being on the group to choose or construct alternative means that impinge less or not at all on the fundamental rights of its members.'[12]

Now, Leader's appeal to democratic principles, civil interests and fundamental rights can sound threatening to many non-liberal groups. They would have great difficulty in subscribing to democratic procedures and in respecting the civil interests or fundamental rights of their members if they came to believe that they might affect the distinctive identity or the established practices of the group. The case cited seems to prove the point: Ms. Lovelace, a Maliseet Indian, had to appeal to the Human Rights Committee of the UN to vindicate her claim to be allowed to return to live in her community. Her claim was based on the rights and guarantees enshrined in the International Covenant on Civil and Political Rights. To many members of her tribe, this looked like an act of interference with their right to autonomy or self-determination. To many others, including the Human Rights Committee, it would appear as an act that would strengthen their autonomy by making the tribe more representative of the views and interests of its members. This contrast of opinion would appear to indicate two things. First, many groups governed by traditional standards or customs are reluctant to accept changes in their identity, however positive they might look to some of their more progressively-minded members. Second, many groups are reluctant to embrace democratic principles, precisely because they appear to threaten their established identity or their distinctive way of life. Thus, contrary to Sheldon Leader, I doubt whether liberals and their opponents would willingly converge in their support for democracy, and thereby in their support for the three types of toleration outlined. As is often the case,

---

[12] "Three Faces of Toleration in a Democracy", pp. 65-6; "Toleration without Liberal Foundations", pp. 161-2.

the commitment to preserve non-liberal forms of life may take precedence over the commitment to uphold democratic principles. We may remain stuck at the point of departure, unable to reconcile the differences between liberals and their opponents by appealing to principles that all can share.[13]

TOLERATION WITHOUT LIBERAL FOUNDATIONS?
LEADER'S REFORMULATION

In the 1996 essay, 'Three Faces of Toleration in a Democracy,' Leader introduces an important extension to his argument about the special right to toleration. The argument centres on the extent to which the state has a right to intervene in the internal affairs of groups and associations located within its jurisdiction. It is not enough, he says, 'simply to apply the earlier distinction between democracy and oligarchy: we must also fix agreement on the proper <u>scope</u> of application for democratic demands. Someone could easily accept everything so far said about the link between toleration and democracy, but still refuse to accept that certain groups within the state, however powerful they may be, should be regulated as internal democracies.'[14] Such people may be perfectly content 'to see churches, corporations, families and tribes run along what we have called oligarchical lines ... claiming that democracy simply has no place in religious or economic or cultural institutions of this sort.'[15] By appealing to the principle of *institutional pluralism* to secure exemption from the reach of the state, such a position seems to be in sharp contrast to the one held by many liberals, who subscribe to what may be called a principle of *symmetry*. On the latter view, 'if a value such as personal autonomy demands respect from the state, then it should ideally be sought across all powerful groups within the state. Any group that unduly restricts that autonomy loses the inherent right to institutional freedom that the first position would assign to it. On this view, a society committed to furthering personal liberty has the right to impose that requirement all the way down, as it were: reaching inside each of its constituent parts.'[16] The disagreement between the two positions thus centres on the proper reach of the state inside civil society: 'the liberal principle of symmetry gives no immunity to any power that impinges too heavily on personal freedom; while the pluralist who wants to preserve non-liberal values and practices inside the group sees no reason for

---

[13] My conclusion thus radically differs from the one put forward by Leader in the final section of his 1997 essay, "Toleration without Liberal Foundations", *Ratio Juris*, op. cit., p. 163. There he claims that: "In working through the nature of these three rights of toleration, we have avoided relying on any of the standard foundations that inform either a liberal position or those of any of the liberal's opponents. Instead we have sought guidance from the cross-cutting principles of democracy ... The solutions that do emerge will often coincide with those that some of these contestants would start out by proposing, but ours is a point of arrival: The point of departure lies in working through the differences between democracy and oligarchy - an effort to which liberals and non-liberals should be committed if, as so often happens, they want to claim their place in society by using the common currency of an appeal to democratic principles." I elaborate on my arguments about the difficulty of reconciling non-liberal groups to democratic principles, and on Leader's reliance on liberal principles to specify the scope and limits of toleration, in the next section of my paper.

[14] "Three Faces of Toleration in a Democracy" , p. 55.

[15] Ibid., pp. 55-6.

[16] Ibid., p. 56.

entitling the state to [enforce] that degree of uniformity.'[17]

Leader tries to overcome this opposition over the special right to toleration by appealing to a common or shared understanding of democracy. His aim is to see whether a proper understanding of democracy yields either a principle of symmetry, or one of institutional pluralism, or even a third possibility. It is at this point that he introduces, drawing on Locke's arguments as set out in *A Letter Concerning Toleration*, the key notion of civil interests: 'These are interests which individuals share with other members of civil society, and which the state is often concerned to protect via fundamental rights. Locke gave as examples, 'life, liberty, bodily health, freedom from pain, and the possession of outward things such as lands, money, houses, furniture, and the like.' Interests in these are the proper business of the state both to guarantee and to regulate.'[18] Leader believes that the protection of such civil interests by the state does not rest on principles to which only liberals could agree. Rather, such civil interests provide a focus 'which should appeal to all parties in debates about the place of groups within the state, so long as they subscribe to the idea that they are in a democratic polity.'[19] This is because 'if they are central enough for the state's legitimacy to ride on protecting them, then ... they must be protected by collateral attack from sources that can potentially be as potent as is the state itself.'[20] Thus if a state 'cannot deprive someone of his life, liberty, or property at its discretion, [it] cannot permit a church—or indeed any other group under its jurisdiction—to do so either.'[21]

This is what Leader calls the *quid-pro-quo* argument: 'in return for allowing the church [or any other group under its jurisdiction] ... the basic right to toleration, [the state] must deny to that church [or group] any arbitrary interference with civil interests.'[22] This *quid-pro-quo* argument, corresponding to the liberal principle of symmetry, applies only to those cases where civil interests are affected. Moreover, such an argument has only *prima facie* validity: it may, in fact, be overridden if the relevant group can demonstrate that the preservation of its identity is at stake. In such a case the special right to toleration comes into force, allowing the group to be exempt from standards that would normally regulate its internal practices. The special right to toleration would correspond to the principle of institutional pluralism: it entitles the group to violate the normal protection given to the civil interests of its members. As Leader puts it: 'it is a claim that a powerful group, because of its special history and structure, is entitled to exercise its own rights to toleration in the wider society on the back of a denial of them to some of its members.' More specifically, 'it is the claim by some within the group to speak on behalf of all when defining the values of the group, and doing so without drawing on the views of a minority of its members.'[23] The special right to toleration, however, is restricted to the central set of beliefs and practices that constitute the identity of the

---

[17] Ibid.
[18] Ibid., pp. 56-7.
[19] Ibid., p. 57.
[20] Ibid.
[21] Ibid.
[22] Ibid.

[23] Ibid., p. 62.

group, and does not extend to the those practices that regulate and secure the evolution of its identity. Such practices have, for Leader, an instrumental—rather than a constitutive—role in the life of the group. If these practices have a negative impact on the civil interests of group members, then society is entitled to intervene to protect their civil interests.

The problem with this argument is twofold: first, as Leader himself admits, it is often difficult to separate in a clear fashion those practices that are constitutive of a group's identity from those that are merely regulative and instrumental. I would venture to say that Leader's liberal credentials emerge most clearly in his attempt to differentiate practices along the constitutive-regulative axis. What makes his position a liberal one is the fact that he sees many of the practices of traditional groups as merely regulative, rather than constitutive, of their identity. This is a liberal position because it presupposes a 'rational revisability' model of group practices, where members are able to critically reflect upon and revise their collective practices in the same way that individuals are able to critically assess and revise their personal ends.[24] But traditional groups are characterised precisely by the lack of such rational revisability vis-á-vis their collective practices: they view many of their practices as constitutive of their identity because they are not open to constant critical revision and amendment. Leader's attempt to view them as regulative, and thus revisable if they affect the civil interests of group members, is perfectly unobjectionable from a liberal standpoint, but cannot be seen to originate in what he claims is a shared endorsement of democratic values.

The second, and related, problem with Leader's argument is that the right of society to protect the civil interests of group members is based not on democratic values that are supposedly shared by all groups in civil society, but on classical liberal principles of personal freedom and autonomy. It is thus hard to believe that non-liberal groups operating along oligarchical lines would willingly accept the imposition of legal restrictions on their internal practices simply because they happen to live in a democratic society. A more consistent position would be to say that non-liberal groups ought to accept such restrictions because they reflect and embody the principles of a liberal constitutional state. Democracy, after all, is not about individual rights, but about collective self-determination or popular sovereignty. Individual rights are best protected by a liberal constitutional framework which protects certain fundamental interests through a series of mechanisms such as a Bill of Rights, a system of checks and balances, the division of powers, and judicial review of the executive and the legislature.

If the above argument is correct, then it becomes clear that Leader's defence of the right of society to protect the civil interests of group members has deep affinities with Kymlicka's liberal defence of minority rights. For Kymlicka, 'a liberal conception of minority rights will not justify (except under extreme circumstances) 'internal restrictions'—that is, the demand by a minority culture to restrict the basic

---

[24] See A. Buchanan, "Revisability and Rational Choice", *Canadian Journal of Philosophy*, vol. 5 (1975), pp. 395-408; W. Kymlicka, *Multicultural Citizenship: A Liberal Theory of Minority Rights* (Oxford: Clarendon Press, 1995), p. 213.

civil or political liberties of its own members.'[25] A liberal conception is more sympathetic to the demands for 'external protections,' which are legitimate 'only insofar as they promote equality between groups, by rectifying disadvantages or vulnerabilities suffered by the members of a particular group.'[26] A system of rights which secures certain external protections but rejects internal restrictions is, as Kymlicka puts it, 'impeccably liberal. It is consistent with, and indeed promotes, basic liberal values.'[27] I would therefore conclude that Leader's conception of the special right to toleration is, like Kymlicka's defence of minority rights, based on the liberal value of personal autonomy, rather than on democratic principles that all can share.

CONCLUSION

My paper has exhibited a sceptical tone regarding the possibility of convincing non-liberal groups to rationally endorse democratic principles and values. I may sum up my reservations as follows: in modern Western democratic societies liberalism is a necessary, though not sufficient, condition for the acceptance of democratic principles. This means that while liberal groups may be more or less democratic depending on the political culture and constitutional traditions of the wider society in which they happen to be located, non-liberal groups are far more likely to be non-democratic both in the way they regulate their internal affairs, and in the way they expect the wider society to respect their special right to exercise power in a non-democratic fashion. The fundamental problem for a theory of toleration remains unsolved, namely, the unwillingness of non-liberal groups to become convinced of the priority of democratic principles over their other constitutive value-commitments. I would therefore conclude that, contrary to Leader's hope of grounding toleration on non-liberal foundations, it is liberalism that provides a necessary, though not sufficient, foundation to toleration.

---

[25] W. Kymlicka, *Multicultural Citizenship: A Liberal Theory of Minority Rights*, p. 152. As Kymlicka puts it: "Liberals are committed to supporting the right of individuals to decide for themselves which aspects of their cultural heritage are worth passing on. Liberalism is committed to (perhaps even defined by) the view that individuals should have the freedom and capacity to question and possibly revise the traditional practices of their community, should they come to see them as no longer worthy of their allegiance."
[26] Ibid.
[27] Ibid., p. 153.

APPENDIX:

A Reply To Peter Jones

Saladin Meckled-Garcia

I am indebted to Peter Jones for offering an additional way to combine toleration and neutrality, with the aim of reconciling these virtues. However, in this brief response, I aim to show why that combination too, falls to the arguments raised in my chapter. If I am right, then this is further evidence for the view that the virtues of political toleration and political neutrality do not happily cohabit.

TOLERATION AS THE GROUND FOR NEUTRALITY

Jones's view is that toleration and neutrality are compatible ideals. Liberal citizens will express their prior commitment to toleration through the development of a neutral state.[1] However, it is this neat flow from having reasons to tolerate to having reasons to uphold neutrality, that I question.

For this argument to work, people must be able rationally to uphold both political toleration and neutrality: in a tolerant society agents need to act on reasons to tolerate and uphold tolerant practices. Similarly, neutral politics is where people reject non-neutral uses of state power, and refrain from advancing them.

As I originally pointed out, the reasons one might have to be politically tolerant are different in structure to the reasons one might have for upholding political neutrality. The pivotal difference is that those who tolerate are lacking a reason which those who uphold neutrality must have. That is a reason to refrain, if the opportunity presents itself, from using state power to obtain positive advantages for their conception of the good. Let us call this type of reason a political-advantage-renouncing-reason (PARR). State power might be used to gain advantage, for example, through the creation of material incentives for adopting certain life-style choices. The state might even sponsor educational programmes for advancing one conception over another. On the account I gave, political neutrality is precisely the view that disagreement about the good life

---

[1] "Toleration comes first and neutrality second: the members of a liberal state have reason to tolerate one another's different and conflicting conceptions of the good and the establishment of a neutral state is the outcome of their commitment to toleration." p. 2

should not by itself ever be a reason to resort to the use of state power, whether that is to repress other's conceptions of the good or, more importantly for this discussion, to give advantages to one's own. Policies should not, then, be formulated on the basis of a ranking of conceptions of the good. So, to seek to employ state power in this way, even when not repressive, is not neutral. To be sure, some conceptions will be disadvantaged, but that is not through ranking the conceptions. Rather, neutrality works across a range of views: those not disposed to use state power to gain advantages for their conception ('reasonable' ones in Rawlsian terminology).

But, as I argued in the original paper, if the reasons an agent has for political action are toleration based, then she does not have this extra type of consideration, leading her to refrain from positively giving advantage to any conception. She does not have a PARR. That is because an agent is tolerant, on the account I gave, only in so far as she has: a) reasons to repress other conceptions of the good, and b) overriding reasons not to act on those reasons to repress. Having these reasons does not prevent her from seeking advantages for the way of life she favours. Thus, as I pointed out, toleration is especially suited to perfectionism. For perfectionism indeed wants to give advantages to those conceptions of the good it favours (without necessarily seeking to repress those conceptions it does not favour).

If we accept Jones' view that tolerant citizens will support a neutral state, we need to know where the extra reason, the PARR, will come from. Yet, the kind of reasons tolerant citizens possess do not seem to involve a PARR.

One way to show tolerant citizens have such a reason would be to show that citizens who have reasons to tolerate each other can only coexist together under neutral state institutions. This is a modus vivendi type solution. It says that citizens realising they are in deep conflict with each other, resolve to establish institutions which do not discriminate between their different conceptions. But this is an option I rule out, for the same reasons that Rawls and other neutralists rule it out: it is too meagre and unstable. It is contingent, as all accommodations are contingent, on a circumstantial alignment of interests, rather than a principled basis for a just conciliation. If the circumstances change, then the same interests can lead to abandoning the modus vivendi, and the neutrality of the state with it.

Consider a situation where citizens only uphold a neutralist state because it suits their reasons to tolerate (say, they prefer peaceful resolution to bloodshed). Conditions may nevertheless emerge allowing one group to bring about changes that will advantage its conception, without bloodshed or strife. What principled reason does this group have for refraining from this action?

More importantly, what reason is there for tolerant citizens, with different conceptions of the good, to accept a neutral state in the full sense of the word? One possibility is that under such a state they fear neither repression nor persecution. But if guarantees against repression, or persecution, is all that is feared, this fails to supply a justification for a *neutral* state. For, should they find themselves in an advantaged position, why should tolerant citizens not seek (non-repressive) advantages for their conception? That in itself requires an independent justificaiton in the form of a PARR.

Peter Jones says of liberal citizens "Their toleration is manifest in their willingness, in spite of their doctrinal commitments, to limit their use of political power...in the ways that Rawls prescribes". But that would only be true if Rawls' description of the limits on the use of political power involved nothing more than refraining from repression. Rawls, however, prescribes neutrality, which means that he believes citizens should be committed to a PARR. That being the idea that it is never appropriate to use state power to give advantage one's conception of the good, positively or negatively (whilst it might be appropriate to use it to protect people in holding their own conceptions of the good).[2]

Jones rightly cites Rawls' burdens of judgement argument, "that there is a limit to what we can reasonably justify to others and that, in turn, makes it unreasonable to use political power to repress comprehensive doctrines we do not share." (p. 12). But, if we happen to be in the majority, why would that give us a reason not to give positive (non-repressive) advantages to our conception? It would only do so if we believed it wrong to use state power for that kind of end. The fact we cannot win over others to our view is irrelevant if we have the power to do this. A PARR is, instead is an independent reason for upholding state neutrality.

In the light of this, consider Jones's further statement: "Thus, given that Rawls' argument for toleration forms part of his political conception of justice, there is a clear case for holding, pace Meckled-Garcia, that...on public or 'political' matters, it provides us with a reason for refraining from acting on reasons of another sort" **(page number)**. This contains an ambiguity as to what kind of refraining toleration supports. As I hope to have shown, it does not give us a reason to do the kind of refraining neutrality requires of us.

My argument poses a dilemma to Jones's position: either his notion of toleration supplies us with a PARR, or it does not. If it does, then it is actually an account of neutrality on my view, and our dispute is about terminology. If it does not, then there is no principled, stable, reason for tolerators to support a neutral state (which would require a PARR). They may have reasons to support the non-repressive character of a neutral state, but no reasons to support the neutral character of such a state, which would have important consequences for disputes over policy.

DEFINING TOLERATION: 'SECOND-ORDER REASONS'

A different argument in Jones' paper is his challenging my analysis of toleration. If Jones' critique is right, then it would be difficult to frame the above mentioned contrast

---

[2] Of course, this neutrality is not unlimited, for there is no such thing as unlimited neutrality, but restricted to a specific range of comprehensive moral doctrines, and it is a neutrality of intention, rather than outcome. J. Rawls, Political Liberalism (New York: Columbia University Press, 1993), pp. 190-195 (especially 195)

between toleration an neutrality. As part of the paper aimed to show that the contrast has been blurred, or ignored, by contemporary political theorists, I need to reply to this point. I have defined toleration using the notion of second-order reasons. A second-order reason is a reason for or against acting on another reason.[3] A reason to tolerate, I propose, is a second-order reason not to act on a first-order reason to repress, which overrides that first-order reason without cancelling it out. Against this view, Jones claims that toleration can be understood in terms of conflicting first-order reasons. He gives three candidate examples of toleration where first order reasons to repress appear to be overcome by first order reasons for not repressing: 1. attempts at repression can lead to bloodshed which is too high a price to pay, 2. citizens can accept some scope for reasonable doubt on the right way to live (a kind of fallibility argument), and so not act on their (fallible) reasons for repressing 3. the value of people living according to their own beliefs overrides the mistake they make in living wrongly, and so we should not force them to live rightly. The claim here is that we have three examples of toleration where no second-order, but only first-order reasons are in play. However, these examples don't seem to challenge my definition. The first is an example of toleration, but is consistent with my definition: the bloodshed supplies a reason not to act on the reason we might have to repress conflicting views (it is thus a second-order reason). The second is not really an example of toleration, for it accepts that disagreement over how to live is not sufficient (given that we have doubts about being in possession of the truth) to justify forcing our view on others. It is, then, an example of not having a sufficient reason for repression. The third is not an example of toleration either: if it is never right to repress people's way of life, given that it is right that they live how they wish, then we do not have an operative reason to repress, we have the claim that we might have a reason to repress were it not for the fact of the value of freedom. That is, the value of freedom cancels out the purported reasons to repress, it does not just override them.

My original examples were not simply examples of disagreements about how to live. One considered a person who refrains from repressing fox hunting, in spite of considering it grievously wrong, but not because her respect for other's way of life is stronger: that might just cancel out the reason she has for repressing it. Respect for different ways of life is a reason not to repress other ways of life. It is not a reason for refraining from acting on reasons one actually has for repressing those ways of life. My example, by contrast, appeals to general repercussions, such as the setting of a bad example, to override the reason to repress. The reason to repress survives the prudential

---

[3] Second-order reasons need not be 'exclusionary'. Jones criticises my example of breaking a promise to meet someone at the cinema. He claim is that I have mis-characterised the reason to help the accident victim as a second-order reason, while it is merely a first-order competing reason. But I do not claim *that* to be the second-order reason. What I say is that, "the fact that helping an accident victim is more important than keeping a promise to go to the cinema is a reason not to act on my first-order reason (the promise)." Thus, my second-order reason is the fact that helping accident victims is more important, not that I have to help an accident victim. That reason is a reason not to act on another reason, my promise, which nevertheless continues to exist. It is therefore a second-order reason (a reason whether to act on another reason).

reason for avoiding the action (setting a bad example), just as a traffic warden's reason to give a parking ticket may survive the prudential reason not to, provided by the possibility of getting a punch in the nose. The punch in the nose supplies a second-order reason not to act on the reason one has for giving a parking ticket. It does not negate that one has a reason to give a ticket, or cancel that reason, it just speaks to the question of whether or not one should act on it.

My analysis of tolerating reasons, then, does not reduce them to second-order reasons: it is rather the possession of a certain combination of first- and second-order reasons.[4] Jones says toleration can be about conflicting first-order reasons. For this to be true, and thereby undermine my account, Jones must show that there are clear examples of toleration that satisfy the following criteria: a) they involve only conflicting first-order reasons (do not involve second-order reasons), b) one of the conflicting reasons gives us a reason not to act on the other, c) it successfully overrides the other, yet d) it does not cancel the other out.

First-order reasons, which do not act as reasons about another reason, but which conflict and do not cancel each other, are reasons that "talk past each other", as it were. That means that they are contingent reasons about incompatible actions. Consider a case where I have a reason to save a child, A, and I also have a reason to save another child, B, but cannot do both at the same time. In such a case one reason does not cancel the other out, but they are competing, in the sense that I cannot act on both. Reasons of this kind cannot engage with each other. We cannot get a conclusion, based on these reasons alone. The only way we can decide is if we were in possession, additionally, of a reason which tells us whether, in the circumstances, we should act on one of our reasons rather than the other. For example, if one reason is stronger than the other (more pressing or more important), together with the rational principle that we should act on the stronger reason, that gives us an additional reason telling us which reason to act on. This, however, would be to invoke a second-order reason: one *about* the first-order reasons in question. If we are not allowed such additional reasons, then first-order reasons can only talk past each other, contingently. But that cannot be toleration, because on any plausible understanding of toleration it will involve definite reasons not to act on our reasons to repress, which would necessarily involve a second-order reason. No one would say that it is toleration, say, for me to leave off repressing you just because my other pressing appointments make it impossible for me to get round to it. No example, in fact, can satisfy all the conditions (a) to (d) above. Which is to say that all examples of toleration, if they are about conflicting non-cancelling, but overriding, reasons, must involve second-order reasons.

---

[4] Plus the other conditions, like it being within one's power to repress, or effectively seek repression.

LOCATION, SCHEDULING, DESIGN
and INTEGER PROGRAMMING

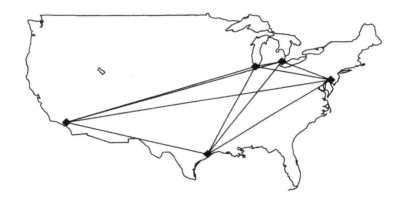

INTERNATIONAL SERIES IN
OPERATIONS RESEARCH & MANAGEMENT SCIENCE

Frederick S. Hillier, Series Editor
Department of Operations Research
Stanford University
Stanford, California

Saigal, Romesh.
The University of Michigan
  LINEAR PROGRAMMING: A Modern Integrated Analysis

Nagurney, Anna/ Zhang, Ding
University of Massachusetts @ Amherst
  PROJECTED DYNAMICAL SYSTEMS AND VARIATIONAL INEQUALITIES WITH APPLICATIONS

Printed by Publishers' Graphics LLC